HANDBOOK
OF
APPELLATE ADVOCACY

REVISED EDITION

Prepared By

UCLA MOOT COURT HONORS PROGRAM

Edited By

BRUCE ERIC DIZENFELD
JOEL D. KUPERBERG
GWEN H. WHITSON

ST. PAUL, MINN.
WEST PUBLISHING CO.
1980

Library of Congress Cataloging in Publication Data

California. University. University at Los Angeles.
    Moot Court Honors Programs.
    Handbook of appellate advocacy.
    Earlier (c1967) ed. by M. S. Josephson, K. A. Kleinberg, and F. Tom.
    Includes index.
    1. Briefs—United States. 2. Oral pleading—United States. 3. Appellate procedure—United States.

I. Dizenfeld, Bruce Eric. II. Kuperberg, Joel D. III. Whitson, Gwen H. IV. Josephson, Michael S. Handbook of appellate advocacy. V. Title.

KF251.J65 1979   808'.066'347   79–23768

ISBN 0–8299–2068–4

Hdbk.App.Advocacy '80 Pamph. MTB

1st Reprint—1980

PREFACE

This handbook is designed to help the beginning appellate advocate—student Moot Court participant and novice attorney alike. Because it is a handbook, certain subjects have been treated in a cursory manner. Throughout the book reference is made to other sources, such as applicable court rules and texts dealing with the specific, discrete elements of a brief.

Because the handbook is designed to assist an advocate who has already decided to file an appeal in his case, rules governing when an appeal may be taken and the various procedural steps necessary to file an appeal are not discussed. Obviously, the initial decision to approach an appellate court determines the tone of the brief, its length, the issues which it emphasizes, and the audience for which it is written. This handbook is designed to assist the inexperienced advocate to write a persuasive brief within this predetermined framework.

The advocate's tools of persuasion are his brief and his oral argument. The importance of each varies substantially from court to court. In some jurisdictions, cases are decided primarily on the briefs with oral argument consisting of little more than a last opportunity to convince the court that it should or should not enter its tentative opinion as a final judgment. For this reason, the basic structure of a brief is carefully reviewed and examples are provided in Chapter One. Chapter Two offers a discussion of the elements of persuasive writing, and the rules governing citation format are detailed in Chapter Three. Some jurisdictions rely heavily upon the face-to-face confrontation of oral argument to set the tone of the case and clarify the main issues prior to any decision. Accordingly, Chapter Four discusses the preparation and presentation of an oral argument.

Throughout the handbook reference is made to the case of *Peggy v. Smith & Jones*. The Petitioner's brief for this case is included as Appendix A. The reader may choose first to read this brief to gain some familiarity with the case as it is used in the examples.

Finally, the advocate should remember that no book can provide the experience necessary for one to become an accomplished advocate. The job of the advocate requires that he be sensitive to every element that may lead to the persuasive quality of his presentation, and experience alone teaches this best. Moot Court provides the student with an opportunity to marshal his talents as an advocate and apply them to a realistic situation. If this opportunity is approached seriously it should prove to be a most valuable experience.

ACKNOWLEDGEMENT

The Editors are indebted to their colleagues in the UCLA Moot Court Honors Program for assistance and suggestions in the preparation of this work. Robert Dawson and Michael Quesnel generously volunteered their time, energy, and expertise to co-author Chapter Four, "The Oral Presentation," and assisted in numerous other ways. This Handbook is in large part the result of their efforts, for which we are greatly appreciative. Douglas Barnes, Shirley Curfman, Marlene Goodfried, and Thomas Mabie kindly assisted the Editors by proofreading and offering stylistic suggestions.

The Editors wish particularly to thank Ms. Mary Burdick of the Western Center on Law and Poverty and Mr. Kent Richland, clerk for the California Second District Court of Appeal, for editing and suggesting revisions of the text. Their substantive and stylistic additions have greatly enhanced the value of this work.

This Handbook had its genesis in the *Handbook of Appellate Advocacy*, published for the UCLA Moot Court Honors Program in 1969 by Michael Josephson, Kenneth Kleinberg, and Franklin Tom. This Handbook would not exist but for their labors, for which we are grateful.

In addition to those who offered substantive and stylistic suggestions, other individuals merit recognition for their help in this project. Ms. Betty Dirstine and the other members of the UCLA Law School secretarial staff patiently typed and revised the numerous drafts of this text, and Ms. Michelle Thrush transcribed the oral argument included in Appendix B to this Handbook.

Many members of the bench and bar, as well as the faculty of the UCLA Law School, gave helpful advice during the various stages of the preparation. Comments and recommendations were solicited from numerous individuals. In particular, we wish to thank Judge Leonard I. Garth, United States Court of Appeal, Third Circuit; Irving R. Kaufman, Chief Judge, United States Court of Appeal, Second Circuit; Harry Phillips, Chief Judge, United States Court of Appeal, Sixth Circuit; Lester Roth, Presiding Justice, California Court of Appeal, Second District; Judge Robert S. Thompson, California Court of Appeal, Second District; Ellis Horvitz; and Michael Josephson.

ACKNOWLEDGEMENT

Finally, we wish to thank Professors Paul Boland, Gail Kass, and Randy Vissar, who generously provided their time and expertise throughout the course of the project.

The Editors wish to note that the pronoun "he" is used throughout the handbook as a matter of convenience. Unfortunately, no widely accepted and stylistically satisfactory pronoun has yet been devised to represent advocates—men and women alike. Whenever particular reference is made to counsel for Petitioner in the case of *Peggy v. Smith & Jones*, the pronoun "she" is used since the brief for *Peggy v. Smith & Jones* was prepared and argued by Gwen Whitson and Kathy Rohwer.

B. E. D.
J. D. K.
G. H. W.

Los Angeles, California
January, 1980

TABLE OF CONTENTS

TABLE OF CONTENTS

ix

TABLE OF CONTENTS

*

HANDBOOK
of
APPELLATE ADVOCACY

Chapter One

STRUCTURE OF THE BRIEF

Although the advocate will have some discretion in determining the writing style of the brief, the physical form of a brief is regulated by the rules specified by the particular appellate tribunal which has jurisdiction over the appeal. The United States Supreme Court has propounded the Federal Rules of Appellate Procedure to govern the presentations of written briefs and appellate arguments in all federal appellate courts. These rules are contained in a published volume entitled Federal Rules of Appellate Procedure. The Supreme Court and various courts of appeal have promulgated rules for their particular courts, which are designed to supplement the Federal Rules of Appellate Procedure. These supplemental rules are published in separate volumes, and are also included in special portions of the encyclopedias which compile decisions of these courts, such as in the "Court Rules" volume of the Supreme Court Digest.

Each state has its own rules. In California, the most convenient source is the "Court Rules" volumes of the *West's Annotated California Codes* and the volume entitled "Rules" in *Deering's California Codes Annotated*. The local legal newspaper may also compile court rules, and publish them in the paper or in a loose leaf publication.

Among the elements of a brief regulated by these rules are the printing or typing format, size and weight of the paper, color of the manuscript cover, maximum length of the brief, and number of copies which must be submitted.

I. TITLE PAGE

The purpose of the title page is to identify the appeal before the court, the parties to the case, and the party submitting the brief. This information is generally conveyed by a formalistic caption. The precise spacing and print required for this caption vary from court to court. Thus, the advocate must check the local rules. In the case of *Peggy v. Smith & Jones* an acceptable title page might look like this:

IN THE

SUPREME COURT OF THE UNITED STATES

OCTOBER TERM 1977

No. 77-1128

JOHN F. PEGGY, DIRECTOR OF REGION 007 OF
THE NATIONAL LABOR RELATIONS BOARD, FOR
AND ON BEHALF OF THE NATIONAL LABOR RE-
LATIONS BOARD,

Petitioner,

- AGAINST -

SMITH & JONES, A PARTNERSHIP,

Respondent.

ON WRIT OF CERTIORARI
TO THE UNITED STATES COURT OF APPEALS
FOR THE TWELFTH CIRCUIT

BRIEF FOR THE PETITIONER

Gwen Whitson
Kathy Rohwer
Counsel for Petitioner
UCLA School of Law
Los Angeles, California
(213) 825-1128

Note that the first statement identifies which court is hearing the appeal. Next, the date of the term and the docket number of the appeal are provided. Following this, the name of the case is given. Petitioner or appellant is always listed first in the United States Supreme Court and the respondent or appellee is listed second. The full names of the petitioner and respondent are given, as well as their procedural designation. Abbreviations of the party's name, such as "Peggy, *et al.*" are not used; generally "against" is used in lieu of "*v.*"

After the name of the case, the title page explains the procedural posture of the case. If the case is an appeal, it is an appeal to the United States Supreme Court; but if the case is being heard on a writ of certiorari, writ is to the United States Court of Appeals for the applicable circuit. Below the procedural posture, the party submitting the brief is identified; and if the brief is a reply brief, that is indicated. All of this information is provided on the cover of the brief and on the first page of the text of the brief, just before the "Opinions Below".

On the cover of the brief, one additional item of information is provided. On the lower right corner of the cover, the names, addresses, and phone numbers of counsel are indicated. Particular attention should be paid to punctuation, spacing, format, and print style.

II. TOPICAL INDEX

The Topical Index of the brief, like the table of contents of any book, is a complete listing of its various parts. It is a recapitulation of the sections, argument headings, and subheadings. Thus, it gives a thorough outline of the argument and enables the reader to secure an initial understanding of the argument and analysis.

TOPICAL INDEX

. . . .

As can be seen from the example, all page numbers are typed "flush-right"; that is, the last digit of each page number is flush against the right-hand margin, and lines up under the last digit of the page number above, with everything backspaced from that point. The page number for each heading of the brief is lined up with the last line of text of that heading, and periods separated by spaces extend from the text up to two spaces before the last digit of each page number. The text of each heading is single spaced and indented in an outline form. Between each separate listing, however, there is a double space. Note that all headings are typed in a style matching a style of the heading in the text. All other items listed in the topical index can be typed either in upper case letters, or in lower case letters with the initial letter of each word capitalized.

III. TABLE OF AUTHORITIES

The Table of Authorities lists all the sources and references cited in the brief. This table is more effective when the references are categorized by groups—cases, constitutional provisions, statutes, and secondary sources. Each category may in turn be subdivided where there are many references. In particular, the advocate may find it effective to subdivide cases and statutes by jurisdiction.

All sources in the Table of Authorities, like those in the body of the brief, should follow proper citation form. For readily available cases, only the official citations must be included. Whenever the official reports may be inaccessible to the court, the unofficial citation should also be given for the court's convenience. Additionally, the advocate should include the subsequent history of any opinion listed in the Table of Authorities.

An abbreviated version of Petitioner's Table of Authorities in *Peggy v. Smith & Jones* follows:

TABLE OF AUTHORITIES

SECONDARY AUTHORITIES

McCulloch, <u>New Problems in the Administra-</u>
<u>tion of the Labor-Management Relations</u>
<u>Act: The Taft-Hartley Injunction</u>, 15
S.W.L.J. 82 (1967) 33

National Labor Relations Board Annual Report 196 (1970) 37

Note that the pages upon which each reference is cited are listed after the references. Here, as with the Topical Index, the page numbers are typed flush-right. When one case or statute is cited on numerous pages throughout the brief the advocate may use the designation *"passim"* in lieu of the page numbers. This designation should, however, be used sparingly.

IV. OPINIONS BELOW

The opinions of the lower court from which the appeal is taken should be listed in "Opinions Below." This allows the reviewing court to become familiar with the previous opinion filed in the case. When the lower court's opinion is published, the citation for that opinion should be given. For example, in petitioner's brief for the appeal to the United States Supreme Court in *Textile Workers Union of America v. Darlington Manufacturing Company*, the Opinions Below section would state:

> The order of the National Labor Rela-
> tions Board is found at 139 N.L.R.B. No.
> 23. The opinion of the United States
> Court of Appeals for the Fourth Circuit
> is found at 325 F.2d 682.

When the lower court's opinion has not been published, as in *Peggy v. Smith & Jones*, reference should be made to the relevant portion of the Transcript of Record.

> The order of the United States Dis-
> trict Court for the Southern District of
> Erewhon is unreported, and contained in
> the Transcript of Record (R. 29-32). The

```
opinion of the United States Court of
Appeal for the Twelfth Circuit is unre-
ported and contained in the Transcript
of Record (R. 33-35).
```

As indicated by the foregoing examples, this section is usually fairly short.

V. JURISDICTIONAL STATEMENT

The United States Supreme Court and some courts of appeal require petitioners and appellants to submit a Statement of Jurisdiction. The respondent or appellee is not required to provide such a statement, but one may optionally be included.

The Statement of Jurisdiction for a court of appeal outlines the basis of jurisdiction for the federal district court, if the case originated there, and the statutory basis for jurisdiction in the appellate court. The Statement of Jurisdiction for United States Supreme Court briefs should also refer to the statutory basis of jurisdiction and the facts which qualify the case according to that statute.

When appealing to a state tribunal, the advocate should check the local rules for the appropriate jurisdictional statement. In Moot Court competition the jurisdictional statement is omitted. This does not imply, however, that issues regarding jurisdiction which are raised by the case are not discussed in the text.

VI. CONSTITUTIONAL PROVISIONS AND STATUTES INVOLVED

The United States Supreme Court Rules require a statement of the Constitutional provisions, treaties, statutes, ordinances and regulations involved in the case, or required for decision of the case. In addition, the text of these applicable laws should be included here or in an appendix. In *Peggy v. Smith & Jones*, Petitioner's brief would include the following statement:

```
    The text of the following constitu-
tional provisions and statutes relevant
to the determination of the present case
are set forth in the Appendices:  U.S.
Const. art. I, § 8; sections 2(7), 8(a)
(1), 8(a)(3), 8(a)(5) and 8(d) of the
National Labor Relations Act, 29 U.S.C.
§§ 152(7), 158(a)(1), 158(a)(3),
```

158(a)(5) and 158(d)(1970); sections
10(a), 10(j) and 14(c)(1) of the Labor
Management Relations Act, 29 U.S.C.
§§ 160(a), 160(j) and 164(c)(1)(1970).

When statutes are known by the title of an act, both this title and the various sections of the act, as well as the pertinent sections of the code, should be given.

VII. QUESTIONS PRESENTED

The "Questions Presented" is the section of the brief in which the advocate first states the issues in the case. The issues are couched as affirmative interrogatories so that an obvious and compelling answer is implied.

QUESTIONS PRESENTED

I. Whether the District Court, pursuant to Section 10(j) of the National Labor Relations Act, as amended, properly issued a temporary injunction restraining Smith & Jones from changing its operational structure.

II. Whether the National Labor Relations Board has established that there is reasonable cause to believe that this labor dispute is within the jurisdiction of the Board.

Note that the questions only describe the primary and determinative issues of the case. Subordinate points should, as much as possible, be incorporated in the questions concerning the main issue. Questions should be phrased to include significant facts relevant to the issue, but caution should be used to keep the question to a manageable length.

VIII. STATEMENT OF THE CASE

The most important of these preliminary statements is the exposition of the material facts in the Statement of the Case. The statement must be objective; it must not state the facts erroneously or in a way which would create misleading or false inferences. In addition, only facts in the record should be cited. It should be remembered that the advocate frequently is bound to accept the facts in a certain light. For example, in a defendant's motion for Summary Judgment for failure to state a cause of action, all the facts must be read in the light most favorable to the plaintiff. Appellate advocates must be familiar with these rules and obey them. By the same token, the advocate should never omit a crucial fact, even though such fact is damaging to his case. Nevertheless, there is room for maneuvering; and the impact which the facts have upon the court can be altered by changing the order in which they are presented, by emphasizing certain facts while merely mentioning others, and by skillfully choosing words and phrases.

In *Peggy v. Smith & Jones*, the Petitioner might state the facts as follows:

When the associates at Smith & Jones first discussed the possibility of unionization, managing partner Rufus Smith told the employees he was "shocked" by their interest in union representation (R. 15, 22). Mr. Smith further stated that the lawyer-associates were "privileged" to work for his firm, and that employees have "no rights" (R. 21, 22).

On June 20, 1977, the Union was certified by the Board as the collective bargaining representative of the lawyer associates at Smith & Jones. Four days later, and before any negotiations had been scheduled between the Firm and the Union, the partners at Smith & Jones decided to reorganize the partnership due to allegedly unfavorable business projections (R. 26, 27). Under the terms of the reorganization agreement, the partnership would be dissolved on August 31, 1977. After that date, the partners and their secretaries would join the firm of Wind & Zephyr, and the lawyer associates who are members of the Union would be unemployed. After the reorganization, the partners of Smith & Jones will render legal services to the clients of Wind & Zephyr as well as to their present clients. Furthermore, the lawyer-associates of Wind & Zephyr

who are not represented by a union will
begin to perform the work formerly performed by unionized Smith & Jones associates (R. 27).

The Respondent, on the other hand, could state these facts in this way:

On May 15, 1977, the Firm's partners
met and the possible dissolution of Smith
& Jones was first discussed. The partners
decided to wait for the conclusion of the
annual Firm audit before reaching a final
decision regarding dissolution (R. 25, 26).
On June 24, based upon the decline in
revenues described in the profit and loss
statement, the projections for future
decline, and the failure of the Firm to
attract new clients of substantial size,
the partners formally decided to dissolve
the partnership. Recognizing the hardship
this decision might cause to the associates
of the Firm, the partners agreed upon a
substantial transition period--until August
31--during which time the associates could
begin to find other employment (R. 26, 27).

During the spring of 1977, while the
partners of Smith & Jones were ascertaining
that the Firm could no longer function in an
economically viable manner, the associates
of the Firm organized a collective bargaining unit. On May 15, the Union, having
secured the signatures of at least 30% of
the lawyer-associates of the Firm, peti-
tioned the National Labor Relations Board
for a representation election for a bargaining unit consisting of all lawyer-associates
(R. 15). The NLRB sent notice of this petition for an election to Mr. Smith, who sup-
plied the NLRB with the requested commerce
data. Following the election on June 15,
the NLRB certified the Union as the collective bargaining representative of the lawyer-associates (R. 16).

In the Petitioner's Statement of the Case the potential anti-union animus is emphasized and the economic weakness of the firm is minimized. In contrast, the Respondent's Statement of the Case highlights the Firm's decline and characterizes the actions of the associates as unjust.

Several other aspects of the Statement of the Case also deserve attention. For every fact used the advocate should include a citation to the record from which the fact is taken. Second, the Statement of the Case should discuss the procedural history of the case. For example, the statement should indicate whether the suit is civil or criminal, what relief is sought, and what the lower court has decided.

IX. SUMMARY OF ARGUMENT

The Summary of Argument is a terse statement of the advocate's main contentions in the same order as they appear in the brief. It contains only those propositions which are crucial to the case, with each argument set forth in separate paragraphs. Minor points should not be presented. Likewise, it is not necessary to cite legal authorities, unless a particular argument rests primarily upon an examination of those authorities.

Many advocates firmly believe the Summary of Argument to be one of the most important sections of the brief. The significance of the Summary of Argument lies in the fact that it is a recapitulation of the central issues in the case. Moreover, judges may not always have read the entire brief prior to oral argument; in such instances, the Summary of Argument is a valuable substitute which the judge can peruse quickly prior to the hearing. The Summary of Argument for Petitioner in *Peggy v. Smith & Jones* appears as follows:

SUMMARY OF ARGUMENT

The fundamental question presented by this litigation is whether the District Court of Erewhon erred in issuing a Section 10(j) injunction, temporarily restraining the contemplated dissolution and reorganization of the Smith & Jones law partnership.

Section 10(j) injunctions were designed to prevent frustration of the National Labor Relations Act pending the National Labor Relation Board's adjudicatory proceedings. These temporary injunctions can be granted

by the District Court upon a petition by
the National Labor Relations Board when
the Board establishes reasonable cause to
believe that an employer is engaging in
an unfair labor practice, and further indicates that the issuance of the injunction will promote the goals of the Act. A
showing of reasonable cause requires both
an indication that the controversy is within the jurisdiction of the Board and, in
addition, a showing of facts which if undisputed would constitute unfair labor
practices. Thus, Petitioner need not
conclusively prove the existence of the
Board's jurisdiction and the liability of
Smith & Jones for unfair labor practices.
Those determinations should be made in
first instance by the NLRB in their upcoming hearings to be held on the unfair
labor practice charges. Nevertheless, in
order to explain fully why the temporary
injunction is essential, petitioner begins
by establishing the case against Smith
& Jones.

. . . .

There is reasonable cause to believe
that Smith & Jones is engaging in a labor
practice that is prohibited by section 8
(a)(5) of the Act. Smith & Jones has
refused and continues to refuse to bargain
about its decision to dissolve and reorganize the partnership. Such a decision is a mandatory subject for bargaining
within the meaning of section 8(d) of
the Act.

Furthermore, there is also reasonable
cause to believe that Smith & Jones is
engaging in a labor practice that is prohibited by section 8(A)(3) of the Act.
Smith & Jones is terminating associates who
have recently unionized so that the firm
may replace them with non-union employees.
Smith & Jones may reasonably foresee that

the proposed reorganization of the firm
will discourage further unionization of
its employees. To discourage this unionization Smith & Jones has decided to
dissolve and reorganize the partnership.

The showing that the Board has jurisdiction and will likely exercise it, and
the evidence that Smith & Jones is reorganizing the operational structure of its law
practice without bargaining about that decision constitute a showing of reasonable
cause to believe that unfair labor practices are occurring. This showing of reasonable cause, coupled with considerations
of public policy and equity, require that a
temporary injunction be issued to promote
the goals of the Act.

In more complicated cases it may be helpful to number the paragraphs
of the Summary of Argument. Usually, however, the caption numbers
may be omitted in the interest of brevity.

X. ARGUMENT

The Argument is the body of the brief where the contentions, legal
analysis, and supporting authority are set forth. The objective of the
structure, design, and presentation of the Argument is to persuade the
reviewing court. Since the various methods of persuasive brief writing
are discussed at length in Chapter Two, this section is devoted to the
structuring of headings and captions.

The purpose of headings is to explain, in a persuasive manner, the
facts and analysis which follow. As a result, the headings should refer
to specific facts of the case, and should be argumentative in tone. To
convey effectively the intended message, captions should not exceed five
lines in length.

The main contention is numbered with roman numerals centered
above the text of the contention. The contention itself is typed in
capitals, and positioned with margins of equal size. The lines of the
caption should be as close in length as possible; and whole phrases
(Smith & Jones, National Labor Relations Board), should be kept, to
the extent possible, on the same line. If the caption cannot be typed as

a perfect block, the text following the first line of the contention should be typed in lines of successively decreasing length. Each line, however, should have margins of roughly equal length.

I.

THE UNFAIR LABOR PRACTICES OF SMITH & JONES
ARE WITHIN THE JURISDICTION ASSERTED BY THE
NATIONAL LABOR RELATIONS BOARD

The contentions, as well as all other captions within the Argument, should be in the form of complete sentences.

The headings are also typed in capitals and are designated alphabetically with capital letters. The first line of the heading is positioned with the capital letter placed five spaces in from the margin, followed by a period and two spaces. The text of the heading is typed in block form with each succeeding line of the heading beginning and ending under the preceding line:

A.   THE DECISION IS DISCRIMINATORY BECAUSE
      IT WILL NOT RESULT IN A COMPLETE LIQUI-
      DATION OF BUSINESS

Headings within a contention should be used only when two or more headings follow the contention; when only one exists, the advocate should eliminate the heading and place the uninterrupted text under the contention. The advocate should be careful always to separate contentions, headings, and subheadings with textual information. A heading should never directly follow a contention.

The subheadings are typed in lower case letters, and the entire subheading should be underlined. Consecutive arabic numerals are used to designate each subheading within a heading. The first line of the subheading is positioned with the arabic numeral placed ten spaces in from the margin followed by a period and two spaces. Like the heading, the subheading is typed as a column, with each succeeding line beginning under the first word in the first line of the subheading:

2.   <u>The NLRB has indicated that labor dis-
      putes at law offices, in general, and
      the controversy at Smith & Jones, in
      particular, should be brought before
      the Board.</u>

Subheadings are not used unless two or more follow the heading. If only one subheading exists it should be eliminated, and the text of the argument should be typed without interruption. Textual information always separates a subheading from another subheading or the preceding heading.

Generally speaking, the advocate should limit subdivision of arguments to three levels of analysis—contentions, headings, and subheadings. Further subdivision tends to decrease persuasiveness of the captions as a whole and may cause confusion to the court reading the brief. Thus, the advocate should consider more detailed levels of analysis with great care.

XI. CONCLUSION

The conclusion of a brief is little more than a restatement of the relief prayed. The advocate should not hesitate to ask for alternative remedies where that is appropriate. In particularly lengthy or complex briefs, the conclusion may also recapitulate the primary arguments which justify the relief sought. The conclusion to Petitioner's brief in *Peggy* is included below:

CONCLUSION

For the reasons set forth above, Petitioner respectfully requests that the judgment of the United States Court of Appeals for the Twelfth Circuit be reversed, and that Smith & Jones be enjoined from changing its operational structure pending final disposition of the matters involved herein present before the Board.

Respectfully submitted,

_____

Gwen H. Whitson

_____

Kathy Rohwer

Attorneys for Petitioner

Note that after the Conclusion the attorneys sign the brief above their typed names. It is not required that all attorneys who have helped to draft the brief sign it. One signature line containing the signature of the senior attorney can be placed above a list of the typed names of the other attorneys who participated in the drafting of the brief.

XII. APPENDICES

Appendices to written briefs are analogous to exhibits attached to trial court pleadings—they refer the court to vitally relevant information which must be set out verbatim.

Appendices to written briefs usually are composed of the constitutional provisions, statutes, and regulations which are the legal foundations for the contentions in the brief. The complete text of the legislative enactments need not be reproduced; the advocate may, for the sake of brevity, provide only those parts of the enactments which relate to the contentions. When excerpting portions of statutes and constitutional provisions, however, the advocate must indicate explicitly that the enactment is not set out in full. A portion of the appendix to Petitioner's brief in *Peggy v. Smith & Jones* is organized as follows:

APPENDIX A

United States Constitutional Provisions

Article 1, section 8, clause 3:

> [Congress shall have the power to] regulate Commerce with foreign Nations, and among the several States, and with the Indian Tribes.

APPENDIX B

National Labor Relations Act

Section 2(7), 29 U.S.C. § 152(7)(1970):

> The term "affecting commerce" means in commerce, or burdening or obstructing commerce or the free flow of commerce, or having led or tending to lead to a labor dispute burdening or obstructing commerce or the free flow of commerce.

Sections 8(a)(3) and 8(a)(5), 29 U.S.C.
§ 158(a)(3) and 158 (a)(5)(1970) provide
in relevant part:

(a) It shall be an unfair labor practice for
an employer

. . . .

(3) by discrimination in regard to hire
or tenure of employment or any term
or condition of employment to encourage or discourage membership in any
labor organization ...

. . . .

(5) to refuse to bargain collectively
with the representatives of his
employees, subject to the provisions of section 159(a) of this
title.

In addition to constitutional provisions and legislative enactments, the
advocate may also use appendices to provide the court with statistics,
graphs, or other information pertinent to the case. Each item should
be placed in a separate appendix, and the appendices should be designated by consecutive capital letters.

Chapter Two

PERSUASIVE BRIEF WRITING

The written brief constitutes the advocate's principal argument of his case before the reviewing court, serving to convince the court that the position advanced by the advocate is the proper one for the court to adopt. As such, the brief is not a scholarly, objective discourse on a specific area of the law. Rather, the brief represents a forceful and eloquent argument that justice is best served by a particular legal result. In this sense, the brief has two functions: to make the court understand fully and sympathetically the facts and legal arguments which the advocate advances, and to persuade the court that the advocate's argument is the correct legal and equitable determination of the case.

Because of the role it plays in persuading the court, the written brief is crucial to the appeal. Particularly in jurisdictions where oral arguments have been restricted or eliminated by the appellate tribunal, the written brief serves as perhaps the only persuasive tool with which the advocate can present his client's case. Moreover, even when oral arguments are not restricted, the brief is the strongest and most effective way to convey the advocate's legal argument to the court, by its careful organization and definition of issues, detailed and forceful legal arguments, and creative articulation of the case.

I. PREPARING TO WRITE THE BRIEF

Before the successful appellate advocate can begin to draft the brief, a number of preliminary steps must first be completed. These include a thorough knowledge of the facts of the case, its procedural posture, extensive research of the law applicable to the case, and a familiarity of the court which will be deciding the appeal.

A. Know the Case

The first step in preparing an appellate brief is to become completely familiar with the case. This can only be accomplished by reading and re-reading the record of the trial court, which includes the pleadings on file, the court's findings of fact and law, and the documents on exhibit. A thorough knowledge of the facts of the case is essential, as the facts will determine not only what areas of the law must be researched, but will also aid the advocate in recognizing the possible issues or reversible errors, and provide him with support for his legal arguments.

In addition, the facts should determine the style or mood in which the brief will be written. Facts indicating that the client has been the victim of unconscionable treatment by the other party to the lawsuit, for example, will dictate quite a different mood from facts which show the client's acts to be technically legal, but morally objectionable. The advocate should remember that appellate courts are as much concerned with the facts and equities of the case as they are with the underlying legal doctrines. A good understanding of the facts will also permit the advocate to develop equitable policy arguments from the interweaving of the facts and legal principles, thus providing a more convincing argument.

A thorough familiarity of the facts of the case allowed the advocate in *Peggy v. Smith & Jones* to establish a distinctly sympathetic tone when discussing the plight of her clients, whose jobs were to be terminated by the dissolution of the law firm:

```
The associates at Smith & Jones have
invested years of their lives special-
izing in the real estate matters handled
by the Firm; one of the associates, for
example, has been with the Firm for
eight years (R. 21). Whether their
special skills are saleable in the present
market is unclear. It is clear, however,
that the Firm's decision to reorganize
the partnership directly threatens their
livelihoods and thus vitally affects their
interests. For this reason, the Firm has
a duty under sections 8(d) and 8(a)(5) of
the Act to bargain with the associates'
representative.
```

In this excerpt, the facts are used to show the unique concerns of the advocate's clients, and the repercussions which the reorganization of the law firm will have upon the individual associates. The use of these facts, in conjunction with applicable statutory authority, enables the advocate to create a strong equitable argument favoring her client's position.

The advocate must not only have a good grasp of the facts of the case, but must also understand fully the procedural posture of the case on appeal. Whether the case is an appeal or on writ of certiorari, or whether the review is of an interlocutory or final decision will determine in large measure the strategy of the brief. In most instances, for example, courts of last resort have complete discretion as to whether or not to hear a case; the same is generally true with respect to the jurisdiction of lower appellate courts to entertain extraordinary writs.

Because these courts are characteristically overworked, they will avoid hearing a new case when possible. For these reasons, the advocate seeking a discretionary appeal must either persuade the court that a severe injustice has been committed or that this particular case presents a vitally important issue of law of widespread impact which should now be decided by the court. Where the court has discretion in accepting the appeal, therefore, the traditional approach of demonstrating only error will be a wasted effort; the court must be persuaded by the gravity of the situation to accept the appeal. Such knowledge will also aid the advocate in determining the substantive and procedural tests applicable in the case. In *Peggy*, for example, the trial court issued a preliminary injunction against the law firm. Knowledge of the procedural posture was necessary to determine the Supreme Court's standard for review, the proper standards which should have been applied by the trial court, and, consequently, the strategy the advocate will use in presenting her legal argument. Were the issues before the trial court or the actions taken by it to change, the court's standards and the advocate's legal strategy would likewise change.

One of the most important reasons for developing a thorough knowledge of the case is to determine whether the client will be characterized in the appellate proceeding as the appellant (petitioner) or appellee (respondent). The advocate's task differs greatly depending upon whether he is appealing from the decision of the lower court or defending the propriety of that decision on appeal. In most cases, the advocate for the appealing party has the heavier burden: he must persuade the appellate court that the trier of fact or legal arbiter below has erred, and that the error is sufficiently significant to warrant a reversal. The appellant's advocate must determine from the facts of his case whether the error committed by the lower court was "harmless" or "prejudicial"; if the error being appealed did not prejudice the client, the appeal will most likely fail.

Appellate courts generally operate under an explicit or implicit presumption that the lower court decision was proper. In this sense, appellate judges are "affirmance-prone," seeking to preserve the lower court decision whenever possible. Counsel for appellate or petitioner consequently must alarm the tribunal that some major injustice has been perpetrated against the client as a result of the lower court decision. This attitude must translate itself both into the tone and substance of appellant's brief, with appellant's counsel capturing that attitude of redressing an injustice with forceful legal and policy arguments based on the facts of the case which evidence the injustice.

While the appellant's counsel has the heavier burden in terms of convincing the court to decide in his favor, he generally does have the advantage of picking the issues to be appealed. As a result, the advocate representing the appealing party need not argue every issue in the record, but can and should confine his arguments to those few issues which are determinative of the case and which he can support with ample legal authority.

By contrast, counsel for respondent must reassure the appellate court that no injustice has been done by the lower court. If the advocate can demonstrate that the error, if any, is harmless, he will succeed in having the lower court decision affirmed. The attitude which counsel for respondent should portray must fit this purpose. The advocate's brief should, in tone and substance, be structured within a calm and rational approach which explains not only the reasonableness of the lower court action, but also emphasizes the fact that whatever errors which might have occurred did not cause the appellant any injustice.

In most jurisdictions, appellee's counsel does not submit his written brief until the reviewing court has received the brief for the appellant. As a result, the appellee or respondent's brief must respond to the issues and legal arguments raised by the appealing party; the appellee's advocate thus does not have quite the same freedom as the counsel for appellant to choose and argue the strongest issues of his case. Nonetheless, the advocate for the respondent certainly may raise and argue determinative issues which favor his client even if they have not been argued by the appealing party.

The knowledge of whether the advocate's client is characterized at the appellate level as petitioner or appellee therefore has a great influence on the strategy, tone, and substance of the advocate's brief.

B. Research

After the advocate gains a thorough understanding of the facts and posture of the case, he is ready to begin the task of researching the relevant legal principles and precedents. Researching can be time-consuming, frustrating, and often tedious, but its importance cannot be over-emphasized. Extensive research enables the advocate to determine the legal issues involved in the appeal, and guides the advocate in developing his strategy and supporting arguments. The research should also indicate to the advocate the relative strengths and weaknesses of his contentions. Additionally, if the advocate represents the appellant or petitioner in the appeal, the research will assist him in anticipating the arguments which will be raised and the facts which will be emphasized by his opponent. This knowledge enables the advocate to dilute those facts and arguments in his brief. Since the court reads petitioner's brief first, the otherwise unfavorable facts and arguments will be read and retained by the court in a light favorable to the advocate. Finally, thorough research will provide him with a sense of the trend of the courts in this area of the law.

It is a waste of time and energy to research "all" of the possible issues generated by the facts of the case. The advocate is best served by engaging in a preliminary issue-determination process prior to commencing his research of the law. Some issues, particularly those pertaining to findings of fact made by the trial court, probably should not be researched in spite of the fact that the advocate believes the finding to be erroneous; this is because appellate courts rarely overturn findings of fact unless no reasonable basis existed upon which to determine the fact in question. Conclusions of law, on the other hand, are worthy of research, particularly if they resulted in prejudice to the client. The advocate should use his discretion and legal training to weed out those issues which appear to be clear "losers," concentrating his research instead on issues and facts which are likely to be of importance to the appellate court.

The advocate should remember to explore not only the legal precedents, but also the applicable statutes or regulations, their histories, and any subsequent amendments or judicial interpretations. He should take pains to shepardize all of the precedents and statutes upon which he intends to rely in his brief. There exists no greater embarrassment to the advocate, nor greater disservice to his client, than to rely on overruled precedents or repealed legislative enactments.

The advocate can discover a great deal of useful knowledge if he takes the time to research decisions issued by the court to which he is appealing. Members of the court may exhibit different prejudices, and changes in the makeup of the tribunal may presage changes in the court's decisions. Knowing this, the advocate can tailor his brief to accommodate these predilections. In addition, a familiarity with the various judges on the bench and their different areas of expertise can be utilized to persuade those whose opinions will be influential when the court decides the case. An understanding of how a particular court views different procedural issues and treats particular types of reversible errors is an invaluable aid in determining which issues to present to the court, and how these issues can be successfully argued. This is particularly true of state or federal supreme courts, and appellate courts in which the advocate knows which judges will be hearing the appeal. In appellate court districts and circuits where the composition of the tribunal is unknown to the advocate until the time of the oral hearing, this information obviously is of much less value.

This is not the proper setting for a detailed discussion of research techniques and procedures. Should the reader feel a need to improve his research skills, the following sources are recommended:

1. M. Cohen, *Legal Research in a Nutshell* (3d ed., 1978).

2. M. Cohen, *How to Find the Law* (7th ed., 1976).

3. J. Jacobstein and R. Mersky, *Pollack's Fundamentals of Legal Research* (4th ed., 1973).

4. M. Rombauer, *Legal Problem Solving*, (3d ed., 1978).

II. SELECTING AND ARRANGING THE CONTENTIONS
TO BE PRESENTED

Having studied the facts in the record and extensively researched the areas of the law which apply to these facts, the advocate must next select and arrange the contentions to be argued in the brief. It is at this point that the advocate must give careful consideration to the means available to convince the court that the outcome which the client favors is the correct one for the court to accept. Depending upon the facts of the case and what has been gleaned from his research, the advocate may decide to argue for a particular construction of a relevant statute or document, the repudiation of a prior judicial principle, or the enunciation of a new doctrine by the reviewing court. The strategy chosen will determine the most persuasive issues to be argued and the most effective order in which they can be presented to the court.

A. Selection of the Issues

Every case will involve a multitude of legal issues. It is the task of the advocate to select only those issues which will effectively persuade the court to accept the advocate's position as the correct legal determination of the case.

The brief, for purposes of persuasion and clarity, should address only a few primary issues. A helpful procedure is to write down all of the possible legal issues involved in the case. The advocate must first determine whether, as a technical matter, the issue can be raised at all. Aside from fundamental constitutional questions, issues which can be raised on appeal must have been first raised in the trial court; if the issue was not raised there, the appellate court may not have jurisdiction even to consider the issue. Nothing can be better calculated to nip an appellate issue in the bud than the fact that the issue was not preserved, by objection or otherwise, in the court below.

After having determined that the issue can be raised on appeal, the advocate should then write beside each issue all of the legal authorities and case facts which bear upon the issue, the anticipated result from arguing those authorities in conjunction with the facts, how a successful determination of the issue aids the client's case, and the ramifications of such a decision on future cases involving the same issue.

Having gone through such a process with every available issue, the advocate should be able to discern the relative value of each. Some issues will be both legally supportable and crucial to a successful determination of the case. Others will be relevant to the facts of the case, but will most likely be decided against the client. Still others, while legally supportable, will not aid the advocate in winning the case. Obviously, those issues which are both central to the case and strongly supported by case law will be retained and included in the brief. The difficulty occurs in deciding the fate of those issues which are weak, irrelevant, inconsequential, or tangential.

A relevant but legally unsupportable issue should either be conceded or discussed briefly. Respondent in *Peggy v. Smith & Jones*, for example, is confronted with such a problem in arguing that the Commerce Clause does not give the National Labor Relations Board jurisdiction over law firms. Because of the jurisdictional hierarchy of the court system, lower courts of appeal are foreclosed from overruling issues which have been determined by the state and federal courts of last resort. And supreme courts generally will not overrule issues they previously have decided. Respondent thus could concede the jurisdiction issue, but concentrate on the subsidiary issue of whether the Board exceeded its jurisdictional discretion in hearing the case. Such fine points and legalistic arguments are often more effective than a broad, general attack which will most likely be decided against the advocate.

An irrelevant issue, which will most likely be decided against the advocate, should never be used, as it may well prove fatal to the advocate's entire case. In determining whether or not a given issue will be decided in his client's favor, the advocate must take a detached, objective view of the issue and its supporting legal authorities. He should attempt to decide the outcome of the issue in the same way as a neutral court, provided with the same facts and law, would make its determination. For example, were Respondent in *Peggy* to weigh dispassionately the outcome of an attack on the constitutionality of the National Labor Relations Act, he would come to the conclusion that the court to which he is appealing would follow previous courts in upholding the Act. Since this argument is neither central to the case nor legally supportable, it should almost always be discarded, unless the issue is being raised in a lower appellate court to preserve it for appeal to a supreme court. Should the advocate decide, however, that this weak issue is crucial to the strategy he has chosen, the better solution is not to try to work around the weak issue, but rather to search for another strategy which does not require this unsupportable yet crucial issue.

Legally supportable, but seemingly irrelevant, inconsequential, and tangential issues should not be dismissed summarily. Instead, the advocate should attempt to weld them into a new issue which retains the legal support but is logical and relevant to the chosen strategy. The formerly valueless facets can then be used as subpoints to provide strength and reinforcement to the new unified issue. But if the valueless issues cannot be combined in an effective manner, they should be discarded. Despite the allure of their sound support, they will only distract and confuse the court if they do not fit within the chosen strategy of the case.

B. Articulating the Issues as Contentions

After the issues have been selected, they must be phrased to state contentions. A contention is an assertive and positive statement of an issue which indicates clearly how the advocate believes the issue should be resolved. These contentions thus should embody the issue under consideration, phrased in such a way as to provide explicitly the desired determination of the issue by the court. Contentions are most effective when they refer to parties and facts involved in the particular appeal, and are articulated in short, direct sentences with verbs in the active voice. Thus the issues of "Whether the N.L.R.B. has jurisdiction over this law firm?" and "Whether the trial court acted properly when it enjoined the reorganization of the law firm?" would be stated as contentions in the following manner:

```
Issue:
    Whether the N.L.R.B. has jurisdiction
    over this law firm?
Contention:
    The unfair labor practices of Smith and
    Jones are within the jurisdiction asser-
    ted by the National Labor Relations Board.

Issue:
    Whether the trial court acted properly
    when it enjoined the reorganization of
    the law firm?
Contention:
    The District Court properly enjoined the
    reorganization of Smith & Jones.
```

These contentions both raise the issues to be considered and indicate to the court their proper determination. The articulation of contentions in the manner suggested serves two purposes. Taken together, the contentions provide a rudimentary outline of the advocate's argument. Moreover, the contentions serve as the headings in the argument section of the written brief.

C. Arrangement of the Contentions in the Brief

Once the issues have been selected and stated as contentions, the advocate must arrange them in a persuasive and logical order. Each contention should be arranged to build upon the preceding one within the structure of the chosen strategy; the individual contentions, when viewed as a unified argument, should persuade the appellate tribunal.

The lead, or first, contention should be both strong and the most logical one with which to commence the argument. In *Peggy v. Smith & Jones*, for example, Petitioner's lead contention—relating to the jurisdiction of the NLRB to hear the case—serves both of these functions. Jurisdiction is a logical contention with which to begin. It allows the advocate to explain the power of the tribunal to hear the case and prepares the court for the remaining issues. The jurisdiction contention is also a "winner" for petitioner; the law clearly indicates that the issue will be decided in his favor.

If the advocate's case depends upon a "threshold issue"—one which, if decided favorably, would compel the court to rule in the advocate's favor—this threshold issue should be used as the lead contention. One example of a threshold issue is whether the injustice complained of was preserved in the lower court. The advocate should commence his argument with a threshold issue because the court can quickly decide the appeal based solely on the threshold issue.

Having chosen a persuasive lead contention, the advocate should then arrange the remaining contentions in a logical and effective manner. One logical approach is to present the contentions so as to complement the chronology of the case. This method is most effective when various legal issues arise out of actions which occurred at different times prior to the commencement of litigation. Another method of ordering the contentions, and hence the argument, is by controlling the scope of the argument by the arrangement of the contentions through the deductive and inductive methods of reasoning. The deductive method proceeds from very general and readily acceptable contentions to those which are very specific and which require a greater amount of persuasion. The inductive method, in contrast, proves narrow, specific contentions first, and then builds upon these, concluding with a general, summary contention.

The deductive method of arranging contentions is demonstrated by the following hypothetical example. Greasy Spoon is a single, non-franchised restaurant in the State of Backwoods. Greasy Spoon services only in-state residents, and buys its cooking oil from Slippery Slide, Inc., a wholesale outlet incorporated under the laws of the State of Backwoods. Slippery Slide buys the oil it sells to Greasy Spoon from various out-of-state manufacturers. The advocate arguing that

Greasy Spoon is sufficiently engaged in interstate commerce to be regulated by congressional agencies established under the Commerce Clause might use the deductive method to establish first that Congress has the power to regulate interstate commerce, then to demonstrate that Slippery Slide, Inc. is subject to the Commerce Clause, and finally to prove that Greasy Spoon's purchases of out-of-state oil from Slippery Slide place Greasy Spoon within the purview of the Commerce Clause.

I.   CONGRESS HAS THE POWER UNDER ARTICLE I, SECTION 8 OF THE UNITED STATES CONSTITUTION TO REGULATE ALL COMMERCE BETWEEN STATES.

II. THE OUT-OF-STATE PURCHASES OF OIL BY SLIPPERY SLIDE PLACES IT WITHIN THE PURVIEW OF THE COMMERCE CLAUSE.

III. BECAUSE GREASY SPOON PURCHASES OUT-OF-STATE OIL FROM A WHOLESALER ENGAGING IN INTERSTATE COMMERCE, GREASY SPOON IS ITSELF SUBJECT TO CONGRESSIONAL REGULATION UNDER ARTICLE I, SECTION 8 OF THE UNITED STATES CONSTITUTION.

The deductive method provides an effective method of arranging the contentions in this case because it permits the advocate to move from a general, easily acceptable contention to contentions which are increasingly narrow and more controversial. The first contention, relating to the power of Congress to regulate interstate commerce, is both a general truism and an unchallengeable legal argument. By applying the Commerce Clause to Slippery Slide, Inc. and its out-of-state purchases of oil, the advocate argue a more specific contention which requires somewhat more detailed legal analysis. In the final contention, in which the advocate extends the Congressional power to regulate to Greasy Spoon because of the restaurant's purchases of out-of-state cooking oil from Slippery Slide, the advocate confronts the issue which is the most detailed and which requires the greatest amount of legal analysis and persuasion. Using the deductive method here to prepare the court for the more detailed and complex arguments by commencing the argument with more general and less controversial contentions, the advocate is both logical and persuasive.

The arrangement of contentions utilizing the inductive method can be demonstrated with the following example: Officer Jones, who is walking down the street, decides for no reason at all to search the

apartment of Mary Renoir. Officer Jones, after demanding admittance
into Mary's apartment, searches the premises and finds a number of
stolen paintings. Upon discovering the works of art, and without
informing Mary of her *Miranda* rights, Officer Jones questions Mary;
and Mary subsequently admits that she stole the paintings from a
museum. The advocate arguing to reverse Mary's conviction might use
the inductive method to argue the various individual acts of Officer
Jones which violated Mary's rights, and culminate with a general contention stating that the cumulative effect of these unconditional acts
requires the court to reverse the conviction:

   I. BECAUSE THE SEARCH OF MS. RENOIR'S APART-
       MENT WAS COMMENCED WITHOUT PROBABLE CAUSE,
       THE SEARCH VIOLATES THE FOURTH AMENDMENT.

  II. THE STOLEN PAINTINGS CANNOT BE INTRODUCED
       INTO EVIDENCE BECAUSE THEIR SEIZURE RE-
       SULTED FROM AN ILLEGAL SEARCH.

III. OFFICER JONES' FAILURE TO ADVISE MS. RENOIR
       OF HER CONSTITUTIONAL RIGHTS RENDERS HER
       SUBSEQUENT CONFESSION INADMISSIBLE UNDER
       THE FIFTH AND SIXTH AMENDMENTS.

 IV. BECAUSE THE ACTIONS OF OFFICER JONES DE-
       PRIVED MS. RENOIR OF HER RIGHTS UNDER THE
       FOURTH, FIFTH, AND SIXTH AMENDMENTS TO THE
       UNITED STATES CONSTITUTION, THIS COURT
       SHOULD REVERSE MS. RENOIR'S CONVICTION.

The inductive method of arranging contentions is effective here because
it permits the advocate to enumerate the specific constitutional violations before aggregating them to argue, in a general contention, that
the conviction should be overturned.

    The various methods of arranging the contentions—chronological,
deductive, and inductive—each vary in effectiveness depending upon the
facts of the case and the legal issues to be argued. As a result, the
advocate should not always use one method to the exclusion of the
others. Instead, the contention should be arranged according to each of
the methods in order that the advocate may examine them and choose
the most persuasive method of argument for his particular appeal.

    There exist two divergent points of view as to the effectiveness of
a strong concluding contention. Some appellate litigators are of the
opinion that an effort should be made to conclude the argument with a

relatively stong contention, as judges often remember best that which they read last. The remaining contentions should then be arranged with the weaker contentions placed, whenever possible, between particularly strong ones. In this manner, the weaker contentions are reinforced and made less vulnerable. The argument, in its entirety, should proceed logically and persuasively as the judge reads through the arrangement of the contentions.

Other attorneys believe that it is unwise to present a strong issue at the end of a brief. A jurist reading the brief naturally will tire and lose some interest as he reads through a lengthy brief, and may miss an important issue if it is not presented early in the brief. Moreover, once a judge has determined that the first contentions are without merit, he may be in a state of mind such that he will attempt to decide the final issues in conformity with the earlier ones. For these reasons, some appellate litigators believe that the strongest and most persuasive contentions should be arranged to be read first, and the weaker contentions should be placed at the end of the brief.

In Petitioner's brief in *Peggy*, the arrangement of the contentions is effective because the issues of statutory violations are discussed prior to the issue of the proper standard for enjoining the law firm:

```
1.   The unfair labor practices of Smith
& Jones are within the jurisdiction
exerted by the National Labor Relations
Board.

2.   The decision to dissolve and re-
organize the partnership is a mandatory
subject for bargaining within the meaning
of Section 8(d) of the Act.

3.   The decision to reorganize the
operations of Smith & Jones, if effect-
uated, will result in a violation of
Section 8(a)(3) of the Act.

4.   The District Court properly enjoined
the reorganization of Smith & Jones.
```

Thus, in *Peggy*, Petitioner's arrangement of contentions leads the court through a series of logically connected steps: Petitioner makes use of the threshold contention relating to jurisdiction to win over the court on the initial issue involved in the case. Thereafter, the statutory violations are discussed so that the court has a sense of the extent of the misconduct alleged. Only after the violations have been detailed is the court presented with the issue of the proper standard to apply in determining whether or not the acts of the law firm are sufficiently grievous to permit the imposition of a prohibitory injunction.

III.   ORGANIZING AND WRITING THE BRIEF

The advocate's task of organizing the brief is not completed with the selection and arrangement of the contentions to be argued. He must next subdivide the contentions into headings and subheadings. These divisions will guide the advocate in arguing logically the contentions; and the subheadings will serve as the basis for the topic sentence for each paragraph in the brief.

A. Subdividing the Contentions

The first break-down of a contention should divide it into a small number of headings which must be demonstrated if the contention is to be proven. Each heading should deal with only one facet of the contention. Headings thus serve as mini-contentions which, when proven, establish the validity of the major contention. The headings are the logical order of the proof of the contention.

In this sense, headings bear the same relationship to the contention as elements of a cause of action do to the cause of action itself. The cause of action for fraud, for example, consists of the elements of representation, falsity of the representation, knowledge or intent, reliance by the victim, and resulting damages to the victim. Assume that Betty sold her car to Bob for $1,000, claiming that she had just installed a new transmission in the car. After Bob drove the newly purchased car for a few hours, the transmission proved defective; the mechanic who charged Bob $400 to repair the transmission told him that the purportedly new transmission was actually five years old. If Bob were to argue at the appellate level that he should recover damages due to the fraudulent misrepresentation by Betty regarding the age of the transmission, his contention and headings might look something like this:

I. BETTY'S FRAUDULENT MISREPRESENTATION OF THE AGE OF THE TRANSMISSION CAUSED BOB DAMAGES IN THE AMOUNT OF FOUR HUNDRED DOLLARS

    A. BETTY REPRESENTED TO BOB THAT THE TRANSMISSION IN THE CAR WAS NEW AT THE TIME THAT BOB PURCHASED THE CAR FROM BETTY

B. BETTY'S REPRESENTATION THAT THE CAR
   CONTAINED A NEW TRANSMISSION WAS FALSE

C. AT THE TIME THAT BETTY REPRESENTED TO
   BOB THAT THE TRANSMISSION WAS NEW,
   BETTY KNEW THAT THIS REPRESENTATION
   WAS FALSE

D. BOB RELIED UPON BETTY'S REPRESENTATION
   THAT THE TRANSMISSION WAS NEW WHEN
   PURCHASING BETTY'S CAR

E. AS A RESULT OF BOB'S RELIANCE ON BETTY'S
   MISREPRESENTATION AS TO THE AGE OF THE
   TRANSMISSION, BOB WAS DAMAGED IN THE
   AMOUNT OF FOUR HUNDRED DOLLARS

In this example, each of the headings must necessarily be proven if
Bob is to be successful in his appeal. The contention that Betty acted
fraudulently can be proven only by Bob proving the headings, which
comprise the elements of fraud. Were any of these headings to be
disproven, the contention itself would fail. The headings thus are
those sub-issues which must be proven if the contention is to succeed.

Counsel for Petitioner in *Peggy v. Smith & Jones* argued in her
brief that the injunction imposed by the trial court to prevent the
dissolution of the law firm should be sustained. Under the provisions
of the National Labor Relations Act, an injunction can issue if the trial
court believes that the employer is engaging in unfair labor practices,
and that restraining those unfair practices is necessary to promote the
goals of the Act. Additionally, implicit in the Act is the understanding
that deference should be accorded by the reviewing court to the findings of the National Labor Relations Board. Given these legal and
factual issues which must be proven if the injunction is to be sustained, counsel for Petitioner in *Peggy* outlined her fourth contention
and its supporting headings as follows:

IV. THE DISTRICT COURT PROPERLY ENJOINED THE
    REORGANIZATION OF SMITH & JONES

   A. THE NLRB HAS ESTABLISHED REASONABLE
      CAUSE TO BELIEVE THAT SMITH & JONES IS
      ENGAGING IN UNFAIR LABOR PRACTICES.

    B. A TEMPORARY INJUNCTION AGAINST THE RE-
       ORGANIZATION OF SMITH & JONES IS ES-
       SENTIAL TO PROMOTE THE GOALS OF THE
       ACT.

    C. THE COURT SHOULD HEED THE EXPERTISE
       OF THE BOARD IN DETERMINING THE PRO-
       PRIETY OF AN INJUNCTION.

So arranged, the contention and its supporting headings provide the advocate with a skeletal outline of the argument of the contention.

Having selected and arranged the headings necessary to prove the contention, each of these headings must then be divided into subheadings. The subheading serves the same function relative to the heading that the heading does to the contention: the subheadings are the detailed elements which must be demonstrated if the heading is to be proven. A detailed version of the contention relating to the injunction in *Peggy* might be constructed as follows:

IV. THE DISTRICT COURT PROPERLY ENJOINED THE
    REORGANIZATION OF SMITH & JONES

    A. THE NLRB HAS ESTABLISHED REASONABLE
       CAUSE TO BELIEVE THAT SMITH & JONES IS
       ENGAGING IN UNFAIR LABOR PRACTICES

    B. A TEMPORARY INJUNCTION AGAINST THE
       REORGANIZATION OF SMITH & JONES IS
       ESSENTIAL TO PROMOTE THE GOALS OF THE
       ACT

       1. A temporary injunction would serve
          the public interest.

          (a) Courts have issued injunctions
             to protect unions in similar
             situations.

          (b) More extensive use of the Sec-
             tion 10(j) injunction guarantees
             additional protection to fledg-
             ling unions.

2. A temporary injunction will prevent
   irremedial violations of the Act.

   (a) The Section 10(j) injunction
       is the most valuable remedy of
       temporary relief.

   (b) Using the applicable test here,
       the injunction must be issued.

C. THE COURT SHOULD HEED THE EXPERTISE OF
   THE BOARD IN DETERMINING THE PROPRIETY
   OF AN INJUNCTION

As can be seen from this outline, each element of the contention is a step in the reasoning process validating the contention. The headings provide the proof of each heading, and additionally serve as the topic, or theme, for each paragraph discussing the contention.

So structured, the contention with its headings and subheadings provides the court with a logical and persuasive argument for deciding the issue in the advocate's favor. To increase the persuasive quality of the contentions, however, the advocate when writing the brief should commence the discussion of each contention with an introductory paragraph setting forth a summary of the argument of the contention, culled from the headings and subheadings. And, after having argued the headings and subheadings, the advocate should conclude his discussion of the contention with a final paragraph summarizing the argument and demonstrating that the proof of the contention is inevitable from the proof of the headings and subheadings.

B. Structuring Paragraphs in the Brief

A paragraph is composed of three elements—an introduction, the development of the topic, and a conclusion. Each paragraph deals with only one discrete topic, which may be one of the subheadings or headings of the contention. In structuring each paragraph to explain and prove a separate topic, the advocate will construct an argument which leads the court logically to the desired conclusion, without distracting the tribunal with tangential arguments or issues.

The introduction of the paragraph should clearly signify a shift or transition from the previous paragraph to a new phase of the contention being developed. The relationship between the previous paragraph and the new topic must be clarified and linked in the introduction of the new paragraph through the use of a transitional device. One transitional device is a connecting word, such as "accordingly," "thus," or "from the foregoing," which links the ideas in the two paragraphs. Another technique is to repeat in the introductory sentence a key word or phrase from the immediately preceding paragraph:

> Conversely, if the employer does not liquidate his business completely, section 8(a)(3) does apply because the employer's discriminatory actions may enable him to reap future benefits.
>
> In the present case there is evidence that Smith & Jones does not intend to liquidate its business completely.

A third transitional device involves a reference in the introductory sentence to the topic discussed in the preceding paragraph:

> Section 8(a)(5) of the Act makes it an unfair labor practice for an employer to refuse to "bargain collectively with the representatives of his employees" with respect to decisions which affect such terms of employment. 29 U.S.C. § 158(a)(5).
>
> The Firm's decision to terminate all union employees pursuant to a plan for reorganization of the partnership falls within the literal meaning of section 8(d) of the Act and within the limitations placed on this section by the Fibreboard decision.

Each of these techniques serves to weld the new paragraph to the preceding one, creating a sense of continuity as the judge reads the brief.

The body of the paragraph is devoted to developing the topic which has been introduced in the introductory sentence. The topic discussed in the body of the paragraph is built around the topic sentence, which is a clear and persuasive articulation of a subheading of the outline. Like the subheading it embodies, the topic sentence should concern itself with a single, discrete idea.

The location of the topic sentence in the paragraph and the method by which supporting sentences reinforce the topic sentence depend upon how the advocate structures the paragraph. The paragraph can be organized in either a deductive or inductive structure. In the following example demonstrating the inductive method of structuring a paragraph, counsel for Petitioner in *Peggy* wished to show that the N.L.R.B. could assert jurisdiction over the law firm because the law firm has an interstate impact on commerce. Utilizing the inductive method, the advocate, after introducing the paragraph, stated the topic sentence and then developed it with specific examples:

> Notwithstanding this, respondent contends that because the effects of the labor dispute will be felt predominantly in Erewhon, the N.L.R.B. lacks jurisdiction to hear the complaint. <u>This contention fails for several reasons.</u> The Firm has a potential for a large interstate practice as indicated by the fact that one of the nation's five hundred largest industrial companies is considering retaining Smith & Jones for all of their real estate work (R. 18). In addition, it is clear that the Firm can affect commerce regardless of the locations of its clients. The writing of a lease for a local apartment house, for example, may affect many commercial variables: the housing market, the economy, and the relocations of our mobile population. Finally, this Court has repeatedly recognized that local transactions can have nationwide commercial implications . . .

The deductive method, in contrast, places the topic sentence at the end of the paragraph, preceded by the specific facts and supporting authorities from which the topic derives. The following example, in which counsel for Petitioner in *Peggy* argues that the N.L.R.B. may assert jurisdiction over law firms, utilizes the deductive method of structuring a paragraph by introducing the paragraph and stating a series of facts which demonstrate that the N.L.R.B. can assert jurisdiction over law firms. The paragraph then culminates with a topic sentence demonstrating that, given the facts, the N.L.R.B. may indeed assert its jurisdiction in this case:

> Because the NLRB's exercise of its jurisdiction is discretionary, all cases

```
falling within its statutory authority
are not heard by the Board.  In this
instance, however, there are significant
indications that the Board will exercise
its jurisdiction--the NLRB recently
asserted jurisdiction over law firms as a
class; the Board has promulgated juris-
dictional standards for law firms; and
in this particular matter, the Regional
Director of the NLRB has issued a complaint
(R. 10-14).  Given these indications, the
district court was correct to defer to the
NLRB's judgment and allow the Board to
assert its jurisdiction.
```

These methods of structuring the paragraph around the topic sentence should be varied throughout the brief, to make the prose read in a more interesting and persuasive manner.

The topic sentence thus does not stand alone in the paragraph. The subpoint articulated in the topic sentence must be developed, supported, and expanded, if it is to have any persuasive effect upon the court.

The paragraph should always end with a concluding sentence which reiterates the topic discussed in the body of the paragraph. The court should not be left with a dangling idea upon completing its reading of the paragraph. The concluding sentence may also be used effectively to prepare the court for the following paragraph and its central theme.

```
     The NLRB's intent to excerise juris-
diction over this labor dispute is evident
from the Regional Director's issuance of
a complaint.  In Hoffman v. Retail Clerk's
Union, Local 648, 422 F.2d 793 (9th Cir.
1970) the court of appeals held that the
district court erred in denying a temporary
injunction because the NLRB had failed to
prove its jurisdiction over a labor dispute
at a retail store.  The Ninth Circuit Court
of Appeals stated that the district court
shoud assume that the NLRB regional
director "proceeds on a knowledgeable
determination that the Board is likely
to assert its jurisdiction." 422 F.2d
```

at 795.   <u>In effect, the issuance of a complaint establishes sufficient reasonable
cause to believe that the NLRB will
assert its jurisdiction.</u>

The NLRB's recent decision in <u>Foley,
Hoag</u> and <u>Eliot, supra,</u> is a further
indication that the Board will assert its
jurisdiction over the labor dispute
at Smith & Jones.

In structuring the paragraphs, the advocate must take care not to bore the court with long and ponderous discussions of a single subpoint. Paragraphs generally should not extend more than one-half page in length. Abnormally lengthy paragraphs often indicate that the advocate is discussing more than one discrete subpoint. If so, the paragraph should be restructured into two paragraphs, each dealing with only one subpoint.

Paragraph length can be used by the advocate to pace the court. Shorter paragraphs tend to speed up the judge's reading pace, while more lengthy paragraphs cause the judge to move more slowly through the advocate's argument. Thus, it is to the advocate's advantage not to structure the brief with paragraphs of uniform length. Subpoints involving ideas incidental to the advocate's argument should be contained in shorter paragraphs, in order to move the judge more quickly through the development of these ideas. Likewise, ideas fundamental to the advocate's contention should be treated in more lengthy paragraphs, which force the court to spend greater time in reasoning through these more important topics.

Often the advocate will argue a complex legal principle which may not immediately be comprehensible to the court. By controlling the length of the paragraphs, the advocate will be able to pace the court and also concentrate the court's attention on this complexity. The advocate should first state the legal principle in a short, direct paragraph. The succeeding paragraph should be longer, to permit a careful analysis of the principle. Finally, in concluding the second paragraph, the principle should be reiterated.

If the advocate must argue a complex, detailed, and technical issue within the structure of one or a number of lengthy paragraphs, it may be to his advantage to conclude the final paragraph with a series of short and direct sentences phrased in the active voice. After having analyzed the mass of substantive analysis, the judge reading the paragraph will not necessarily pay attention to a lengthy concluding sentence. If the conclusion is phrased in short sentences, however, it will catch the attention of the judge and demonstrate that the simple rationale embodied in the conclusion underlies the complex analysis.

C. Structure and Use of Sentences

The use of sentences and words provides the advocate with the greatest opportunity to develop a unique and creative style of persuasive brief-writing. No established formula exists for using words and sentences; they must be individually tailored to fit the needs and requirements of the topic being argued and the particular writing style of the advocate.

Just as paragraphs serve a purpose in developing a contention, so sentences have their proper place within paragraphs. All sentences should be linked somehow to the topic sentence in order to provide continuity and flow within the paragraph. Frequently, this can be accomplished with conjunctives and adverbs:

```
accordingly      furthermore      moreover
although         hence            nevertheless
as a result      however          similarly
but              in addition      such
consequently     incidentally
for example      likewise
```

The use of these transitional words effectively bridges sentences, creating a more lyric flow within the paragraph.

The stylistic goal of sentence structuring is to pace the court in its reading of the argument with long, short, and medium-length sentences. The desired blend depends upon the message or mood which the advocate wishes to convey to the court. A short sentence is an effective means of emphasizing an important thought, especially if it appears at the end of a string of longer sentences, or at the conclusion of a lengthy paragraph. The lack of descriptive words makes the sentence stand out, stating clearly and concisely the intended idea. The following example demonstrates how a series of short sentences implies a cold and hostile emotion while listing clearly the objectionable actions of the law firm:

```
    Evidence of the Firm's anti-union motive
is abundant:  During the years prior to
certification of the Union, the Firm re-
fused to accept any suggestions by the as-
sociates that changes be made in the terms
and conditions of employment offered by the
Firm (R. 21).
```

```
The Firm objected to the union election
(R. 16). All of the associates who have
paid their union dues will be terminated.
And at least one of the associates who
has refused to pay dues to the Union will
not be terminated (R. 18).
```

As this example indicates, short sentences can forcefully articulate an advocate's point.

Short sentences can also be used to minimize an opponent's argument. Choppy sentences, devoid of any descriptive or qualifying words, can imply a cold quality to the subject being discussed. Thus, the advocate may draft a series of short, plain sentences when discussing a precedent or fact detrimental to his case. Counsel for Respondent in *Peggy* might distinguish a case favorable to Petitioner in the following manner:

```
The Board in Ozark Trailers, Inc., 161
N.L.R.B. 48 (1966), held that the
decision of a single employer to close
down one of its three plants violated
Section 8(a)(5) of the Act. In so
concluding, the Board relied on this
Court's decision in Fibreboard. This
conclusion by the Ozark Board represents
a misreading of Fibreboard. The holding
in Fibreboard did not rely upon the
incidental termination of employees.
Instead, Fibreboard examined management-
related issues to determine that the
employer would not be unduly hampered
by the requirement of bargaining with
the Union.
```

In this example, the unfavorable holding in *Ozark* is discussed in short sentences. This discussion is characterized by a cold tone, whereas the analysis of *Fibreboard*, as a result of the lengthier sentences, creates a mood more favorable to the respondent. These longer, more descriptive sentences should be used to promote a warmer quality as they slow the reading pace. Longer sentences may be effective when arguing equitable and policy considerations, as counsel for Petitioner in *Peggy* demonstrates in the following excerpt discussing the effects of the proposed dissolution and reorganization of the law firm:

```
Finally, it is foreseeable that, given
the timing of the Firm's decision to
```

reorganize, the employees who remain will
fear that they also would be terminated
if they unionized. Respondent may argue
that under the terms of the proposed
partnership agreement with Wind & Zephyr
the partners of Smith & Jones will have
no formal control over personnel matters
(R. 27). However, even if the partners
have no formal control, the employees will
still fear that their views will be reflected in the policies of the reorganized
firm because there already exist close
personal and working relationships between
members of the respective firms (R. 26).
More important, if the Firm's "dissolve
and reorganize" tactics enable it to
discriminate against union employees with
impunity, it is foreseeable that the
employees will fear that if they unionized,
the partners would immediately call for
another "dissolution and reorganization,"
which this time would result in their
termination.

While there exists no standard length for a sentence, a common error involves drafting overly long and complex sentences. Most sentences should be simple for the sake of clarity. Judges are much more favorably disposed to arguments which they can grasp without having to read and re-read. If the advocate really understands the argument, he will be able to articulate it clearly and simply. A sentence should contain only one main thought; the advocate should not attempt to stuff into a sentence material which should be spread throughout the paragraph. It is better to err in favor of too many short sentences. When redrafting the brief, the advocate will find it considerably easier to combine simple sentences than to tear apart lengthy ones replete with dependent clauses and descriptive phrases.

Persuasive brief writing necessarily entails colorful writing. One way to achieve this is to use varying sentence structures. This makes the paragraph, as a whole, more interesting to read. The advocate who can maintain the court's attention is in a better position to persuade the tribunal to adopt the contentions being advanced. Numerous techniques can be used to vary sentence structure.

Dependent clauses (subject and verb which do not create a complete thought) can be introduced as an important idea which the advocate wants to impress upon the court:

> <u>Inasmuch as the labor dispute at Smith &</u>
> <u>Jones affects both a private law practice</u>
> <u>and the services rendered at a federally</u>
> <u>funded community legal center (R. 19)</u>, the
> dispute is within the NLRB's statutory
> jurisdiction.

The dependent clause can also be used effectively to convey an idea related to the main thought in the sentence:

> Bargaining about these matters in the pres-
> ent case could substantially change the
> Firm's financial situation, <u>eliminating the</u>
> <u>reasons given by the Firm for reorganiza-</u>
> <u>tion</u>.

And the dependent clause can be used as a technique to advance a detrimental argument which is then refuted in the remainder of the sentence:

> <u>While the NLRB declined to assert its ju-</u>
> <u>risdiction in Evans and Bodle</u>, the Board
> has recently reversed these earlier deci-
> sions in part by acknowledging its statu-
> tory jurisdiction and asserting it.

The dependent clause thus can be used in a number of ways to highlight legal points and increase the readability of the brief.

Phrases can be used in a variety of ways to add color to a sentence. Phrases generally serve as an introductory device:

> <u>Given these indications</u>, the courts should
> defer to the NLRB's judgment and allow the
> Board to assert jurisdiction.

Phrases also can be used to add persuasive description or to qualify the main thought in a sentence:

> <u>Few courts</u>, however, have been as thorough
> as the court in <u>Douds</u> discussing what con-
> stitutes a showing of reasonable cause.

Finally, phrases are effective as transitional devices to link the present sentence with the one immediately preceding it:

```
This Court recognized in Fibreboard that
such a decision vitally affects the inter-
ests of employees in the unit. In that
case, an employer's decision to contract
out maintenance work previously performed
by employees in the bargaining unit result-
ed in termination of the employees. Upon
these facts this Court concluded that the
subject of contracting out was within the
meaning of Section 8(d) with respect to
terms and conditions of employment.
```

In the preceding example, counsel for Petitioner in *Peggy* uses phrases as introductions to all of the sentences in the excerpt, thus providing a smooth transition from one thought to another in the paragraph.

In structuring sentences to provide variety and enhance persuasion, the advocate also has at his disposal a number of forms of punctuation. The most commonly used punctuation is the comma which, in addition to separating words in lists, can be used to set off words and phrases from the rest of the sentence:

```
In short, the Firm has refused and con-
tinues to refuse to bargain about a deci-
sion which, for all practical purposes, in-
volves a simple reorganization of its busi-
ness operations. As the facts indicate,
Smith & Jones have no intention of discon-
tinuing their practice of law or liquidat-
ing the assets of the Firm.
```

Used in this manner, the comma has the effect of slowing the pace of the reading, in much the same way as a speaker pauses while talking.

The semicolon, on the other hand, serves to speed up the pace of the reading. Semicolons are used to join together two short sentences into a single compound sentence. This is a particularly useful technique when the advocate wants the court to move rapidly through similar facts touching upon the same topic:

```
Public policy requires such a holding; un-
less the Board is allowed to exercise its
jurisdiction, the merits of the unfair la-
bor practice will never be determined.
```

The semicolon can also be used advantageously when coupled with a conjunction or adverb to weaken or strengthen a thought. Accordingly counsel for Respondent might write:

```
This Court held in Darlington that the em-
ployer had violated Section 8(a)(5) of the
Act; however, the Darlington court recog-
nized that the employer there was in a sub-
sidiary relationship with another firm.
Such is not the case here.
```

In this manner, the semicolon functions to color the thought in the desired manner, by de-emphasizing the portion which precedes the semicolon.

Colons and dashes are additional tools available to vary sentence structure. The colon is usually used to introduce a list or to set off ideas necessarily implied by words earlier in the sentence. The dash is an effective means of setting off a parenthetical idea. The dash can also be used at the end of the sentence to set off a new and important fact or to show a different interpretation of previously discussed facts:

```
Thus the foreseeable effect of the Firm's
decision to reorganize is exactly the same
as the Firm's purpose in reorganizing--to
discourage unionization of its unrepresented
employees.
```

In this example, the dash is particularly effective, because it separates a powerful conclusion from the supporting reasoning.

Certain persuasive devices are best used infrequently, if at all. These include exclamations, rhetorical questions, parentheses, and underlining, italics, boldface print, or capitalization for effect. The persuasiveness of the argument should result from effective legal analysis and persuasive writing, not from artificial signals denoting intended effect. In addition, the techniques recommended for varying sentence structure are most effective when used with discretion. Overuse of any or all of these techniques decreases the persuasiveness of the writing. The advocate should guard against the use of these techniques when they have the effect of distracting or confusing the court. Remember, the techniques are valuable to convey persuasively the advocate's argument, and should not be used as an end in themselves.

D.　Persuasive Use of Words

Like sentences, words play an important role in providing the advocate with the opportunity to develop creative means of persuasion. Through the choice, use, and positioning of words in the sentence, the advocate can articulate arguments in a colorful manner and direct the court to pay close attention to the ideas being advanced.

One of the simplest methods of calling attention to an idea is by the positioning of words in the sentence. Normal word order in a sentence is subject-verb-object. In order to add color to a sentence, or emphasize the object of the sentence, the order may be inverted:

Normal word order:
        The District Court properly enjoined the
        reorganization of the law firm.

Inverted word order:
        The reorganization of the law firm was
        properly enjoined by the District Court.

In this example, the placement of the object at the beginning of the sentence focuses greater attention on this portion.

The advocate's choice of words also permits him to be creative in his means of persuasion. Words serve two functions in a sentence: they convey information and set a mood or emotional tone for the reader. Persuasive words are chosen both to connote and denote the precise idea intended by the advocate.

In conveying information through words, the advocate must be careful to use the precise word to communicate what he wishes the court to understand. The advocate who uses "comprise" when he means "constitute" will do his client and his reputation a disservice, for such mistakes distract the court when reading the brief. The only certain, albeit tedious, method of avoiding the misuse of words is to consult the dictionary for each word whose meaning is uncertain. Similarly, many words have both general and legal meanings. Words of art within the legal community, such as "negligence", "intent", "offer", and "negotiate" are usually recognized as such by attorneys. But care should be taken to use words of art for their precise legal meaning, rather than as part of the general vocabulary. The brief is written for a select audience which will read these terms for their legal, rather than usual meaning. And other terms, while not words of art, nevertheless contain specialized meanings when used in legal writing. For example, when courts "say" something, dicta is inferred; a reference to a court's "holding" indicates the rule of law enforced by the case.

Besides conveying information, words also create an emotional setting which can be manipulated by the advocate to aid in persuading the court. Many words, for example, have synonymous substantive meanings, but convey entirely different emotional qualities. The advocate, when writing about his client's statements, should never use the word "allege", but rather "assert" or "declare". "Allege", "assert", and "declare" all have substantively similar meanings; but the emotional quality of "allege" is defensive, while "declare" and "assert" connote positive, forceful, and direct qualities. Needless to say, the advocate would want to color his opponents explanations with the word "allege". Other sets of words with similar denotations but which convey distinctly different emotional qualities are "agree-admit", "avoid-evade", and "difference-discrepancy".

Some words express emotional qualities because of their sounds. Harsh-sounding words, such as "attack" and "quash" convey harsh qualities to the reader; a few words, because of their soft sounds, convey gentler emotions. Still other words, such as "scheme", "inexcusable", and "alibi" express disparaging or pejorative qualities because of their sounds.

The advocate must, of course, avoid using harsh language to characterize all of the opposition's actions. The overuse of this technique could have an effect upon the court opposite of that planned by the advocate, causing the judges to sympathize with the opponent as the victim of a verbal attack and overstatement. Thus, the use of harsh and harsh-sounding words, like all writing techniques, is most effective when used sparingly and with discretion.

Words should be carefully chosen for their desired effect, both informational and emotional. Utilizing a thesaurus is helpful when choosing words to convey the quality intended by the advocate. The thesaurus will aid the advocate in finding synonymous words with different emotional shadings, and can also be used to prevent unseemly repetition of words throughout the brief. Colorful, different and vivid words persuade the court by attaching emotional qualities to the text. As a result, judges may become more involved with the arguments of the advocates.

When using words to create a desired effect, however, the advocate must remember that the brief is a formal document. Slang words and vernacular terms should be avoided, as they create an informal mood which is inconsistent with the purpose of the brief. Furthermore, judges may be so distracted by such informal uses of language that they will concentrate on these words rather than the argument being made. Thus, while the advocate should strive to make the brief an interesting and compelling document to read, he should not do so at the expense of proper English.

The advocate must also be conscious of the fact that persuasion results from the use of particular types of words. The most common use of words to persuade is the employment of adjectives and adverbs to provide description. These descriptive words are an effective tool so long as they are not over-used. The advocate's use of verbs is another means of making the written brief more persuasive. One technique is to use the active voice when discussing facts and law relating to the client:

> On August 18, 1977, Petitioner requested the District Court to issue an injunction pursuant to Section 10(j) of the Act, enjoining the reorganization of Smith & Jones pending final disposition of the proceedings on the Complaint which are now pending before the Board (R. 3-7).

The active voice is strong and direct. On the other hand, the weaker-sounding passive voice colors those same points in a less favorable light.

> On August 18, 1977, the District Court was asked by Petitioner to issue an injunction. Section 10(j) of the Act was the basis of Petitioner's request, which was designed to stop the reorganization of Smith & Jones until the proceedings on the Complaint are ultimately decided. These proceedings are now pending before the Board.

The advocate thus has at his disposal two verb voices which can be used to evoke different emotions from otherwise neutral words and sentences.

In addition to their use in strengthening or weakening the content of sentences, verbs can also be used in different forms for persuasive effect. The present participle form of the verb (verb + ing) can be used in different forms for persuasive effect. The present participle form of the verb serves in a variety of ways to add strength or action to descriptions. Present participle used as a noun:

> A <u>showing</u> of reasonable cause requires an <u>indication</u> that the controversy is within the jurisdiction of the Board . . . ,

Present participle used as an adjective:

> Petitioner submits that the Firm may rea-
> sonably have foreseen that the decision to
> reorganize would have a <u>chilling</u> effect
> upon unionization . . . ,

Present participle used as an introductory word:

> In <u>deciding</u> to assert its jurisdiction, the
> Board stated . . . .

Present participle used as a connective:

> <u>Considering</u> all of these facts and the cir-
> cumstances involved in the present case,
> Petitioner submits that these facts demon-
> strate that the Firm's purpose in reorgan-
> izing the partnership is the discouraging
> of unionization of its unrepresented em-
> ployees.

The present participle thus can be used in a number of ways to add color to the advocate's writing style. Similar uses, however, can be made of the past participle (verb + ed or en) and the infinitive (to + verb) forms of verbs.

   In using words to catch and maintain the court's attention, the advocate must be careful not to use words in an incorrect or distracting manner. Two common word use mistakes involve indefinite relations of pronouns and failure of agreement between subjects and verbs. Indefinite relation occurs when a pronoun does not clearly relate to an antecedent noun:

> <u>Messrs.</u> Smith and Ludley argued in the
> <u>office</u> for some twenty minutes before <u>he</u>
> asked <u>him</u> to leave.

Whenever two or more persons or things are mentioned in a sentence, or whenever the antecedent to which the pronoun refers is not in the immediately preceding sentence, the advocate must take care that the meaning of the pronoun is clear.

The error of failing to provide the proper agreement between words in the sentence occurs when the subject and verb are inconsistent in number:

> The <u>continuation</u> of such violations <u>are</u> repugnant to the purposes of the Act.

Typically, this problem occurs with words such as "each", "every", and "any"—all of which "sound" plural, but are in fact singular.

Other types of word usage may not be grammatically incorrect, but are equally distracting to the court. The use of some legal-sounding words, for example, is both pretentious and distracting to a court seeking a clear and concise articulation of the advocate's legal argument. "Assume arguendo", "ergo", and "aforementioned" retain the mystique of eighteenth century legal parlance, but add nothing to the advocate's persuasive skills. The word "said" should not be used when the words "the", "these", or "those" would convey the same message:

> <u>Said</u> violations of the Act justify the imposition of the Section 10(j) injunction.

can be better and more clearly stated as:

> <u>These</u> violations of the Act justify the imposition of the Section 10(j) injunction.

The advocate should try to avoid repeating key words and phrases throughout the brief. While repetition may be used occasionally as a persuasive technique to remind the court of some particular fact or legal principle, it is often the result of the advocate's inability to find another, similar word. Use of the thesaurus will normally remedy this problem, providing the advocate with a more diversified vocabulary.

Finally, the advocate should be careful never to over-state his case. The use of hyperbole or superlatives rarely is persuasive; instead, overstatement often proves to be detrimental to the advocate's argument. Courts confronting superlatives and overstated arguments will tend to be skeptical of the advocate's presentation, and will lose confidence in his reasoning and judgment. The better technique is to understate slightly the arguments being made and then, by use of the facts, legal precedents, and logical reasoning, demonstrate to the court just how compelling the argument is.

IV. PERSUASIVE WRITING TECHNIQUES

While it is important to develop technically sound legal propositions in accordance with a general strategy, the effective advocate is one who can develop those contentions in such a way as to convince the court that it should decide in his favor. The purpose of persuasive brief writing is to advocate a particular position through sound substantive analysis and structured writing.

Generally speaking, persuasive writing is achieved through the careful adherance to three principles: clarity, brevity, and accuracy. Clarity is the keystone to a persuasive written argument; the court can only be persuaded if it can comprehend the arguments and reasoning presented. In order to be understood, the advocate must avoid turgid writing and tortuous reasoning. This is not an easy task. Most legal issues are by their nature complex, and the language of the law abounds with highly technical terms which, when strung together, may be unintelligible to all but the most skilled legal mind. Clarity can be achieved only through a continual process of drafting and re-drafting the brief, with the intent to communicate the argument in the simplest, clearest terms possible. Persuasive brief writing thus necessarily entails numerous drafts. In testing the clarity of his writing, the advocate may find it helpful to allow his colleagues or employees to read the brief and critique it. Still another method of spotting unclear writing is to read aloud portions of the brief; if the material cannot be spoken with ease, it should be re-written.

When drafting his written argument, the advocate must be prepared to edit out superfluous passages. The quality of a brief is not related to its length. The successful advocate recognizes that courts are persuaded not by the sheer mass of material presented to them, but rather by the selective use and analysis of the relevant law. Brevity enhances clarity, and clear arguments are what persuade judges. The following example shows the difference that prudent editing can make in the clarity and tone of a written argument:

```
Unedited version:
     On June 20, 1977, the Union was offi-
cially certified by the local office of the
National Labor Relations Board, acting in
accordance with the National Labor Rela-
tions Act.  The local office certified the
Union as the collective bargaining repre-
sentative of the lawyer-associates at the
law firm of Smith & Jones.  Four days after
the Union was certified by the Board to
```

represent these associates, and before any
negotiations had been scheduled between the
law firm and the nascent associates' Union,
the partners of the Smith & Jones law firm
convened and decided to reorganize the
partnership. The reason given by the partners of Smith & Jones for this action was
the unfavorable prospects for future business for the law firm.

Edited version:
    On June 20, 1977, the Union was certi-
fied by the Board as the collective bargaining representative of the lawyer-associates at the Firm. Four days later, and
before any negotiations had been scheduled
between the Firm and the Union, the partners of Smith & Jones decided to reorganize the law firm, allegedly due to unfavorable prospects for future business.

By merely removing superfluous words the size of the paragraph may
be reduced by one-half. The resulting text lacks none of the substance
of the unedited argument, yet reads more clearly and logically.

To be sure, editing is a painful process—no one enjoys chopping up
a seemingly perfect brief in which he has invested so much time and
effort. But the process must be undertaken. Swamped with appeals,
courts are becoming increasingly hostile to lengthy, unedited briefs.
The unwillingness of the advocate to sacrifice any portion of what is
perceived to be a masterpiece may well jeopardize the appeal.

When editing, many advocates find that they are too close to their
own work to be able to exercise sound discretion. By setting aside the
completed draft and leaving it untouched for a day or two, however,
the advocate will gain a different perspective on the argument he has
written, and should be able to find passages in the brief which can be
excised without doing damage to the structure of the legal argument.
As with clarity, brevity can best be achieved through a process of
drafting, examining, and re-drafting the brief.

The third principle to be kept in mind when drafting the brief is
accuracy. Courts will not be persuaded by the advocate's argument if
they cannot trust him to present a fair and accurate version of the
facts and law. An advocate who conveys inaccurate information to the
court risks alienating the judges who will be deciding his case. To
insure the accuracy of the law and facts in the brief, the advocate

should verify that all quotations and citations are correct and used in the proper context. In addition, the advocate should examine the facts he discusses in the brief to be sure that they can be traced to the record and are an accurate depiction of the factual setting presented therein.

Although it may appear an unnecessary warning, nothing can be more distracting to the court than faulty spelling, grammar, or syntax. Mistakes of this sort interrupt the smooth flow of the written argument. Instead of concentrating on the advocate's presentation of the case, the court will ponder the advocate's errors. Elementary errors can be corrected easily by referring to dictionaries and English usage texts. The following books are useful as handy references to proper grammer syntax, and style:

1. W. Strunk and E. B. White, *The Elements of Style* (3d ed., 1979).
2. J. M. and A. K. Walsh, *Plain English Handbook* (5th ed., 1966).
3. H. Weihofen, *Legal Writing Style* (2d ed., 1980).

V. PRESENTING THE ARGUMENT

Persuasive brief writing involves more than the careful selection and arrangement of contentions, and the proper structuring of paragraphs and sentences. The stuff of the brief is the persuasive analysis which weds the legal authorities supporting the contentions to the facts of the case and public policy considerations. In order to achieve such an effect with the facts and law at his disposal, the advocate must be able to apply these tools of persuasion to a reasoned analysis of his legal authorities.

A. Persuading the Court

The advocate should always keep in mind that he is writing for a very select audience. Appellate court judges and their law clerks are generally well-versed in the law, skilled in the reasoning process, and unusually sophisticated in their ability to perceive logical inconsistencies in superficially sound arguments. Extreme caution must be taken never to underestimate the intellectual capacities of the court—the result will more often than not prove fatal to the advocate's case.

Despite their skills, however, appellate court judges may be unfamiliar with the specific area of the law upon which the advocate's legal strategy rests. Until informed by the advocate, the court is likely to know nothing of the specific facts of the case on appeal. In order to convince the court that his client should prevail, the advocate must not only persuade, but also inform.

The task of effectively informing the court of the applicable law and relevant facts can be very difficult. The advocate must be careful neither to insult the court with overly simplistic analysis, nor to lose the court in a maze of esoteric and highly complex points of law. One method of avoiding these two extremes entails making an effort to simplify and clarify the arguments while drafting and re-drafting the brief. Another method involves inviting others to read and criticize portions of the brief. Generally speaking, it is preferable to favor simplicity over complexity. The advocate must, however, guard against any inference of intellectual condescension; the advocate's goal is to convince the court, not to alienate it.

Advocates often forget that courts are composed of human beings, with the same concerns and frailties as other members of society. Like the advocate, judges can be moved by eloquent arguments and clear evidence of injustice, or find themselves bored by dull, unimaginative briefs. Judges will understand the advocate's argument only if they carefully read the entire brief. Thus, the advocate must write a brief which captures the judge's attention.

When reviewing a case, courts of appeal generally have as their objective a fair and just result consistent with established legal principles. In order to persuade the court to adopt his argument as the proper determination of the case, the advocate must weave into the brief three components: the facts of the case, the legal principles bearing on those facts, and the equitable consequences resulting from combining the facts with the law.

B. Combining Facts and Law

The winning brief is a successful welding together of persuasive facts and compelling legal principles. Courts rarely decide cases strictly on grounds of *stare decisis*, as no two cases ever involve identical factual situations. As a result, the advocate should never argue legal principles in the abstract; rather, he should use the facts of his case to interpret and explain legal principles. The following example shows the abstract nature of an argument based solely on law:

```
     Section 8(d) of the N.L.R.A., 29 U.S.C.
§ 158(d), defines collective bargaining as
"the performance of the mutual obligation
of the employer and the representatives to
meet at reasonable times and confer in good
faith with respect to wages, hours and
other terms of employment." Section 8(a)
(5) makes it an unfair labor practice for
```

an employer to refuse to "bargain collectively with the representatives of his employees" with respect to decisions which
affect such terms of employment. 29 U.S.C.
§ 158(a)(5). Furthermore, this Court recognized in <u>Fibreboard</u> that an employer's
decision to <u>terminate</u> all employees in a
bargaining unit vitally affects the interests of employees. Because the Firm has
refused to bargain with the lawyer-associates, the Firm has violated § 158(a)(5)
of the Act.

Contrast the preceding example with the following analysis which com-
bines the law with the facts of the case:

Section 8(a)(5) makes it an unfair labor
practice for an employer to refuse to "bargain collectively with the representatives
of his employees" with respect to decisions
which affect such terms of employment. 29
U.S.C. § 158(a)(5). Furthermore, this
Court recognized in <u>Fibreboard</u> that an employer's decision to <u>terminate</u> all employees in a bargaining unit vitally affects
the interests of employees.

The associates at Smith & Jones have invested years of their lives specializing in
the real estate matters handled by the
Firm. Whether their specific skills are
saleable in the present market is unclear.
It is clear, however, that the Firm's decision to reorganize the partnership directly threatens their livelihoods and this
vitally affects their interests. As a result, the Firm has a duty under sections
8(d) and 8(a)(5) of the Act, as well as
this Court's holding in <u>Fibreboard</u>, to bargain with the representative of the associates.

The use of facts to interpret and explain the abstract legal principles not only clarifies the law, but permits the judge reading the brief
to apply the law in a manner favorable to the advocate and his client.

This is because courts are composed of human beings; and, given their concern for just results, courts are more likely to be moved by the application of the facts of the case to the law than by the mere recitation of legal principles in the abstract.

C. Presenting Favorable Precedents

Legal precedents are worthless standing alone; their only value lies in supporting a principle of law which the advocate espouses. By drawing analogies between the facts of the precedent case and facts of the case on appeal, the advocate can demonstrate the application of the precedent.

Favorable precedents are handled in various ways depending upon their function. A general rule is that the greater the importance of the principle being advanced, the greater the attention devoted to the precedent which supports that principle. Thus, when using a precedent in support of a proposition which is fundamental to his contention, the advocate would provide the appellate tribunal with a terse statement of the facts of the precedent which relate to the espoused principle, as well as the holding in the precedent case. The advocate should then blend the reasoning of the holding with a favorable comparison between the facts of the precedent and the instant case, as counsel for Petitioner in *Peggy v. Smith & Jones* has done:

> In Fibreboard Paper Products Corp. v. NLRB, 379 U.S. 203 (1964), this Court concluded that Section 8 does not require an employer to bargain about every business decision which results in termination of employees or which is suitable for discussion at the bargaining table. As Justice Stewart explained in his concurring opinion in Fibreboard, some decisions are so basic to the scope and direction of the employer's enterprise that to require bargaining about them would interfere with the "prerogatives of private business management." 379 U.S. at 223. As an illustration of such a decision, Justice Stewart noted that Section 8(d) does not require an employer to bargain about a decision to liquidate its assets and go out of business. 379 U.S. at 223.
>
> In the present case the Firm's decision to reorganize the partnership will result in neither a dissolution of the business

```
nor a liquidation of assets.  Rather, upon
termination of the existing partnership
agreement, the partners of Smith & Jones
will simultaneously enter into a new part-
nership agreement with the partners of Wind
& Zephyr.  Thereafter, the partners will
continue to carry on their business "as
usual."  Notably, they will continue to
work in the same building, use the same law
library, serve the same clients, and spe-
cialize in the same area of the law (R. 26-
27).  The only significant change in oper-
ations will be the assistance by associates
who are not represented by a union (R. 13).
In this respect the situation in the pre-
sent case is remarkably similar to that in
Fibreboard.  Here, as in Fibreboard, the
decision to reorganize will not result in
a major change in the nature and direction
of the employer's business:  "the same work
will be done at the same location under
similar conditions of employment."  379
U.S. at 215.
```

Petitioner here uses the holding and reasoning in *Fibreboard* as a basis for alleging violations of the National Labor Relations Act, and to demonstrate the similarity between the facts in the two cases. By using a quotation from Justice Stewart's concurring opinion, Petitioner establishes a standard against which she measures the respondent's actions to prove that the facts in the case require the same legal conclusion as that reached by the Supreme Court in *Fibreboard*.

When concluding his analysis of the precedent, the advocate may also wish to direct the court to other cases which contain similar holdings, based on closely-related facts. This technique is an effective and concise means of showing the court that the legal principle being advanced is recognized in other jurisdictions and contexts. Because these concluding cases will not be binding upon the court, they should not be analyzed at length. The advocate should merely cite the cases and describe them briefly so the court may investigate them if it wishes. Counsel for Petitioner in *Peggy* utilized this technique when, after a lengthy analysis of the *Eisenberg* case, she invited the court's attention to a number of other cases involving injunctions against employers issued to protect unions:

```
. . . The court in Eisenberg held that the
public interest in ongoing collective bar-
```

gaining--one of the cornerstones of the National Labor Relations Act--and the predomi-
nating interest of the majority of workers
who favored the currently certified representative militated against issuance of an
injunction.

In a number of cases the same considerations of protecting the membership of a
particular union have caused the courts to
issue injunctions.　In Brown v. Pacific
Telephone and Telegraph Co., 218 F.2d 542
(9th Cir. 1954), an injunction was issued
requiring the employer to bargain with the
designated representative to prevent union
members from "drifting away" from the
union.　The court granted an injunction to
prevent the employers from giving non-negotiable pay raises to certain employees
pending the adjudication of refusal-to-
bargain charges in American Gypsum Co. v.
Price, 81 Lab. Cas. ¶ 13,142 (10th Cir.
1977).　And, in Kennedy v. Telecomputing
Corp., 43 Lab. Cas. ¶ 17,297 (S.D. Cal.
1961), the court enjoined the employer from
paying union scale wages after unilaterally
removing the union's representative.

In this example, counsel used *Brown*, *American Gypsum*, and *Kennedy*
to supplement her analysis of *Eisenberg*. Because the cases are generally consistent, but not exactly on point, with *Eisenberg*, she provides the
court with the citation and a synopsis of these cases, to permit the
court to examine them at its discretion.

When providing the tribunal with additional cases, however, the
advocate should be careful not to string cite merely to demonstrate to
the court the extent of his research. Long lists of citations are not a
particularly effective method of persuasion, as judges often ignore what
appears to be a mass of cases thrust upon them in this manner. Citing
only one or two significant decisions following the analysis of an important and favorable precedent will often be far more effective than a list
of similarly-decided cases.

Courts often create explicit standards or tests with which to determine the outcome of cases; the advocate should always employ these
tests when they appear in a favorable precedent. The most effective

way to make use of the test is to articulate the holding and facts of the precedent, quote or paraphrase the test, and use the facts of the instant case to show that each of the requisite factors are met:

> The court in Douds explained the precise requirements for the issuance of a Section 10(j) injunction in this matter:
>
>> The requirements of a prima facie case are met when the factual jurisdictional requirements are shown, and credible evidence is presented which, if uncontradicted would warrant the granting of the requested relief . . . . Douds v. International Brotherhood of Teamsters, Local 294, supra, 75 F.Supp. at 418.
>
> The opinion further emphasized that the court should not be concerned with finding ultimate facts, since the actual adjudication of the charges is the exclusive domain of the Board itself. Douds, supra; accord, National Licorice Co. v. NLRB, 309 U.S. 350 (1940).
>
> Measured by the criteria set forth in Douds, the NLRB has clearly met its burden of proof.

This technique reminds the court of the test to be applied, explains the factual context in which the test was originally created, and aids the court by applying the test to the facts under review. In addition, the application of the test will show that the legal principle being advanced should be adopted by the court in accordance with the precedent case.

If the court test to be applied by the advocate is a lengthy one, it is usually preferable to paraphrase the test rather than quoting it verbatim. The test applied by the United States Supreme Court in *Textile Workers Union of America v. Darlington Mfg. Co.*, 380 U.S. 263 (1965), to determine a violation of § 8(a)(3) of the N.L.R.A. is as follows:

> . . . the persons exercising control over the plant that is being closed for anti-union reasons (1) have an interest in an-

other business, whether or not affiliated with or engaged in the same line of commercial activity as the closed plant, of sufficient substantiability to give promise of their reaping of a benefit from the discouragement of unionism in that business; (2) act to close their plant with the purpose of producing such a result; and (3) occupying a relationship to the other business which makes it realistically foreseeable that its employees will fear that such business will be closed down if they persist in organizational activities . . .

The length and wording of the *Darlington* test makes it a somewhat clumsy standard to be applied as an effective test. In such a case, the advocate should paraphrase and simplify the test, retaining its substance while using language which makes the test easier to apply to the facts of the case:

The Court in Darlington established a three-prong test to determine if an employer who closes his plant for anti-union purposes has violated section 8(a)(3) of the Act.

1. The person exercising control over the plant must have an interest in another business sufficiently connected to the plant being closed such that the employer would benefit from the discouragement of unionism at the second business;

2. The employer must close the plant with the purpose of producing this result; and

3. The employer must be so related to the other business that it is realistically foreseeable that the employees of the other business will fear that it will be closed if they persist in organizational activities.

Darlington, supra, 380 U.S. at 275-276.

By paraphrasing and restructuring the court test, the advocate makes the test more comprehensible and, therefore, more persuasive, when applied to the facts of the case on appeal.

In determining which cases are favorable to his contentions, the advocate should remember that few precedents are ever "on all fours" with the facts of the case on appeal. The facts of precedent cases must be carefully studied and compared to those in the instant case, so that the advocate knows in exactly what ways the two cases are similar, and how they differ. This additional study will prevent the advocate from presenting a case as "on point," only to have the opposition counsel distinguish it and render the precedent inapplicable.

All points of law discussed in the brief, no matter how basic they may seem to be to the advocate, should be supported by legal authority. When a precedent case is used in support of a collateral point in the advocate's argument, however, it is sufficient to cite the case after articulating the point of law involved, without engaging in the more detailed analysis reserved for precedent cases supporting more important legal principles:

> The federal courts agree that for the NLRB to obtain a Section 10(j) injunction, it must demonstrate reasonable cause to believe that an unfair labor practice has occurred. See, e.g., Eisenberg v. Hartz Mountain Corp., 519 F.2d 138 (3rd Cir. 1974); Boire v. International Brotherhood of Teamsters, 479 F.2d 778 (5th Cir. 1973); Angle v. Sacks, 382 F.2d 655 (10th Cir. 1967).

The advocate may, of course, decide that the precedent deserves a somewhat more extended analysis, and discuss it accordingly.

Should the advocate be fortunate enough to be in a position to choose from a number of precedents supporting the same principle of law, the case from the highest court within that jurisdiction should be selected. If a state law principle is involved, the advocate should select a state supreme court precedent. If no state supreme court precedent exists, a precedent from the appellate court of the local jurisdiction should be used. This same analysis holds true for federal courts when discussing federal law principles. Thus, in *Peggy*, the advocates support their principal legal contentions with holdings from the United States Supreme Court.

Precedent cases may also be grouped together to reinforce a legal principle espoused by the advocate, or to show the history and development of a point of law. When grouping together precedents, the advocate should articulate each precedent's holding and the relevant facts in a manner such that the court can easily follow the development of the analysis. This is particularly important when the advocate weaves into this analysis the facts of the instant case. Counsel for Petitioner in *Peggy* used this technique when she demonstrated that intrastate law firms come within the jurisdiction of federal regulations:

> This Court has repeatedly recognized that local transactions can have nationwide commercial implications. In N.L.R.B. v. Jones and Laughlin Steel Corp., 301 U.S. 1 (1937), this Court held that steel production that is completely intrastate affects the nation's commerce. Likewise, in N.L.R.B. v. Fainblatt, supra, 306 U.S. 601 (1939), this Court held that one small sewing shop engaged in stitching together precut fabric for a larger manufacturer affects commerce. Similarly, in Polish National Alliance v. N.L.R.B., 322 U.S. 643 (1944), this Court concluded that a labor dispute in an intrastate business affects commerce if it is representative of other, similar disputes nationwide.
>
> Furthermore, the N.L.R.B. has recently held that labor disputes affecting federally funded community legal service offices affect commerce sufficiently to invoke the Board's jurisdiction. Wayne County Neighborhood Legal Services, Inc., 229 N.L.R.B. No. 171, Lab. L. Rep. (CCH) ¶ 18,229 (1977); Camden Regional Services, Inc., 231 N.L.R.B. No. 47, Lab. L. Rep. (CCH) ¶ 18,430 (1977). Inasmuch as the labor dispute at Smith & Jones affects both a private law practice and the services rendered at a federally funded community legal center (R. 20), the dispute is within the N.L.R.B.'s statutory jurisdiction.

By grouping together the legal precedents in this manner, counsel for Petitioner in *Peggy* shows how the legal principle evolved over the years, and applies the principle to the facts of her case.

D. Confronting Unfavorable Precedents

The advocate should deal with unfavorable precedents in the same manner as favorable precedents—the more damning the precedent, or the more important the legal principle threatened by the unfavorable precedent, the greater the effort in dealing with it.

If the advocate is confronted with a major precedent which calls into question the validity of a legal principle fundamental to the advocate's contentions, he cannot ignore the unfavorable precedent. The advocate has a duty as an officer of the court to inform the tribunal of all the relevant law. And, much as the advocate may wish it, the unfavorable precedent will not go unnoticed. The opposition counsel will most likely rely upon the case in his brief, and the court will distrust the advocate for attempting to conceal the precedent. Because the court's confidence in the advocate is a necessary prerequisite to his ability to persuade, the advocate must confront the precedents, no matter how damaging they may be to the argument.

By confronting these unfavorable precedents in his brief, the advocate not only preserves his credibility with the reviewing court, but also provides himself with the opportunity to place the potentially damaging precedent in the context most favorable to his argument. By confronting the case and distinguishing it in some manner in his brief, the advocate dilutes the effect of the unfavorable precedent, rendering the precedent much less damaging than it would be if it were discussed only in the opposition brief.

Unfavorable precedents which directly threaten a fundamental legal principle can be dealt with in two ways. The easiest and most effective method of countering such unfavorable precedents is to distinguish their facts from those of the instant case. One way to distinguish factually is to demonstrate to the court that, because the facts of the two cases are different, different legal principles apply to each factual situation. Thus, counsel for Respondent in *Peggy* might distinguish two unfavorable precedents in this manner:

```
The facts in the instant case show Smith &
Jones to be an independent partnership, and
not part of a single employer enterprise,
as in Darlington or Lees.  Unlike Smith &
Jones, Darlington was a subsidiary corpora-
tion, completely controlled and in an "al-
ter-ego" relationship with the parent cor-
poration.  No such "alter-ego" relationship
exists between Smith & Jones and Wind &
Zephyr.  Likewise, the relationship be-
```

tween the three businesses in Lees bears no
resemblance to the two law firms in the instant case. The businesses in Lees are
horizontally integrated, with the businesses, despite their separate formal entities,
controlled by the same entrepreneur. In
this case, the two law firms are not horizontally integrated, and no partner in
either firm has any financial interest in,
or managerial control over, the other.

The unfavorable precedent can also be distinguished from the case on
appeal by showing that, while the same legal principles apply to both
sets of facts, discrepancies between the two factual situations require
that a different conclusion be drawn from the legal principle when
applied to each case:

Furthermore, the Firm's decision to reorganize is not based upon considerations
which would tend to make bargaining meaningless. In this respect the Firm's decision is distinguishable from those of several employers who have been found by lower
courts to have no statutory duty to bargain
about terminating or relocating parts of
their ongoing businesses, because "[n]o
amount of collective bargaining could erase
the economic facts that gave rise to the
[employer's] decision. . . ." NLRB v.
Thompson Transport Co., 406 F.2d 698, 703
(8th Cir. 1969). In Thompson Transport the
employer decided to close one of his two
oil terminals after losing the major part
of his business in the town where one of
them was located. See also, NLRB v. Transmarine Navigation Corp., 380 F.2d 933 (9th
Cir. 1967) (where, in order to avoid losing
his principal customer due to the physical
inadequacies of his shipyard facilities,
the employer decided to close his Los
Angeles shipyard and to enter into a joint
venture to provide expanded facilities in
the Long Beach Harbor); NLRB v. Royal Plating and Polishing Co., 350 F.2d 191 (3d
Cir. 1965) (where the employer was charged
with an unfair labor practice after he ac-

cepted a "take it or litigate it" offer
from a housing authority which had condemned the property on which one of his
plants was located).

There is no evidence in the present case
that collective bargaining could not erase
the economic facts giving rise to the
Firm's decision to reorganize. For this
reason, and because the considerations involved here are particularly suitable for
discussion at the bargaining table, the
decision to reorganize the partnership is
subject to the collective bargaining requirements of the Act.

Since the court seeks legal principles applicable to the facts of the case
on appeal, such distinctions will remove much of the power of the
unfavorable precedent.

Should the unfavorable precedent threaten a less fundamental or
collateral point of law, the precedent can be distinguished in a summary
fashion. If a collateral point of law has been both favorably and un-
favorably analyzed by the courts, the unfavorable precedent can be
used to show the veracity of the favorable one. Contrasting favorable
and unfavorable precedents can be achieved through the use of con-
junctive adverbs. Respondent in *Peggy v. Smith & Jones* could use
this technique advantageously by writing:

While the distinction between managerial
and operational decisions has frequently
been discussed by courts during the past
decade, the trend is toward finding operational decisions which are subject to mandatory bargaining. In NLRB v. Adams Dairy,
Inc., the Eighth Circuit Court of Appeals
determined that a decision to terminate delivery employees and subcontract the services to independent contractors was a managerial decision; as a result, the court
held that the decision to terminate was not
subject of mandatory bargaining. In Fibreboard, however, this Court held that the
employer-manufacturer was required to bargain concerning the termination of maintenance employees. The Fibreboard court thus

distinguished managerial decisions from
those which affect only working conditions.

An even more effective method of using the unfavorable precedent to the advocate's advantage is to dispose of the unfavorable case in an introductory subordinate clause, to be followed by a more extensive analysis of the favorable precedent in the independent clause and succeeding sentences. Accordingly, Respondent in the *Peggy* case might phrase the argument as follows:

The distinction between managerial and operational decisions has frequently been
discussed by courts during the past decade.
The trend is toward finding operational decisions which are subject to mandatory bargaining. While the court in NLRB v. Adams
Dairy, Inc. determined that the decision to
terminate the delivery end of its operations and subcontract those services was
not a mandatory subject of bargaining, the
Fibreboard court distinguished that reasoning on the basis of managerial control involved. This Court in Fibreboard held that
the employer-manufacturer was required to
bargain concerning the termination of maintenance employees at the plant. In so doing, the Court drew a distinction between
decisions which are inherently managerial,
and those which do not go to the "core of
entrepreneurial control." Fibreboard Paper
Products v. NLRB, supra, 379 U.S. at 223.

The advocate thus is able to point out the unfavorable precedent to the court, distinguish it, and use the unfavorable case to introduce a precedent which supports the advocate's legal contentions.

A less desirable means of dealing with an unfavorable precedent is to attack directly the validity of its holding. One of two methods of attacking a precedent is usually employed. The advocate can either demonstrate that the precedent was decided incorrectly, pointing out flaws in the reasoning and analysis in the case; or the precedent can be attacked by a showing of changed circumstances. The latter means of discrediting an unfavorable precedent requires the advocate to examine the subsequent history of the holding enunciated in the case in order to show that the underlying justification for the holding no longer exists.

If the advocate can develop a strong argument that the holding in the precedent, while valid when written, has become an anomoly, he may be successful in convincing the court to overrule or distinguish the prior case.

Since both methods of directly attacking the unfavorable precedent require the appellate court to void the precedent, the advocate should realize that he is fighting an uphill battle. Courts are very reluctant to overrule cases. The burden imposed on the advocate who argues for such a result may, for all practical purposes, be insurmountable. Given the choice, the advocate should always opt for distinguishing the unfavorable precedent on the facts, and thus not force the court to void the precedent. It is only when the facts cannot be distinguished that the advocate should consider a direct attack on the unfavorable precedent.

E.   Effective Presentation of Statutes

Statutes are employed in much the same manner as precedent cases to support legal propositions. If the statute clearly supports the affected proposition, the advocate should quote from or paraphrase the statute, interpret the statute while reiterating the contention being advanced, and demonstrate how the facts of the case on appeal bring the case within the scope of the statute:

> There is reasonable cause to believe that Smith & Jones is engaging in a labor practice that is prohibited by section 8(a)(5) of the Act. Section 8(a)(5) declares that it is an unfair labor practice for an employer "to refuse to bargain collectively with the representatives of his employees . . ." Section 8(d) of the Act defines collective bargaining to include bargaining over wages, hours and other terms and conditions of employment or any question arising thereunder. The decision by Smith & Jones to dissolve and reorganize the partnership is a term and condition of employment to those associates who will be terminated, yet the Firm steadfastly refuses to bargain with the Union over this decision. This refusal to bargain thus constitutes an unfair labor practice under section 8(a)(5) of the Act.

By quoting from the applicable statute, defining its terms through the use of another statute, and applying the statute to the facts of the case, the advocate not only provides the court with an interpretation of the legislation, but also shows how the statute bears upon the case on appeal.

On occasion, the advocate will be fortunate enough to find support for his legal proposition in both case and statutory form. This usually occurs when a statute has been interpreted and upheld by subsequent court decisions. Counsel for Petitioner in *Peggy* was able to use a statute in conjunction with caselaw to argue that the law firm had reorganized in order to discourage union membership:

> Section 8(a)(3) of the Act provides that it
> shall be an unfair labor practice for an
> employer "by discrimination in regard to
> hire or tenure of appointment to encourage
> or discourage membership in any labor orga-
> nization." 29 U.S.C. § 158(a)(3). In
> Textile Workers Union of America v. Dar-
> lington Mfg. Co., 380 U.S. 263 (1965), this
> Court held that section 8(a)(3) is violated
> when an employer may reasonably foresee
> that discrimination in regard to tenure of
> employment will discourage union membership
> and discriminates between union and non-
> union employees for that purpose.
>
> The plan to reorganize the operation of
> the Firm discriminates between union and.
> non-union employees in terms of employment,
> in violation of section 8(a)(3) and the
> holding in Darlington, as Petitioner sub-
> mits that the Firm may reasonably foresee
> that the plan will have a chilling effect
> upon unionization. Furthermore, the Firm's
> purpose in dissolving the partnership and
> executing a new partnership agreement is to
> discourage further unionization of employ-
> ees . . ..

This combination of statutory and case analysis provides the advocate with a compelling foundation upon which to build his proposition. By positing the legal contention, supporting it with both statutory and case law analysis, and demonstrating the interrelationship between the proposition, legal support, and the facts of the case, the advocate provides the court with a virtually unassailable argument in favor of the contention.

While statutes can provide valuable support for a legal argument, they may also threaten legal arguments crucial to the advocate's strategy. An unfavorable statute is dealt with in a manner similar to that employed in refuting unfavorable precedents. The most successful method of discounting the effectiveness of an unfavorable statute is to show that the statute does not control the subject matter of the case, either because the statute relates to a different jurisdiction, or because the statute governs conduct not relevant to the case on appeal. Thus, in *Peggy v. Smith & Jones,* a hypothetical state statute permitting management to lock out workers during periods of national security crises could be distinguished on grounds of both jurisdiction and subject matter.

If the unfavorable statute cannot be distinguished, the advocate must either interpret the statute in a manner favorable to his strategy, or attempt to convince the court to void the statute. Voiding a statute usually requires an analysis showing that the unfavorable statute is somehow in conflict with the applicable constitution. This is the least favored means of confronting an unfavorable statute. Unless the statute impinges upon a fundamental civil right or liberty, courts traditionally impose an almost irrefutable presumption in favor of a legislative enactment.

The advocate will find that attempting to re-interpret the statute is preferable to challenging its constitutionality. Particularly when the statute is drafted in ambiguous terms, the advocate may be able to demonstrate to the court that the statute does not mean what it purports to say. The general rule of statutory construction requires the advocate to search within the statute for its meaning. But when the language of the statute affords more than one interpretation, the legislative history and subsequent construction of the act should be examined. In this manner, the advocate may be able to develop an alternate interpretation of the statute and its effect on the facts of the instant case which mitigate the previously unfavorable effect of the statute.

F. Effective Use of Quotations

Quotations from cited cases or statutes can be an effective means of showing legal support for a proposition. But it must be remembered that the purpose of the brief is to persuade the court with logically reasoned arguments, not to provide the court with a digest of applicable quotations. Appellate court judges frequently read cases on their own, but they should not be required to conjure up the legal propositions and arguments which should be in the brief.

Quotations are best used in a limited number of circumstances. One effective use is to provide an eloquent statement of a point of law which cannot be more persuasively articulated by the advocate, as counsel for Petitioner in *Peggy* demonstrates when discussing why employees must be permitted to bargain over the effect of the reorganization:

> The profound significance of this issue as a mandatory subject for bargaining is recognized by the Board. In explaining its approach to section 8(d) problems the Board has stated:
>
> > [J]ust as the employer's interest in the protection of his capital investment is entitled to consideration in our interpretation of the Act, so too is the employee's interest in the protection of his livelihood.
> >
> > For, just as the employer has invested capital in the business, so the employee has invested years of his working life, accumulating seniority, accruing pension rights, and developing skills that may or may not be salable to another employer. Ozark Trailers Inc., 161 N.L.R.B. 561, 566 (1966).
>
> The associates at Smith & Jones have invested years of their lives specializing in the real estate matters handled by the Firm. One of the associates, for example, has been with the Firm for eight years (R. 21). Whether their special skills are salable in the present market is unclear. It is clear, however, that the Firm's decision to reorganize the partnership directly threatens their livelihoods and thus vitally affects their interests. Consequently, the Firm has a duty under sections 8(d) and 8(a)(5) of the Act to bargain with the representative of the associates.

Also effective is the use of quotations to present to the court a succinctly worded test which has been applied by past tribunals:

> In that matter, the Board decided to assert jurisdiction over a California corporation engaging in processing, addressing and mailing materials submitted to it by customers. The Board explained the application of the standard in this manner:
>> [J]urisdiction is asserted over all non-retail enterprises which have an <u>outflow or inflow across State lines of at least $50,000, whether such outflow or inflow be regarded as direct or indirect</u>. . . . In applying this standard, the Board will adhere to its past practice of adding direct and indirect outflow, or direct and indirect inflow. <u>Siemons Mailing Service</u>, <u>supra</u>, 122 N.L.R.B. at 85 (emphasis in original).

Finally, quotations can be used to add emphasis to a heavily relied-upon precedent. Usually only the holding of the case is quoted:

> In <u>Camden Regional Legal Services, Inc.</u>, 231 N.L.R.B. No. 47 (1977-1978) Lab. L. Rep. (CCH) ¶ 18,430 (1977), the Board set out the jurisdictional guideline to be applied to law firms. In <u>Camden</u>, the employer was a nonprofit legal corporation with gross annual revenues of $900,000. In asserting its jurisdiction, the Board stated:
>> We have examined the most recent empirical data collected by the Bureau of the Census and the American Bar Association and are of the opinion and find that it will effectuate the policies of the Act to limit our assertion of jurisdiction over law firms in general and legal assistance programs such as those involved herein to those that receive at least $250,000 in gross annual revenues. (1977-1978) (CCH) NLRB ¶ 18,430 at 30,615.

Misuse or ineffective use of quotations is less persuasive than not using any quotations at all. The advocate should be careful that he reproduces the quotation verbatim or clearly indicates to the court where changes have been made. In addition, quotations should never be used when they can be read out of context. Courts recognizing such misrepresentation will suspect all other quotations and citations. Only those portions of the quotation absolutely necessary to the brief should be reproduced, as lengthy quotations are almost never read by the courts. And the advocate should be careful not to overuse the technique of quoting from precedent cases. Overuse decreases the impact of the technique, as the court will come to think that the advocate is relying on the words of prior courts, rather than his own reasoning, to persuade.

The advocate will often desire not to quote verbatim from a precedent case, either because the ideas can be conveyed more succinctly and persuasively by the advocate himself or because the quotation, when read apart from the text of the decision, takes on a different meaning. In these instances, the court's discussion should be paraphrased, with a citation to the text of the precedent where the original language can be found:

> As an illustration of such a decision, justice Stewart noted that Section 8(d) does not require an employer to bargain about a decision to liquidate its assets and go out of business. *Fibreboard*, *supra*, 379 U.S. at 223.

The use of paraphrasing also has the effect of decreasing the number of quotations in the brief, adding to the smooth flow of its reading. But, when paraphrasing, the advocate must take great care not to misrepresent the decision.

Persuasive brief writing is thus an art which cannot be mastered without much time and effort. The successful appellate advocate must be able to select and arrange contentions in an effective manner. In addition, he must be skilled in the various methods of structuring sentences and paragraphs and know how persuasive word use enhances his legal propositions. Finally, the advocate must have the ability to analyze persuasively those precedents and statutes which support his contentions and be able to diminish the effect of unfavorable legal authorities. When used properly, these elements of persuasive brief writing will enable the advocate both to make the court understand the facts and legal contentions which he advances, and persuade the court that the advocate's argument is legally and equitably required.

Chapter Three

GENERAL RULES OF STYLE AND
CITATION OF AUTHORITIES

Just as it is important to be persuasive in the style and presentation of a brief, it is also important to supplement such arguments with proper, clear, and informative citations. This chapter is designed to give the reader an understanding of the proper use of citation forms and to provide him with a quick reference to the rules governing basic citation forms for legal pleading.

The citation to authorities in the text of a brief must complement the persuasive style of the argument without interrupting its flow. With this in mind, the standard citation forms described in this chapter should be followed as the generally accepted method of citation. Explanations and suggestions follow the presentation of many of the basic rules, so that these rules may be adapted to citation of authorities not commonly used, or for use in non-standard presentations in a brief.

I. GENERAL RULES OF STYLE

A. Abbreviations

Abbreviations generally should be avoided unless substantial space is saved and the resulting abbreviation is not ambiguous. However, well-known statutes, agencies and organizations may be designated by initials or other appropriate abbreviation once the full name has been presented and the proposed abbreviation introduced.

```
The injunction restrained Smith & Jones from
changing its operational structure pending
final disposition of certain proceedings
presently before the National Labor Rela-
tions Board (hereinafter referred to inter-
changeably as "the NLRB" or "the Board").
```

Generally, every abbreviation in which the last letter of the original word is not included and set off from the rest of the abbreviation by an apostrophe should be followed by a period (*thus*: Bldg., Co., Corp., Ry.; *but*: Ass'n, Dep't, Gov't, Nat'l). But widely recognized initials which are generally read as initials rather than as the words they represent (*e.g.*, FTC, NLRB, UCLA; *but*, N.L.R.A.,N.Y.) may be used without periods in the text of the brief and in case names. Names of states and the "United States" should not be abbreviated, except as they may appear in the citation to a case or statutory reporter.

Abbreviations in citations must be used to designate the title of a reporter, a code abbreviation, or the name of the court of decision. The proper abbreviation for the citation of a particular authority is usually given in the front pages of that source. When initials are used in the citation, periods are required to separate the initials. Thus:

<u>Ozark Trailers Inc.</u>, 161 N.L.R.B. 561 (1966).

Note that periods are always used in a citation, inasmuch as the citation is a formal designation. Textual abbreviations, however, are less formal and may be presented without periods. Often these decisions—whether to abbreviate a certain word—will be left to the advocate's discretion. Clarity and purpose should guide the advocate in making this decision.

B. Capitalization

The function of capitalization is to give distinction, importance, and emphasis to words. Thus the first word of a sentence is capitalized to indicate distinctively and emphatically that a new sentence has begun. Moreover, proper nouns are capitalized to signify the special importance of these words as the official names of particular persons, places, and things. A number of words, however, may function either as proper nouns or as common nouns—for example, terms like "petitioner" or "court." Capitalization practices vary widely. This variation reflects the relative importance each writer assigns to the word in question.

1. Capitalization of Specific Words

The following words are capitalized only in the following situations:

"Act"—when part of a proper name given in full: The National Labor Relations Act ... the Act.

"Bill"—when part of a proper name given in full.

"Circuit"—when used with the circuit number: Ninth Circuit.

"Code"—when referring to a specific code: The 1939 and 1954 Tax Codes.

"Constitution"—when referring to the United States Constitution. *Exception*: federal constitution. This is because reference to the Constitution merely as the federal constitution is usually only used in distinguishing a state constitution rather than directly referring to any particular provision of the Constitution. When referring directly to the Constitution, do not use "federal constitution." Parts of the Constitution are not capitalized individually or in connection with a citation to the Constitution: article III, fifth amendment. U.S. Const. art. I. § 9, cl. 2, U.S. Const. amend. XIV, § 2; *but*: Bill of Rights, Commerce Clause, or First Amendment rights (*i.e.*, when using a part of the Constitution as a proper noun).

"Court"—when naming any court in full: The Supreme Court of California; but, this state's supreme court. The Court of Appeals for the Second Circuit or the Second Circuit Court of Appeals; but, the court of appeals. Always capitalize "Court" when referring to the United States Supreme Court. Also, when referring to the court to which the brief is being submitted, "Court" should be capitalized.

Thus:

```
"This Court is urged to find that
sufficient jurisdiction exists for the
NLRB to petition the Court for an
injunction."
```

"Federal"—when the word it modifies is capitalized, and when discussing particular rules in the text of the brief: Federal Rules of Civil Procedure. However, both "Constitution" and "federal" are not capitalized when used together.

"Government"—when it is an unmodified noun standing alone meaning the United States government.

"Justice"—when referring to a Justice of the United States Supreme Court.

"National"—when the word it modifies is capitalized.

"Rule"—when part of a proper name given in full.

"Section"—only when used as a proper noun designation; *thus*: "Petitioner seeks a Section 10(j) injunction," *but*: "Petitioner seeks an injunction pursuant to section 10(j) of the Act." Likewise, "Petitioner alleges a Section 8(a)(5) violation," *but*: "Respondent acted in violation of section 8(a)(5)."

2. Capitalization of Famous Old Statutes and Rules

The names of famous old statutes and rules, such as the Statute of Frauds and the Rule Against Perpetuities, are customarily capitalized. Note, however, that "statute of limitations" is not capitalized.

3. Words Denoting Groups or Officeholders

Certain words are capitalized when used to refer to a specific group, officeholder, or government body. For example: the Agency, the Commission, the Congress, the Legislature, the President. On the other hand, these words are not capitalized when used as adjectives. For example: legislative decision, agency administration.

4. Title of Parties

Titles are often used as pronouns to denote the parties to an action. This serves two purposes: it reminds the court of the procedural posture of the case, and the party bringing the appeal; and it is used to group a number of individual parties aligned on one side of the action. Thus, the terms Appellant, Appellee, Plaintiff, Defendant, Petitioner, and Respondent are capitalized when used to identify parties to the appeal. These terms, however, are never capitalized when referring to a party in another action (*i. e.*, in discussing the facts of an authority cited in the brief):

```
In that case, the court held that the peti-
tioner did have reasonable cause; similarly,
Petitioner in this case has reasonable cause
to believe unfair labor practices were com-
mitted.
```

5. Capitalization Within Quotations

The first word of a quotation is usually capitalized to indicate distinctively and emphatically that a new sentence has begun. However, quotations are often most effective in a brief when they are woven into the context of a textual sentence or introduction. In those cases, capitalization of the first word of the quotation will vary. The following examples from Petitioner's brief in *Peggy v. Smith & Jones* demonstrate the change in capitalization in relation to how the quotation is used.

a. Quotation of a complete sentence following an introductory statement and a colon (whether the quotation is indented or not):

```
The Act provides:

    The Board shall have power, upon issuance
    of a complaint . . . charging that any
```

> person has engaged in or is engaging in
> an unfair labor practice, to petition any
> United States district court, . . . for
> appropriate temporary relief or restrain-
> ing order.

and:

> The Act provides: "The Board shall have
> power, upon issuance of a complaint . . .
> charging that any person has engaged in or
> is engaging in an unfair labor practice, to
> petition any United States district court,
> . . . for appropriate temporary relief or
> restraining order."

The first word of a quotation following a colon is always capitalized, because the quotation is a complete sentence intended to stand on its own. In addition, a quotation should only follow a colon when the advocate intends the quotation to stand on its own as a complete sentence.

   b. Quotation of less than a complete sentence following a colon which excludes the first portion of the sentence quoted:

> The Act provides that upon filing a petition:

> [T]he court . . . shall have jurisdiction
> to grant to the Board such temporary re-
> lief or restraining order as it deems just
> and proper.

Since the quotation follows a colon and is intended to stand on its own as a complete sentence, the first word must be capitalized. The first letter of the first word is capitalized and placed in brackets to indicate that in its original context it was not capitalized.

   c. Quotation of a complete sentence not intended to stand on its own as a complete sentence:

> In addition to the power granted the Board
> by section 10(j) of the Act, "[u]pon the
> filing of any such petition the court . . .
> shall have jurisdiction to grant to the
> Board such temporary relief or restraining
> order as it deems just and proper."

Although the first word of the quoted sentence is capitalized in its original form, the quotation has been woven into the text and is not intended to stand on its own. In this context, the first letter of the first word of the quotation is changed to a lower case letter and placed in brackets to indicate the change from its original form. Using a quotation in this manner can be very effective since a closer connection seems to be drawn by the interchangeability of language from the authority to the presentation of the case being argued.

d. Quotation of an incomplete sentence which includes the first word of the sentence:

```
In addition to the power given the Board to
petition the court for temporary relief or
restraining order by section 10(j), the
court was given jurisdiction to grant such
relief "[u]pon the filing of any such peti-
tion".
```

In this context, although the first word of the quotation is capitalized in its original form, it is merely a clause in the textual sentence. As a result, the first letter has been changed to lower case and put in brackets to indicate the change. A quotation is used in this manner merely to show the exact wording.

e. Quotation of an incomplete sentence which does not include the first word of the sentence:

```
Section 10(j) of the Act provides the Board
with the power "to petition any United
States district court" for such temporary
relief or restraining order as the court
deems just and proper.
```

In this context the quoted portion is merely used as a clause in a textual sentence. It is not intended to stand on its own and there have been no changes made. A quotation is used in this manner to show the exact language of the authority cited. The case on appeal and the authority cited are made to appear so closely related that the reasoning as well as language used in the cited authority may be used interchangeably with the case being argued to the court.

C. Use of Italics or Underscoring

Underscoring in a typewritten brief is the counterpart to italics in a printed brief. For purposes of this chapter underlining, underscoring, and italics will be used interchangeably. This method of providing special emphasis is used in the following instances.

1. Case Names

The names of both parties and the "v." between them should be underscored with one continuous line. Italics are also used in abbreviated references to cases in the text.

Thus :

Fibreboard Paper Products Corp. v. NLRB,
379 U.S. 203 (1964).

Also :

In Fibreboard this Court recognized that
such a decision vitally affects the interests of employees in the unit.

Although case names are generally not underlined when they appear in a footnote, in a brief all case names are underscored. The entire brief is considered textual. Even though a citation may physically appear in a footnote, its inclusion in either a footnote or the body of the brief is for the singular purpose of persuading the court. Thus, even references in a footnote are central to the purpose of the brief; as such, they are underscored in the same manner as in the body of the brief.

[3]In recent years, the Board has refused
to require bargaining when the decision
would significantly abridge the employer's
freedom to manage his own affairs. Kingwood Mining Co., 210 N.L.R.B. 344 (1974),
aff'd sub nom., U.M.W.A. v. NLRB, 515 F.2d
1018 (D.C. Cir. 1975). Such is not the
case here, however.

As the example indicates, Latin words appearing in a case name, whether in the text or footnote, are underlined.

2. Introductory Signals

All introductory signals are underlined ("e.g.," "see", "but see", "see also"). However, if any of these words are used in their ordinary sense rather than as an indicator, they are not to be underlined.

3. Foreign Words and Phrases

Some foreign words always underlined: ex parte, ex rel., in re, inter alia, inter se, passim, quare, sic., sub nom., and supra.

Foreign words which are not underlined include: ad hoc, a fortiori, amicus curiae, arguendo, bona fide, certiorari, de nova, dictum, ipso facto, mandamus, per curiam, per se, prima facie, pro rata, quo warranto, res judicata, stare decisis, and subpoena.

The use of foreign words, however, should generally be avoided because it is pretentious and draws attention to the legalistic contributions of the advocate over the equitable concerns of the client represented in the brief.

4. Terms of Art

When it is necessary to use terms of art, they should be enclosed in quotation marks to indicate the word or phrase has a special meaning given its context. In labor conflicts, for example, the phrase "dissolve and merge" has acquired a particular meaning:

```
Thus, it is evident that Smith & Jones is
using the device of "dissolve and merge"
as an economic weapon against the associ-
ates who have joined the union.
```

When read literally, terms of art may appear cumbersome in the sentence. They are useful, however, to convey a precisely defined idea. Quotation marks indicate that the word or phrase is used in this manner.

5. To Provide Emphasis

Underscoring may be used to emphasize words or phrases in a quotation or in the text of the brief. This use of underscoring is similar to the use of quotation marks to highlight a word or phrase in the text of the brief. The decision to use one or the other is often aesthetic and as such, is at the discretion of the advocate.

```
[J]urisdiction is asserted over all nonre-
tail enterprises which have an outflow or
inflow across state lines of at least
$50,000, whether such outflow or inflow be
regarded as direct or indirect. (Emphasis
in original.)
```

Although the emphasis was provided in this instance, the advocate used the underscored portion to draw attention to the standard applied in the particular decision.

6. Headings

Underscoring is also used to identify and emphasize subheadings. *Thus:*

1.   The Board's exercise of jurisdiction
     is discretionary.

As can be seen, underscoring the subheading distinguishes it from the body of the argument.

The use of these techniques to emphasize a word or phrase is superficial and should be used sparingly. The brief should be written in such a way that the key words and phrases stand out without the aid of additional emphasis.

D. Numbers and Symbols

1. Numbers

The rules for expressing numbers would be quite simple if writers would all agree to express numbers entirely in figures or entirely in words. But in actual practice the exclusive use of figures is considered appropriate only in tabulations and statistical matter, whereas the exclusive use of words to express numbers is found only in very formal documents. In writing that is neither formal nor technical, most style manuals call for the use of both figures and words in varying proportions. Numbers from one to ten should be written. Although authorities do not agree on details, there are two basic number styles in wide use for larger numbers: the *figure* style (which uses figures for most numbers above 10) and the *word* style (which uses figures for most numbers above 100).

There is a significant difference between using figures and using words to express numbers. Figures are big (like capital letters) and compact and informal (like abbreviations); when used in a sentence, they stand out clearly from the surrounding words. By contrast, numbers expressed in words are unemphatic and formal; they do not stand out in a sentence. This functional difference between figures and words underlies all aspects of number style.

Unless referring to a statistical study, the word style is used in appellate briefs, because the brief is of a more formal and literary nature and the use of figures would give numbers an undesired emphasis and obtrusiveness. The basic rules for the word style are as follows: Spell out all numbers that can be expressed in one or two words. (A hyphenated compound number like *twenty-one* or *ninety-nine* counts as one word.) In effect, spell out all numbers from 1 through 100 and all round numbers above 100 that require no more than two words (such as *sixty-two thousand* or *forty-five million*). However, the word style, as a matter of practicality ordinarily uses figures when more than two words are required. Numbers in the millions or higher that require more than two words when spelled out may be expressed as "231 million" (in place of 231,000,000). The style that is ultimately followed by the advocate will depend on the substance of the brief, the advocate's own style and whether words or numbers will help highlight the argument by maintaining the flow of the sentence or emphasizing the numbers involved. In Petitioner's brief in *Peggy v. Smith & Jones*, one contrasting example appears as follows:

```
The firm specializes in real estate matters
and annually provides legal services valued
in excess of $250,000.  The firm presently
consists of three partners and employs an
additional twenty-five people, including
ten people who are employed as lawyer-advo-
cates.
```

The use of a numeral to express the amount of business is highlighted because this figure is relevant to the jurisdictional issue. The number of employees is not of any special importance; these figures, therefore, are expressed by words which maintain the flow of the presentation.

2. Symbols

When referring to dollars or percentages, the appropriate terms should be spelled out whenever the number is written out (*thus*: fifty dollars, or thirty percent) and the appropriate symbol should be used when the arabic numerals are used (*thus*: $50,000, or 45%). Note, the dollar sign comes before the numeral and the percent sign follows the numeral. Out of custom and usage in non-legal materials, there is no space between the symbols "$" and "%" and the numeral. Whether the advocate uses words or numerals and signals to express the figure will depend on the nature of the brief and the advocate's own style.

When referring to a particular section of an authority, the word "section," unless appearing as part of a full citation, should be used rather than merely a section sign (§).

```
Because the NLRB has satisfied both of these
criteria, a Section 10(j) injunction should
be issued.
```

But:

> Because the NLRB has satisfied both of these
> criteria, the Court should issue an injunc-
> tion. 28 U.S.C. § 160(j)(1970).

When the "§" sign is used there should be a space between the "§" and
the numeral. The space makes reading the numeral easier.

The same rules that apply to "section" and "§" also apply to
paragraph references and the symbol "¶". References to paragraphs
are generally in connection with a citation; thus, usually only the "¶"
is used. Note, as with the "§", there is a space between the "¶" and
the numeral.

Thus:

> <u>American Gypsum Co. v. Pine</u>, 81 Lab.Cas.
> ¶ 13,147 (10th Cir.1977).

E. Quotations

Quotations may be very effective in a brief to emphasize the
particular language of a court opinion or the language of an applicable
statute. Because the exact wording is the primary reason a quotation
is used, it should be accurate and clearly identified.

In the text of a brief a quotation of three or more typographical
lines may be indented and a quotation of over fifty words in length
must be indented. Such indented quotations are not set off by quotation marks, and unless the applicable rules of court require otherwise,
indented quotations are single spaced. Indented quotations are usually
preceded by a colon at the end of the textual sentence used to introduce
the quotation, because a quotation of three or more lines is usually
intended to stand on its own as a complete sentence:

> In <u>Goldfarb</u>, the Court wrote:

> > [T]he exchange of such a service for mon-
> > ey is "commerce" in the most common usage
> > of that word. It is no disparagement of
> > the practice of law as a profession to
> > acknowledge that it has this business as-
> > pect. 421 U.S. at 787.

Note that double quotation marks are used within an indented
quotation.

Shorter quotations or quotations under approximately fifty words may be incorporated into the regular flow of the sentence and set off by quotation marks. *Thus:*

> Section 8(d) of the Act, 29 U.S.C. § 158(d) (1970), defines "collective bargaining" as "the performance of the mutual obligation of the employer and the representative of the employees to meet at reasonable times and confer in good faith with respect to wages, hours, and other terms and conditions of employment."

This latter example was incorporated into the regular flow of the sentence rather than being indented for a number of reasons. The quotation was not indented because it followed immediately after a primary heading. In addition, since the longer quotation was preceded by a shorter quotation, each served to complement the other.

Note, the citations to the quotations in the two examples appear in different locations—one after the quotation, one before the quotation. The location of the citation is not determined by whether the quotation is indented or not, it depends on how it is being introduced.

The paragraph structure of a quotation is not indicated unless the quotation is indented (*i.e.*, over three lines or fifty words). Where the quotation is indented, the first sentence of each paragraph is further indented to show the paragraph structure of the material quoted. Do not, however, indent the first sentence of the first paragraph unless the first word of the original paragraph is included in the quotation.

1. Placement of Quotation Marks

Periods and commas should always be placed inside quotation marks. All other punctuation marks should be placed outside the quotation marks unless they are part of the material quoted. However, when a word, short phrase, or the exact wording and sentence structure of a decision or statute is quoted, periods and commas are placed outside the quotation marks. *Thus:*

> Specifically, this Court held that inclusion of this subject within the meaning of section 8(d) "would promote the fundamental purpose of the Act by bringing a problem of vital concern to labor and management within the framework established by Congress as most conducive to industrial peace." Fibreboard Products Corp. v. NLRB, supra, 379 U.S. at 204.

But:

> More important, if the firm's "dissolve and
> reorganize" tactics enable it to discrimi-
> nate against union employees with impunity,
> it is foreseeable that the employees will
> fear that if they unionized, the partners
> would immediately call for another "disso-
> lution and reorganization", which this time
> would result in their termination.

Note that in the latter example there was no citation. This is because the advocate was using the phrase for effect, not in relation to any specific authority.

2. Omissions from Quotations

Omissions are indicated by insertion of three evenly spaced periods set off by a space before the first and after the last period to take the place of the word or words omitted. This ellipsis signal should never be used to begin a quotation. The specific manner in which an omission should be indicated depends upon the character of the fragment quoted. When one edits material from the source quoted, the quotation reflects the advocate's own interpretation of what the source intended. The integrity of the source should not be threatened in the process.

a. Phrases or clauses. When the quotation of a phrase or clause is not intended to stand by itself as a complete sentence, do not indicate the omission of surrounding words.

> Specifically, this Court held that inclu-
> sion of this subject within the meaning of
> section 8(d) "would promote the fundamental
> purpose of the Act by bringing a problem of
> vital concern to labor and management with-
> in the framework established by Congress as
> most conducive to industrial peace."

To indicate the omission of material within the phrase or clause; the advocate could rephrase this statement in the following manner:

> Specifically, this Court held that inclu-
> sion of this subject within the meaning of
> section 8(d) "would promote the fundamental
> purpose of the Act by bringing a problem of
> vital concern to labor and management with-

```
in the framework . . . most conducive to
industrial peace."
```

Such an omission is always indicated when it occurs in the middle of the quotation. When, however, the omission comes at the end of the quotation, it is not always indicated. When the quoted phrase or clause is in the middle of a textual sentence, the omission at the end of the quotation usually is not indicated.

```
Specifically, this Court held that inclu-
sion of this subject within the meaning of
section 8(d) "would promote the fundamental
purpose of the Act" and be conducive to in-
dustrial peace.
```

If, however, this quotation is used at the end of a textual sentence, an omission from the end of the quotation should be indicated.

```
Specifically, this Court held that inclu-
sion of this subject within the meaning of
section 8(d) "would promote the fundamental
purpose of the Act . . .."
```

Note, when the ellipsis signal appears at the end of the quoted sentence there is a space before the three periods, as usual. There is, however, no space between the last period of the ellipsis and the period indicating the end of the sentence. This variation in the rule clearly indicates not only the end of the quoted sentence, but the end of the textual sentence as well.

   b. Quoted sentences intended to stand on their own. If the quoted language is intended to stand by itself as a complete sentence, but the language beginning the original sentence has been deleted, capitalize the first letter of the remaining quoted portion and place it in brackets:

```
In explaining its approach to Section 8(d)
problems the Board has stated:

    [J]ust as the employer's interest in the
    protection of his capital investment is
    entitled to consideration in our inter-
    pretation of the Act, so too is the em-
    ployee's interest in the protection of
    his livelihood.
```

An omission of language in the middle of a quoted sentence is indicated in the same manner as such omissions are indicated in a quoted phrase or clause:

> ```
> [J]ust as the employer's interest in the
> protection of his capital investment is en-
> titled to consideration . . . so too is the
> employee's interest in the protection of
> his livelihood.
> ```

When deleting language at the end of a quoted sentence, insert the ellipsis between the last word and the period or final punctuation. Unless there is an intervening sentence or part thereof, no space is necessary between the end of the ellipsis and the final punctuation.

> ```
> [T]he employer's interest in the protection
> of his capital investment is entitled to
> consideration in our interpretation of the
> Act . . ..
> ```

Notice, by omitting a different portion of the quotation, the interests implied by the contents of the quotation are changed. This shows why the ellipsis is important—to indicate that "interpretive editing" may have occurred.

When language is deleted from the end of a quoted sentence and the beginning portion of the following quoted sentence; four spaced periods are used. Likewise, when an entire sentence is deleted from the middle of a quotation, the omission is indicated by four spaced periods. The first three periods indicate an omission from the end of the quoted sentence. The fourth period, being spaced rather than closed in, indicates that language following the ending punctuation in the original sentence has also been omitted. The four spaced periods are used only when the quotation continues beyond the omitted portion.

> ```
> The indication that the Board has jurisdic-
> tion and will likely exercise it, . . . .
> coupled with considerations of public pol-
> icy and equity, require that a temporary
> injunction be issued to promote the goals
> of the Act.
> ```

If the omitted language comes after the end of a quoted sentence, but is followed by further quotation, the ending punctuation of the quoted sentence is retained. Depending on the amount of material omitted a three or four-period ellipsis is inserted before the remainder of the quotation. Note that two spaces must intervene between the ending punctuation of the quoted sentence and the ellipsis.

```
[J]urisdiction is asserted over all nonre-
tail enterprises which have an outflow or
inflow across State lines of at least
$50,000, whether such outflow or inflow be
regarded as direct or indirect. . . . add-
ing direct and indirect outflow, or direct
and indirect inflow. (Emphasis in origi-
nal.)
```

Capitalization of the first letter of the remainder of the quotation following the period will depend on whether the remainder begins at the beginning of a new quoted sentence or whether the remainder can stand on its own. In both of these cases the first letter is capitalized, either by leaving it as it appears in the original sentence or changing it to a capital letter and placing it in brackets. Otherwise, the remainder begins with a lower case letter, as in the example.

c. Paragraphs. When deleting language that would otherwise be indented to indicate the beginning of the second or any subsequent paragraphs within a single quotation, insert and indent a spaced, three-period ellipsis signal. When deleting one or more entire paragraphs, insert and indent a spaced, four-period ellipsis, and begin the next paragraph on the next line. The omission of a subsequent paragraph is only indicated if the quotation continues after the omitted paragraph.

If an advocate were to quote from Petitioner's brief in *Peggy v. Smith & Jones*, the quoted material would appear as follows:

```
Smith & Jones has refused and continues to
refuse to bargain about its decision to
dissolve and reorganize the partnership.
Such decision is a mandatory subject for
bargaining within the meaning of section
8(d) of the Act.

     . . . .

     . . . [A] showing of reasonable cause to
believe that unfair labor practices are oc-
curring. . . . coupled with considerations
of public policy and equity require that a
temporary injunction be issued to promote
the goals of the Act.
```

3. Alterations Within Quotations

Alterations are made in a quotation to emphasize a particular point, to clarify the language of the quotation, or to omit material that is unnecessary or cumbersome within the context and usage of the quotation within the argument.

a. Adding emphasis. Altering a quotation by underscoring some portion of the language of the quotation for emphasis is indicated by a parenthetical statement at the end of and as part of the citation to the quotation. If the citation precedes the quotation, the parenthetical statement appears by itself at the end of the quotation. This parenthetical statement should indicate the nature of the change made to the quotation.

> [J]ust as the employer's interest in the protection of his capital investment is entitled to consideration in our interpretation of the Act, so too is the employee's interest in the protection of his livelihood. Ozark Trailers Inc., 161 N.L.R.B. 561, 566 (1966)(emphasis added).

If portions of the quotations were italicized in their original context, this should be indicated in a similar fashion.

> [J]urisdiction is asserted over all non-retail enterprises which have an outflow or inflow across State lines of at least $50,000, whether such outflow or inflow be regarded as direct or indirect. 122 N.L.R.B. at 85 (emphasis in original).

Note, when the parenthetical appears independent of the citation, the first letter is capitalized and the period is inside the parenthesis.

b. Omitting unnecessary or cumbersome material. The omission of footnotes or citations from a quotation is also indicated by a parenthetical statement at the end of the quotation which reflects the nature of the omission. Were an advocate to quote from Petitioner's brief in *Peggy v. Smith & Jones*, the quotation would appear as follows:

> Thus, even though the NLRB declined to exercise jurisdiction over law firms in the first two matters raising the issue, the Board was able to exercise jurisdiction in the more recent cases concerning law practices. (Citations omitted).

Also commonly used is "(footnotes omitted)". This type of material is often omitted because it interrupts the flow of the quotation as it applies to the situation presented in the brief. Such references usually refer to material outside the scope and purpose for which the quotation was used.

    c. Clarification of material or language within the quotation. When the first letter of a word within a quotation must be changed, this should be indicated by placing the changed letter in brackets.

```
[I]t is not possible to say whether a sat-
isfactory solution could be reached . . ..
```

When inserting a word to replace a noun or pronoun or to change the tense or number of a verb, the word or words inserted should be placed in brackets.

```
No amount of collective bargaining could
erase the economic facts that gave rise to
the [employer's] decision . . ..
```

The word "[employer's]" is added to modify the word "decision" in the quotation.

    d. Citation of quoted materials. The page on which a quotation begins and, if it continues to another page, the page on which it ends, should be indicated. Even if the source of the quotation is indicated to introduce the quotation (*e.g.*, "In *Goldfarb*, the court stated . . .") citation to where the quotation actually appears is indicated immediately following the quotation (*e.g.*, 421 U.S. at 787). The citation should be presented as an independent sentence following the quotation, indented where the quotation is indented or in the regular flow of the paragraph where the quotation is not intended. *Thus:*

```
For, just as the employer has invested
capital in the business, so the employee
has invested years of his working life,
accumulating seniority, accruing pension
rights, and developing skills that may
or may not be salable to another employ-
er. Ozark Trailers Inc., 161 N.L.R.B.
561, 566 (1966).
```

and:

> Specifically, this Court held that inclu-
> sion of this subject within the meaning of
> section 8(d) "would promote the fundamental
> purpose of the Act by bringing a problem of
> vital concern to labor and management with-
> in the framework established by Congress as
> most conducive to industrial peace." 379
> U.S. at 211.

F. Use of Footnotes

Although footnotes are not used in a brief for the citation of authority, the use of footnotes in a brief should not be overlooked. Footnotes may be used sparingly to provide the reader with additional information that may be of interest but would unnecessarily disrupt the flow of the brief. Analogous laws, statistical information, and discursive secondary authorities are more appropriate in a footnote than in the text. But it should be remembered that the brief is written persuasively. Footnotes are to be used to this end, and not as an excuse to write a law review article on the subject area of the law.

Footnotes are indicated by consecutive arabic numerals set off on a typewriter by an underline beneath the numeral and a slash after it "2/". This may also be accomplished by raising the footnote number above that of the text. *Thus:* "²". When a footnote is indicated in the middle of a sentence, it should be followed by one space, and a footnote indicated at the end of the sentence should be placed after the period and should be followed by two spaces.

> In the most recent decision, however, the
> Board partially reversed itself by acknowl-
> edging its statutory jurisdiction <u>and</u> as-
> serting it.[1]

The footnote itself should appear at the bottom of the page on which the footnote indicator appears. A line should appear above the foot-note to indicate that the material beneath the line is not part of the text. The footnote should be preceded by an arabic numeral corre-sponding to that appearing in the text of the brief and it should be typed in the same manner (*i.e.,* "2/" or "²").

---

[1]The Board has never questioned that
lawyers can be employees. <u>See</u> <u>Lumberman's</u>

Mutual Casualty Co. of Chicago, 75 N.L.R.B. 1132 (1948). Their status as professionals as defined by section 2(2) of the Act, 29 U.S.C. § 152(12)(1970), does not exclude them from the Act's protections. Rather, professionals are distinguished from other employees only insofar as they may not be included in a bargaining unit of non-professional employees.

G. Use of the Dash and the Parenthetical

Although the use of proper punctuation is important, the rules governing punctuation will not be treated exhaustively. Nevertheless, two punctuation marks deserve special attention: the dash, because of its seldom but effective use; and the parentheses, because of its common but often incorrect use.

Although the dash has a few specific functions, it most often serves in place of the comma, the semicolon, the colon, or parentheses. When used as an alternative to these other marks, it creates a much more emphatic separation of words within a sentence. Because of its versatility, careless writers are tempted to use a dash to punctuate almost any break within a sentence. However, the indiscriminate use of dashes is inappropriate; moreover, it serves to destroy the special forcefulness of this mark. Use the dash infrequently—and then only for deliberate effect.

Use dashes in place of commas or parentheses to set off a parenthetical element that requires special emphasis. Single words may also be given special emphasis by the use of dashes to set it off. The dash is constructed by placing two hyphens together with no spaces before, between, or after the hyphens. When using the dash, it should always follow a word; it should never be used to begin a new line.

The issuance of an injunction would protect the second of the stated goals of the Act-- it would prevent the employer from accomplishing an illegal objective pending the resolution of the charges.

In this instance, the dash is used instead of a semicolon to provide a stronger but less formal break.

Parentheses and dashes serve many of the same functions, but they differ in one significant respect. Parentheses can set off only nonessential elements, whereas dashes can set off essential and nonessential elements. In setting off elements, dashes emphasize; parentheses de-emphasize. Parentheses should not be used to include additional, unnecessary information. Generally, if it cannot be worked into the text, then it probably does not belong in the text. If the information to be put in parentheses is important but too lengthy, it is more appropriate in a footnote.

Parentheses enclose explanatory material which is independent of the main thought of the sentence. They are used when dashes would be too emphatic and commas would be inappropriate or might prove confusing. The material within parentheses may be a single word, a phrase, or even an entire sentence. The parentheses should enclose only what is truly parenthetical, and not words essential to the construction of the sentence.

> Since this meeting the Firm has made no effort to conceal the fact that Smith & Jones (minus the associates who are Union members) plans to merge with Wind & Zephyr (R. 18).

If the parenthetical is within a sentence, make sure that any punctuation falls outside the closing parenthesis.

On occasion a signal is used within the parentheses to indicate the relationship between the text and the substance of the parentheses. Two of these signals are "e. g.," and "i. e.,". Technically these mean "for example" (e. g.,) and "that is to say" (i. e.,). These, however, are informal references and are generally not appropriate in a brief, just as the use of "viz.," and "etc." should be avoided.

H. Reference Words

1. "Infra," "Ibid." and "Id."

These reference words, although used in other scholarly works, should not be used in a brief. The nature of the brief dictates that textually oriented rather than footnote oriented references be used. The term "infra" is inappropriate because each point in the brief builds upon the preceding points raised. Using "infra" would refer the reader to a subsequent point in the brief, ignoring the logical progression which had painstakingly been developed by the advocate as the most persuasive order of presentation.

2. "Supra"

"Supra" is used only in connection with a citation and then, only after the complete citation has previously been given within the same general contention. "Supra" provides the advocate with a short form method of citing an authority while preserving the natural flow of the argument.

The term "supra" is used only when it would be clear to the reader which authority is being referred to by the writer, thus making a complete citation unnecessary. Depending on how the authority is being used, "supra" indicates to the reader that certain elements of the citation have been omitted (*e. g.*, the date, subsequent history, or the page on which the authority begins). Technically, "supra" refers the reader to information in the full citation previously presented. It should only be used in the brief when the reader will not need to refer back to find the information for which "supra" has been substituted.

The extent of the citation and the use of "supra" depend on the location of the citation in relation to the text and other citations. The advocate should also consider what information is to be conveyed by the citation, and whether the abbreviated citation clearly identifies the authority. There are generally four ways in which a particular authority may be cited in a brief.

a. As a textual reference. A complete citation of the name and location is given upon initially referring to a particular authority; thereafter, the authority may be referred to by its most common identification (case name, statute section number, or common title). If reference to a particular authority is separated by several pages from the previous citation to that authority, it may be necessary to provide the reader with the full citation. The word "supra" is never used in connecton with an authority which is being used in the text as a proper noun rather than as a citation. As a guide, assume that the reader is following the discussion of the particular authority by reading the authority itself. When the discussion or reference to that authority is discontinued in the brief, the reader closes or puts away the volume containing the authority cited. Any further reference to that authority again in the brief should inform the reader which volume and page to consult; in other words, a complete citation should be given.

Cases abbreviated for use in the text should still be underscored, and the abbreviated name should be clearly distinguishable from other case names. Using the name of only one of the parties to identify a case can often be confusing if it is a common name or the particular case is not commonly known by that name.

This Court recently concluded in Goldfarb v. Virginia State Bar, 421 U.S. 773 (1975) that the practice of law affects interstate commerce. In Goldfarb, the Court held that the Sherman Act applies to attorneys because the title searches performed by attorneys incident to the sale of property are crucial to commercial activities.

Note, "supra" is not used after the second reference to *Goldfarb*.

When referring to a statute number, always spell out the word "section."

> Because this Court has not previously considered the issue of when a Section 10(j) injunction is appropriate, the requirements imposed by this provision are unclear.

b. As a general authority. When an authority is cited for a general proposition, the citation of the beginning page is given. Internal citations are not necessary. Thereafter, within the context of any general contention in which the citation appears in full the complete name is given followed by a comma and "supra". This form of citation is common when several authorities are listed in a "string cite."

> See, e.g., Camden Regional Legal Services, supra; Bodle, Fogel, Julber, Reinhardt and Rothschild, supra; and Evans and Kunz, Ltd., supra.

When stating a general proposition, the full name of the authority is given even though the location reference has been replaced by "supra". In the foregoing example, the complete, official citations of the Board decisions do not contain the names of the petitioners. When citing court decisions, the complete, official citations usually contain the names of both parties.

c. As a footnote. A complete citation should always be given in a footnote to the brief because there is no danger of interrupting the flow of the text.

d. As a location reference. Even after an authority has been cited in full, citation to a particular location in that authority will involve more than a mere reference to the name. The information included in the location portion of the citation is determined by the citation's proximity to any previous citation to the same authority within the general contention.

If the complete citation is not on the same page as the internal citation, it should contain the complete name of the case, the reference "supra" within commas, the volume number and name, and the location. The term "supra" in this instance indicates that the citation is not complete, and serves as a replacement for the reference to the page on which the authority begins, the date, and any relevant history.

Fibreboard Paper Products Corp. v. NLRB,
supra, 379 U.S. at 211.

If the complete citation is on the same page, the internal citation should include the complete name of the case, the reference "*supra*" preceded by a comma, and, with no intervening punctuation, the location. Because the volume number and name appear on the same page it is unnecessary to repeat such information.

Fibreboard Paper Products Corp. v. NLRB,
supra at 211.

On occasion, the citation may be further abbreviated. When a case is referred to in the text, a citation following that reference need only contain the volume and page number on which the relevant material is located. This form of citation is most often used in connection with the introduction and citation of a quotation. For example:

> For example, as Justice Stewart explained in his concurring opinion in *Fibreboard,* some decisions are so basic to the scope and direction of the employer's enterprise that to require bargaining about them would interfere with the "prerogatives of private business management." 379 U.S. at 223.

This shortened citation form should be used only when the case has been cited in full on the same page as this abbreviated reference. When the internal citation is given with the complete citation, a comma is placed after the number indicated as the beginning page of the authority, followed by the internal citation. Next, the date and any subsequent material is provided. There is no comma between the location reference and the date.

See, e.g., NLRB v. Reliance Fuel Oil Corp.,
371 U.S. 224, 226 (1963).

Whenever referring to the name of a case in a citation, the full name must be given, although it would have been appropriate to use an abbreviated version in the text.

Although these are the rules generally applicable, abbreviated citation forms are discretionary. The advocate need only keep in mind the reasons behind these rules and the purpose which each citation serves.

For example, if only one case is being discussed in the context of a general contention, then within that contention the following abbreviated citation form may be used.

> Certainly the chances for resolution of the problems involved in the present case are as good as, if not better than, the chances for resolution of the problems as they existed in <u>Fibreboard</u>. In that case, high labor costs were the primary factor in the employer's decision to contract out the maintenance work. This Court concluded that matters which relate to fringe benefits, overtime payments, and other labor costs are peculiarly suitable for resolution by collective bargaining. 379 U.S. at 213. Bargaining about these matters in the present case could substantially change the Firm's financial situation, and thus eliminate the reasons given by the Firm for reorganization.

This short form can be used within points and subpoints as well, because it is clear to the reader which case is being discussed and its location.

I.   References to the Record and Appendix

References to the record of the case should immediately follow an assertion of fact. Such references, or citations, are placed in parentheses with a capital letter "R." and the page number of the record where the information can be found (R. 35). Note, the record reference is considered part of the sentence, and precedes sentence punctuation.

Citations to the record can and should be used effectively. Facts of the case which the advocate feels are determinative should be supported by a citation to the record, thus highlighting this fact as something more than mere rhetoric. Unnecessary references to the record, however, interrupt the flow of the argument and destroy the persuasive effect such citations can have.

If there is an appendix to the brief, citation to it will depend upon how the appendix is organized. When the appendices are lettered separately, refer to the letter of the appendix. *Thus*: "Appendix B". If the reference is to a particular page of a general appendix, then cite as follows: "Appendix at p. 6". The appendices are paginated independently of the pagination provided for in the brief. This gives the reader a clear indication when the text ends and the appendix begins.

If lengthy appendices are necessary, a "Table of Appendix" may be used immediately preceding the appendix and should identify the contents and location of those items contained therein.

J. Reference to the Briefs

Reference to the briefs in the case should appear as follows: Brief for Appellant at 20.

K. Table of Authorities

The format of this section of the brief is set forth in Chapter One of this Handbook, at page 6. A description of the rules regarding the form of the individual citations listed in the Table of Authorities is included here. The proper order of presentation will be determined by the particular requirements of each case. Therefore, the order suggested in this section is merely to aid in the process of determining which authorities should be listed first.

1. Citation of Cases

The names of cases and the "v." are underlined in the Table of Authorities by one continuous line.

```
Goldfarb v. Virginia State Bar,
421 U.S. 773 (1975). . . . . . . . . 8, 9, 13
```

The cases are listed according to their jurisdiction and then in alphabetical order. When the brief is being submitted to a federal tribunal, federal cases should be listed first, state cases second, and administrative cases third. When submitting the brief to a state tribunal, list the state cases from that jurisdiction first, any applicable federal cases second, and cases from any other jurisdiction last. Any of these jurisdictional categories may be subdivided further. Hence, federal cases may be subdivided into United States Supreme Court cases and lower federal court cases.

When listing cases in the Table of Authorities, give the relevant history; for decisions from out-of-state state courts, the advocate should give parallel citations. This provides an easy cross-reference for the reader without adding unnecessary parallel references to the body of the brief.

```
Abercrombie v. Davies,
36 Del. Ch. 371, 130 A.2d 838 (1957) . . . .
Spivak v. Sachs,
16 N.Y.2d 163, 263 N.Y.S.2d 953, 211 N.E.2d
329 (1965) . . . . . . . . . . . . . . . . . .
```

2. Citation of Statutes

Statutory authority is listed immediately following the cases in the Table of Authorities, under the general heading "Statutes". When more than one section of a particular statute is being listed, the title of the act or code can be used as a subheading. Beneath the subheading the individual sections should be listed in numerical order.

As with the cases listed in the Table of Authorities, federal statutes are listed first in a federal brief; and the state statutes are listed first in a brief submitted to a state tribunal.

3. Constitutional Provisions

If there are constitutional provisions cited in the brief, either state or federal, then a separate list with an independent general heading "Constitutional Provisions" should precede the "Statutes" list.

4. Administrative Regulations

If there are any regulations cited in the brief, these regulations should be listed under the general heading "Administrative Regulations". Beneath the general heading there should be a subheading which indicates the agency issuing the regulations or their source, for example:

Administrative Regulations

Treas. Reg.:
    § 1.61-3 . . . .
    § 1.119-1 . . . .
    § 1.162-1 . . . .

or

42 C.F.R.:
    § 450.80 . . . .
    § 450.310 . . . .

5. Citation of Secondary Authority

All secondary authority should be grouped under the general heading "Secondary Authority" in the Table of Authorities. Secondary authorities should be listed in alphabetical order, as the weight of the authority is indicated by the title.

If several categories of secondary authorities are used in a brief (*i.e.,* legislative history, treatises, books, articles), then subheadings should be used to differentiate types of authorities. Subheadings for secondary authorities are usually unnecessary because these writings are not persuasive enough to warrant extensive citation.

6. Page References

For every authority cited in the body of the brief the page or pages on which that authority is cited should be listed in the Table of Authorities. The relevant page reference is placed against the right-hand margin opposite the authority to which it relates.

If an authority is cited often throughout the brief, this is indicated by use of the word "passim". It is placed against the right hand margin in lieu of the page references. Note, the word "passim" should be underscored. Although "passim" does not indicate clearly where the authority is cited, it does inform the reader that the particular authority is central to the decision of the case, and that it may be found throughout the brief.

L. Spacing the Type Within the Citations

The rules concerning the proper spacing of citations have not always been consistently applied in various legal writings. The primary principle that should be followed is to space the citation in such a manner as to avoid any confusion or potential misreading of the citation. Whatever spacing is adopted should be applied consistently throughout the brief

The system set forth in *A Uniform System of Citation* (12th ed. 1976) provides useful guidelines for spacing citations. In the abbreviated titles of volumes, there are no spaces between capitalized initials, or between capitalized initials and a single numeral. For example: "N.L.R.B.", "N.W.2d", "F.2d". Otherwise, there should be a space between any abbreviation of one letter or more, and the following letter, number, or word. For example: "49 Cal. App. 2d 1, 120 P.2d 910 (1942)"; "42 Wash. L. Rev. 1117 (1969)".

M. Spacing on the Page

Avoid splitting up a heading between pages. Splitting any material between pages affects the impact of that statement. When a quotation or heading will not fit completely at the bottom of the page, begin the quotation or heading at the top of the next page. This principle holds true with respect to splitting paragraphs also. If a paragraph would begin within three lines from the bottom margin of the page, start the paragraph on the next page.

Most jurisdictions require typewritten briefs to be double spaced. Nevertheless, the advocate should always consult the local court rules.

Generally. four lines should precede and follow a heading in order to highlight the assertive summary of the discussion which follows.

It satisfies the selective jurisdictional criteria delineated by the Board, as well as the single statutory requirement.

A. THE BOARD IS EMPOWERED TO ASSERT ITS JURISDICTION OVER SMITH & JONES BE- CAUSE THE FIRM'S UNFAIR LABOR PRAC- TICES AFFECT COMMERCE.

The sole statutory limitation upon the Board's jurisdiction is that the Board may only prevent those unfair labor practices that affect commerce.

N. Enumeration

When the advocate enumerates legal or factual elements in the brief, these elements may be introduced and identified by independently numbering each element. This technique is commonly utilized where the legal theory advanced by the advocate is established by the proof of certain requisite factors.

In its supplemental decision on remand from this Court's decision in Darlington, the Board concluded that foreseeability of a chilling effect is established if the following criteria are met:

(1) It was foreseeable that news of the employer's decision to terminate union employees would be communicated to his non-union employees;

(2) It was foreseeable that the employer's non-union employees would be aware of the connection between the business operation in which the union members

were employed and the business operation
in which the non-union employees are employed; and

(3) It was foreseeable that the circumstances surrounding termination of the
union employees would cause the employer's non-union employees to fear that
they also would be terminated if they
unionized. Darlington Mfg. Co., 165
N.L.R.B. 1074, 1084-86 (1967).

These criteria were approved by the circuit
court of appeals in Darlington Mfg. Co. v.
NLRB, 317 F.2d 760, 772 (4th Cir. 1968).

In this manner, the advocate can direct the court's attention to the test
or standard to be applied, and draw a nexus between each of those
elements and the facts of the case.

The use of enumeration permits the advocate to paraphrase the
standard established by the courts, while instilling in the paraphrased
material the emphasis of a quotation. When any one of the enumer-
ated items or factors consists of more than one typed line, each element of the enumeration should be indented and in paragraph form.
If none of the elements are lengthy, the entire enumeration should be
contained within the textual paragraph and preceded by a colon. Different forms of enumeration are acceptable, but it is suggested that
arabic numerals enclosed by parentheses be used to identify the various
elements. The use of parentheses distinguishes the enumeration from
the headings and sets the enumeration off from the text of the paragraph when the enumeration is not indented. Arabic numerals are
suggested as they are easier to read and provide a more effective
means of referring to the elements.

II. CITATIONS

A. Citation of Cases

Case citations should identify the name of the case, the court rendering the decision, where that decision can be found, and any subsequent history that may be relevant to the citation. As discussed in the
other parts of this chapter, those elements necessary to any one citation may depend on its use in the text of the brief.

1. Case Names

a. Procedural phrases. When citing cases where adversary parties are named, omit all procedural phrases from the case identity. Such procedural phrases include: "<u>In re</u>", "<u>ex rel</u>."

When including procedural phrases in a citation, abbreviate "on behalf of" and similar expressions as "<u>ex rel</u>." Abbreviate "in the matter of", "petition of", and similar expressions as "<u>in re</u>". For example, <u>Ozark Trailers, Inc.</u>, could have been cited <u>In re Ozark Trailers, Inc.</u>, 161 N.L.R.B. 561 (1966). The procedural phrase was dropped, however, because it was not an essential element of the citation as used in the brief in *Peggy v. Smith & Jones.*

b. State names. "State of", "Commonwealth of", and "People of" are omitted except when citing decisions to a court sitting in the state which is identified as a party to the action. In that instance, only "State", "Commonwealth", or "People" should be retained. For example cite: <u>State v. Swanson</u>, 307 Minn. 412 (1976), when citing this case to a court sitting in Minnesota; but, this same case would be cited <u>Minnesota v. Swanson</u>, 307 Minn. 412, 240 N.W.2d 822 (1976), were this case to be cited to a court in New Mexico.

c. Abbreviations in case names. When the entire name of a party is commonly abbreviated to widely recognized initials, the initials may be used in the citation. *Thus*:

<u>Fibreboard Paper Products Corp. v. NLRB</u>, 379 U.S. 203 (1964);

But: <u>Minnesota Mining and Manufacturing Co. v. Meter</u>, 385 F.2d 265 (8th Cir. 1967).

Even though the appellant company is commonly referred to as 3M, for the sake of clarity and to avoid any possible confusion this name is spelled out in full. This will be true for most private parties.

A word which is commonly abbreviated may be shortened in a citation if it is not the first word of the name of a party. Some words in this category are: Association (Ass'n), Commissioner (Comm'r), Company (Co.), Consolidated (Consol.), Corporation (Corp.), Department (Dep't), Insurance (Ins.), Mutual (Mut.), National (Nat'l), Society (Soc'y).

Note, when the last letter of the word appears in its abbreviated form, no period should be placed following that word (*e. g.*, Ass'n and Nat'l).

2. Citation to the Court of Decision and Appropriate Reporter

a. Federal cases. When citing United States Supreme Court decisions, citation to the official reports *United States Reports* (U.S.) is all that is required.

Goldfarb v. Virginia State Bar, 421 U.S. 773 (1975).

The complete parallel citation given in the following example is not necessary.

Goldfarb v. Virginia State Bar, 421 U.S. 773, 95 S.Ct. 2004, 44 L.Ed. 2d 572 (1975).

Parallel citation to the *Supreme Court Reporter* or to the *Lawyer's Edition* need not be included when citing a United States Supreme Court case that has been published in the official reporter. This additional information is superfluous, and unnecessarily interrupts the flow of the text.

If the official reporter containing the case has not been published, then citation should be to the *Supreme Court Reporter* (cited: S.Ct.), or, if not therein, to the *United States Law Week* publication (cited: U.S.L.W.). Citation to "U.S.L.W." should contain the full date of the decision.

NLRB v. Local Union No. 103, 46 U.S.L.W. 4081 (January 17, 1978).

Citation to these unofficial reporters will indicate that the case cannot, as yet, be found in the official reporter. Therefore, this fact need not be indicated separately in the brief by using "—— U.S. ——".

When citing the decisions of the federal courts of appeal, refer to the *Federal Reporter* series. Since the *Federal Reporter* (F., F.2d) compiles decisions from all the circuit courts and, prior to 1932, from federal district courts as well, the specific court deciding the case must be indicated in parentheses.

Boire v. International Brotherhood of Teamsters, 479 F.2d 778 (5th Cir. 1973).

And: The Court of Appeal for the District of Columbia is cited:

> International Ladies' Garment Workers Union
> v. NLRB, 463 F.2d 907 (D.C. Cir. 1972).

The *Federal Supplement* (F. Supp.) contains decisions of the United States district courts and courts of claims. Therefore, the particular court issuing the decision cited as authority should be indicated in parentheses.

> Davis v. Huttig Sash & Door Co., 288 F.
> Supp. 82 (W.D. Okla. 1968); Johnson v.
> Evans, 223 F. Supp. 766 (E.D.N.C. 1963).

Some states may have only one district. In such a case, the citation should read:

> Dooley v. Highway Truckdrivers and Helpers
> Local 107, 192 F. Supp. 198 (D.C. Del.
> 1961).

This citation indicates that the decision was rendered by the United States District Court in Delaware—a state with only one federal court district.

When a lower federal court decision has not been reported in the *Federal Reporter* or *Federal Supplement*, either because it is too recent or because the case has not been chosen for publication, it may appear in one of the unofficial topical reporters.

> Hoban v. Connecticut Foundry Co., 53 Lab.
> Cas. ¶ 11,255 (D.C. Conn. 1966).

The proper abbreviation for these topical reporters is:

Administrative Law Reporter Second (¶) _____ Ad. L.2d (P & F)
All State Sales Tax Reporter (¶) _____ ALL STATE SALES TAX
                                                    REP. (CCH)
American Stock Exchange Guide (page) _____ AM. STOCK EX. GUIDE
                                                    (CCH)
Antitrust & Trade Regulation Report
  (page and section letter) _____ ANTITRUST & TRADE
                                                    REG. REP. (BNA)

Atomic Energy Law Reporter (¶)------------ATOM.EN.L.REP. (CCH)
Automobile Law Reporter (¶)--------------AUTO.L.REP. (CCH)
Automobile Insurance Cases (¶)------------AUTO.INS.CAS.(CCH)
Aviation Law Reporter (¶)----------------AV.L.REP. (CCH)
　Aviation Cases------------------------ AV.CAS.
Bankruptcy Law Reporter (¶)--------------BANKR.L.REP. (CCH)
Blue Sky Law Reporter (¶)----------------BLUE SKY L.REP.
　　　　　　　　　　　　　　　　　　　　(CCH)
Commodity Futures Law Reporter (¶)-------COMM.FUT.L.REP.
　　　　　　　　　　　　　　　　　　　　(CCH)

Conditional Sale—Chattel Mortgage
　Reporter (page)-----------------------CONDIT.SALE—CHAT.
　　　　　　　　　　　　　　　　　　　　MORT.REP. (CCH)
Consumer Credit Guide (¶)----------------CONS.CRED. GUIDE
　　　　　　　　　　　　　　　　　　　　(CCH)

Consumerism (page and ¶, in different
　sections)----------------------------- CONSUMERISM (CCH)
Corporation Guide (¶)--------------------CORP. GUIDE (P–H)
Corporation Law Guide (¶)----------------CORP.L. GUIDE (CCH)
Cost Accounting Standards Guide (¶)-------COST ACC'G. STAND.
　　　　　　　　　　　　　　　　　　　　GUIDE (CCH)
Criminal Law Reporter (page)-------------CRIM.L.REP. (BNA)
Economic Controls (¶)--------------------ECON.CONT. (CCH)
Employment Practices Guide---------------EMPL.PRAC. GUIDE (CCH)
　Employment Practices Decisions----------- Empl.Prac.Dec.
Energy Users Report (page and section
　letter)-------------------------------- EN. USERS REP. (CCH)
Environment Reporter (page)--------------ENVIR.REP. (BNA)
Equal Employment Opportunity------------EEOC COMM.MAN.
　Commission Compliance Manual (¶)------- (CCH)
Family Law Reporter (page)--------------FAM.L.REP. (BNA)
　bound in same name------------------- Fam.L.Rep.
Federal Banking Law Reporter (¶)----------FED. BANKING L.REP.
　　　　　　　　　　　　　　　　　　　　(CCH)
Federal Carriers Reporter (¶)-------------FED.CARR.REP.
　　　　　　　　　　　　　　　　　　　　(CCH)
　Federal Carriers Cases------------------ Fed.Carr.Cas.
Federal Estate and Gift Tax Reporter (¶)----FED.EST. & GIFT
　　　　　　　　　　　　　　　　　　　　TAX REP. (CCH)
Federal Excise Tax Reporter (¶)------------FED.EX. TAX REP.
　　　　　　　　　　　　　　　　　　　　(CCH)
Federal Securities Law Reporter (¶)--------FED.SEC.L.REP.
　　　　　　　　　　　　　　　　　　　　(CCH)
Federal Taxes (¶)-----------------------FED. TAXES (P–H)

Federal Taxes: Estate and Gift Taxes (¶)____FED. TAXES EST. &
                                        GIFT (P–H)
Federal Taxes: Excise Taxes (¶)_____FED. TAXES EXCISE
                                        (P–H)
Food Drug Cosmetic Law Reporter (¶)_____FOOD DRUG COS.L.REP.
                                        (CCH)
Government Contracts Reporter (¶)_____GOV'T CONT.REP. (CCH)
    Board of Contract Appeals Decisions_____ Bd.Cont.App.Dec.
    Contract Cases, Federal_____ Cont.Cas.Fed.
Government Employee Relations Report
    (page and section letter)_____GOV'T EMPL.REL.REP.
                                        (BNA)

Housing & Development Reporter (page)_____ HOUS. & DEV. REP.
                                        (BNA)
Industrial Relations (¶)_____IND.REL. (P–H)
Insurance Law Reporter (page)_____INSUR.L.REP. (CCH)
    Automobile Cases 2d_____ Auto.Cas.2d
    Fire & Casualty Cases_____ Fire & Casualty Cas.
    Life (Health, Accident) Cases 2d_____ Life Cas.2d
    Negligence Cases 2d_____ Negl.Cas.2d
Labor Arbitration Awards (¶)_____LAB.ARB. AWARDS
                                        (CCH)
    bound in same name_____ Lab.Arb. Awards
Labor Arbitration Service_____LAB.ARB.SERV.
                                        (P–H)
Labor Law Reporter (¶)_____LAB. REP. (CCH)
    Labor Cases_____ Lab.Cas.
    NLRB Decisions_____ NLRB Dec.
Labor Relations Reporter_____ LAB.REL.REP.
                                        (BNA)
    Fair Employment Practices
        Cases_____ Fair Empl.Prac.Cas.
    Labor Arbitration and Dispute
        Settlements_____ Lab.Arb. & Disp.
                                        Settl.
    Labor Relations Reference Manual_____ L.R.R.M.
    Wage and Hour Cases_____ Wage and Hour Cas.
Mutual Funds Guide (¶)_____MUT.FUNDS GUIDE
                                        (CCH)
New York Stock Exchange Guide (page)_____NYSE GUIDE (CCH)
Pension Plan Guide (¶)_____PENS.PLAN GUIDE
                                        (CCH)
Poverty Law Reporter (¶)_____POV.L.REP.
                                        (CCH)
Private Foundations Reporter (¶)_____PRIV.FOUND.REP.
                                        (CCH)

Products Liability Reporter (¶)------------PROD.LIAB.REP.
(CCH)
Public Utilities Reports (¶)----------------PUB.U.REP. (PUR)
Radio Regulation (¶)----------------------RAD.REG. (P–H)
Securities Regulation & Law Report
 (page and section letter)----------------SEC.REG. & L.REP.
(BNA)
Securities Regulation Guide (¶)------------SEC.REG. GUIDE
(P–H)
Selective Service Law Reporter
 (page and ¶, in different sections)--------SEL.SERV.L.REP.
(PLEI)
Standard Excess Profits Tax Reporter (¶)----STAND.EX.PROF.
TAX REP. (CCH)
Standard Federal Tax Reporter (¶)---------STAND.FED.TAX
REP. (CCH)
 U.S. Tax Cases---------------------------- U.S. Tax Cas.
State and Local Taxes (¶ by section)--------STATE & LOC. TAXES
(BNA)
State Motor Carrier Guide (¶)--------------STATE MOT.CARR.
GUIDE (CCH)
State Tax Cases Reporter (¶)---------------STATE TAX CAS.REP.
(CCH)
 State Tax Cases---------------------- State Tax.Cas.
Tax Court Reported Decisions (page)--------TAX CT.REP.DEC.
(P–H)
Tax Court Reporter (decision number)-------TAX CT.REP.
(CCH)
Tax Court Memorandum Decisions (page)----TAX CT.MEM.DEC.
(CCH)
 bound in same name------------------ Tax Ct.Mem.Dec.
Tax-Exempt Organizations (¶)-------------TAX-EXEMPT ORGS.
(CCH)
Tax Management (section number)----------TAX MNGM'T (BNA)
Trade Regulation Reporter (¶)-------------TRADE REG.REP.
(CCH)
Unemployment Insurance Reporter (¶
 within section)---------------------------UNEMPL.INS.REP.
(CCH)
United States Law Week (page)------------U.S.L.W.
United States Patent Quarterly (page)------U.S.P.Q. (BNA)
Urban Affairs Reporter (¶)----------------URB.AFF.REP.
(CCH)
Utilities Law Reporter (¶)----------------UTIL.L.REP.
(CCH)

Workmen's Compensation Law Reporter (¶)__WORKMEN'S COMP.
                                        L.REP. (CCH)
Wills, Estates, Trusts (¶)------------------WILLS, EST., TR.
                                        (P–H)

Those titles listed beneath those of a looseleaf service are of the set of bound volumes containing those materials previously published in the looseleaf service. These bound volumes are cited independent of the looseleaf service, as set forth on the above list.

Decisions of administrative boards, like court decisions, should be cited to the official report if the case is included there.

Evans & Kunz, Ltd., 194 N.L.R.B. 1216 (1972).

If the official report of a decision has not yet been bound and paginated, citation should be by case number and include the full date of the decision. In such cases, citation should be to an official release, and, whenever possible, a parallel citation to an unofficial reporter or service should be provided so that the court can more easily locate the opinion.

Foley, Hoag & Eliot, 229 N.L.R.B. No. 80,
Lab. L. Rep. (CCH) ¶ 18,116 (May 4, 1977).

In the text of the brief, either citation may be used, or both. The following is a list of official administrative reporters.

Administrative Decisions under Immigration and Nationalization Laws	1940–date	I. & N. Dec.
Agricultural Decisions	1942–date	Agric.Dec.
Atomic Energy Commission Reports	1956–1975	A.E.C.
Civil Aeronautics Board Reports (Vol. 1 by C.A.A.)	1940–date	C.A.B.
Copyright Decisions	1909–date	Copy.Dec.
Court of Customs Appeals Reports	1919–1929	Ct.Cust.App.
Cumulative Bulletin	1919–date	C.B.
Customs Bulletin and Decisions	1967–date	Cust.B. & Dec.
Decisions of the Comptroller General	1921–date	Comp.Gen.

Decisions of the Employees' Compensation Appeals Board	1947–date	Empl.Comp.App.Bd.
Decisions of the Department of the Interior	1881–date	Interior Dec.
Decisions of the Federal Maritime Commission	1947–date	Dec.Fed.Mar.Comm'n
Decisions of the United States Maritime Commission	1919–1947	Dec.U.S.Mar.Comm'n
Department of the Interior, Decisions Relating to Public Lands	1881–date	Pub. Lands Dec.
Federal Communications Commission Reports	1934–date	F.C.C.
Federal Power Commission Reports	1931–date	F.P.C.
Federal Reserve Bulletin	1915–date	Fed.Res.Bull.
Federal Trade Commission Decisions	1915–date	F.T.C.
Interstate Commerce Commission Reports	1931–date	I.C.C.
Interstate Commerce Commission, Valuation Reports	1929–date	I.C.C. Valuation Rep.
Motor Carrier Cases	1936–date	M.C.C.
National Labor Relations Board Decisions and Orders	1935–date	N.L.R.B.
National Railroad Adjustment Board, 1st–4th Div.	1934–date	*e.g.,* N.R.A.B. (1st Div.)
National Transportation Safety Board Decisions	1967–date	N.Trans.S.Dec.
Official Gazette of the United States Patent Office		Off.Gaz.Pat. Office
Official Opinions of the Solicitor for the Post Office Department	1878–1951	Op.Solic.P.O. Dep't
Opinions of the Attorney General	1789–date	Op.Att'y Gen.
Patents, Decisions of the Commissioner and of U.S. Courts	1869–date	Dec.Com.Pat.
Securities and Exchange Commission Decisions and Reports	1934–date	S.E.C.
Treasury Decisions Under Customs and Other Laws	1943–date	Treas.Dec.

Treasury Decisions Under
Internal Revenue Laws   1942   Treas.Dec.Int.Rev.

The *Federal Rules Decisions* (F.R.D.) includes selected opinions from all federal courts deciding cases which interpret and apply the *Federal Rules of Criminal and Civil Procedure*. If the same case is printed in both the *Federal Rules Decisions* and the *Federal Supplement* or *Federal Reporter*, the advocate should cite to the *Federal Supplement* or *Federal Reporter* only. When citation is to the *Federal Rules Decisions*, the specific court rendering the decision should be noted specially in parentheses.

Huk-A-Poo Sportswear, Inc. v. Little Lisa, Ltd., 74 F.R.D. 621 (S.D.N.Y. 1977).

Federal court citations should specifically indicate the court deciding the case, to indicate to the reviewing court the precedential or persuasive value of the decision. For example, the reviewing court may be more philosophically or geographically aligned with a particular circuit or district court. Thus, the court will want to know the particular court rendering a decision. The astute advocate will use this information to his advantage.

The *American Law Reports* (A.L.R., A.L.R.2d, A.L.R.3d, A.L.R. Fed.) contain selected state and federal cases, some of which are extensively annotated. If a decision reported in the *American Law Reports* is also contained in one of the other federal or state reporters, citation should always be to these latter sources. The *American Law Reports* should not be given as a parallel citation to a case unless the annotation to the particular case provides a survey of authorities which indicates an established point of law especially advantageous to the point the advocate is making.

City of Beloit v. Wisconsin Employment Relations Commission, 73 Wis. 2d 43, 242 N.W. 2d 231, 84 A.L.R.3d 221 (1976).

If the advocate were more interested in the annotation associated with the case cited above than with that particular case, the citation would be as follows: Annot., 84 A.L.R.3d 22 (1976).

American Law Reports annotations are similar to secondary authorities in weight, and citation to the annotations alone as authority is weaker than a citation to a court decision discussing the same principles of law. Thus, if the advocate has a choice, he should always cite to a court opinion instead of an A.L.R. annotation.

On occasion, it may be beneficial to refer to the *American Law Reports* as a source for locating additional cases on the stated principle. Nevertheless, it is better to make the point rather than invite the court to discover the information for itself. If additional cases are thought to be necessary, select them from among those cited in the *American Law Reports* and cite to them in the brief.

b. State cases. State court cases within the jurisdiction of the reviewing court should be cited to the official reporter only, if there is an official reporter for that state. The advocate, however, may want to include a parallel citation to the unofficial reporter when listing the cases in the Table of Authorities. This provides the reader with a cross-reference should he wish to review the unofficial citation or should the reader not have access to an official reporter. If the state in which the court sits does not have an independent official reporter, then citation is necessarily to the unofficial reporter.

When citing a state court case from outside the jurisdiction of the reviewing court as authority, the advocate should include a citation to both the official reporter and the applicable unofficial reporter. This cross-reference is essential in the Table of Authorities.

Reece Shirley & Ron's Inc. v. Retail Store Employees Union & Local 782, 222 Kan. 373, 565 P.2d 585 (1977).

The advocate may also want to indicate the location of the opinion in both the official and unofficial reporters when first citing the case in the body of the brief. This is unnecessary, however, and citation to the unofficial reporter alone will suffice for out-of-state cases. It is more likely that the court will have the National Reporter System's unofficial versions than those versions contained in the official reporters from each state. Should the reader want to review the official version, a cross-reference is provided in the Table of Authorities. This also serves to preserve the flow of the text by avoiding unnecessarily long citations.

In states without an independent official state reporter, the regional reporter is cited. This citation should include a reference in parentheses to the state court which rendered the opinion,

School District of Kansas City v. Clymer, 554 S.W.2d 483, (Mo. App. 1977).

In Missouri, however, cases reported in the regional reporter are considered to be the official reports of the case.

The following list compiles the abbreviations that should be used in the citation to the most current, independently bound, official state reporters:

Alabama	Ala., Ala. App.
Arizona	Ariz., Ariz. App.
Arkansas	Ark.
California	Cal., Cal. 2d, Cal. 3d, Cal. App., Cal. App. 2d, Cal. App. 3d
Colorado	Colo.
Connecticut	Conn.
Delaware	Del.
Georgia	Ga., Ga. App.
Hawaii	Haw.
Idaho	Idaho
Illinois	Ill., Ill. 2d, Ill. App., Ill. App. 2d, Ill. App. 3d.
Indiana	Ind., Ind. App.
Iowa	Iowa
Kansas	Kan.
Kentucky	Ky.
Louisiana	La.
Maine	Me.
Maryland	Md., Md. App.
Massachusetts	Mass., Mass. App. Ct.
Michigan	Mich., Mich. App.
Minnesota	Minn.
Montana	Mont.
Nebraska	Neb.
Nevada	Nev.
New Hampshire	N.H.
New Jersey	N.J., N.J. Super.
New Mexico	N.M.

New York	N.Y., N.Y.2d, App. Div., App. Div. 2d, Misc., Misc. 2d.
North Carolina	N.C., N.C. App.
Ohio	Ohio St., Ohio St.2d, Ohio App., Ohio App. 2d.
Oregon	Or., Or. App.
Pennsylvania	Pa., Pa. Super. Ct., Pa. Commw. Ct.,
Rhode Island	R.I.
South Carolina	S.C.
South Dakota	S.D.
Tennessee	Tenn., Tenn. App.
Utah	Utah, Utah 2d.
Vermont	Vt.
Virginia	Va.
Washington	Wash., Wash. 2d, Wash. App.
West Virginia	W. Va.
Wisconsin	Wis.

In most jurisdictions, the official reporter covers only the decisions of the highest appellate court of the state. But, in some states, there is more than one official reporter; one set reports the highest court of the state, and the other set covers the decisions of a lower appellate court of that state. Where this occurs, the court rendering the cited opinion is indicated within the citation reference itself, and need not be indicated in parentheses:

Anderson Federation of Teachers, Local 519 v. School City of Anderson, 252 Ind. 558, 251 N.E.2d 15 (1969), reh. denied, 252 Ind. 558, 254 N.E.2d 329, cert. denied, 399 U.S. 928 (1970); Gary Teachers Union, Local No. 4 v. School City of Anderson, 152 Ind. App. 591, 284 N.E. 108 (1972).

In other jurisdictions, the decisions of the various appellate levels are reported in a single reporter. Where this occurs, it is necessary to indicate the particular court which rendered the decision. If no court is expressly indicated, the implication is that the court rendering the decision is the highest court in the state:

> Alaska v. City of Petersburg, 538 P.2d 263 (Alaska 1975); City of Artesia v. United Steelworkers of America, AFL-CIO, 87 N.M. 134, 529 P.2d 1255 (N.M. Ct. App. 1974); Goodyear Tire & Rubber Co. v. Sanford, 540 S.W.2d 478 (Tex. Civ. App. 1976).

Note, the following states do not presently have independent official state reporters: Alaska, Florida, Mississippi, Missouri, North Dakota, Oklahoma, Texas, and Wyoming. Hence, citation to recent cases arising in these state courts will be to one of the unofficial reporters.

> Alaska v. City of Petersburg, 538 P.2d 263 (Alaska 1975); Maxwell v. School Board of Broward County, 330 So. 2d 177 (Fla. App. 1976); Masonite Corp. v. International Woodworkers of America, AF1-CIO, 215 So. 2d 691 (Miss.), cert. denied, 394 U.S. 974 (1968); Missey v. City of Cabool, 441 S.W. 2d 35 (Mo. 1969); West Fargo Public School District No. 6 of Cass County v. West Fargo Education Association, 259 N.W.2d 612 (N.D. 1977); Midwest City v. Cravens, 532 P.2d 829 (Okla. 1975); Goodyear Tire & Rubber Co., v. Sanford, 540 S.W.2d 478 (Tex. Civ. App. 1976); Retail Clerks Local 187 AFL-CIO v. University of Wyoming, 531 P.2d 884 (Wyo. 1975).

The following is a list of the most commonly cited unofficial reporters, all of which are part of the West National Reporter System.

Atlantic Reporter
    Connecticut, Delaware, Maine, Maryland,
    New Hampshire, New Jersey, Pennsylvania, Rhode Island, Vermont
	A. ; A.2d

California Reporter	Cal. Rptr.
New York Supplement	N.Y.S. ; N.Y.S.2d

Northeastern Reporter   N.E.; N.E.2d
     Illinois, Indiana, Massachusetts, New York, Ohio

Northwestern Reporter   N.W.; N.W.2d
     Iowa, Michigan, Minnesota, Nebraska, North Dakota, South Dakota, Wisconsin

Pacific Reporter   P.; P.2d
     Alaska, Arizona, California, Colorado, Hawaii, Idaho, Kansas, Montana, Nevada, New Mexico, Oklahoma, Oregon, Utah, Washington, Wyoming

Southern Reporter   So.; So. 2d
     Alabama, Florida, Louisiana, Mississippi

Southeastern Reporter   S.E.; S.E.2d
     Georgia, North Carolina, South Carolina, Virginia, West Virginia

Southwestern Reporter   S.W.; S.W.2d
     Arkansas, Kentucky, Missouri, Tennessee, Texas

Where the case has not yet been published in either an official or unofficial reporter, the case should be cited by its docket number, the court rendering the decision, and the full date of the decision.

Comden v. Los Angeles Superior Court, Doc. No. L.A. 30787 (April 11, 1978).

3. Case History

Within the citation of a case, only subsequent case history is given. Whenever the case is cited in full, this information becomes a part of the citation. The subsequent history of the case is preceded by underscored explanatory words.

Darlington Manufacturing Co. v. NLRB, 397 F.2d 760 (4th Cir. 1968), cert. denied, 393 U.S. 1023 (1969).

The subsequent history is offset by commas and is followed by a citation to the location.

Moreover, if the date of the subsequently published history is printed in the same year as the opinion cited, the date is indicated only at the end of both citations.

Masonite Corp. v. International Woodworkers
of America, AFL-CIO, 215 So. 2d 691 (Miss.),
cert. denied, 394 U.S. 974 (1968).

B. Citation of Statutes and Constitutions

1. Federal Statutes

Citation of United States statutes should be to parts of the *United States Code* or *United States Code Annotated.*

29 U.S.C. § 160(j)(1970) or 29 U.S.C.A. § 160(j)(1970). If the statute has a commonly used title, this should precede the citation to the code compilation in the Table of Authorities, and may be used as a reference in the text. For example, in the Table of Authorities, the citation is as follows:

Labor Management Relations Act § 10(j), 29
U.S.C. 160(j)(1970).

In the text of the brief, this statute is referred to as section 10(j). However, citation to this statute is to 29 U.S.C. § 160(j)(1970). These different forms exist because this statute is commonly known by a section number related to the Act, but it will be easier for the court to locate this statute by its codified reference. The advocate may want to include both references in the citation.

a. Amended statutes. In certain circumstances it may be persuasive to show how the statutory language cited differs from an earlier or later version of the statute. For example, the advocate may want to show a trend in the law or a subtle change in legislative intent. This information must be conveyed in the citation to the statute.

When a section is amended so that the subsequent version completely supersedes and repeals the earlier version, the version presently in force is cited to the code and the version no longer in force is cited to the session laws. When discussing the repealed version, cite:

Clayton Act § 7, ch. 25, § 7, 38 Stat. 631
(1914), as amended, 15 U.S.C.A. § 18 (1964).

When discussing the present version, cite:

Clayton Act § 7, 15 U.S.C.A. § 18 (1964),
formerly Clayton Act, ch. 25, § 7, 38 Stat.
631 (1914).

However, the former version need not be cited unless there is a comparison being made and inclusion of the former citation is important to the point being made.

When an amendment makes additions to, but does not repeal the statute as enacted, cite both versions to the code. This indicates a trend in the development of the statute for purposes of statutory construction. If the statute is being cited only for a proposition wholly contained in either the original portion of the statute or in the supplementary portion, and the portion cited is unaffected by the supplementary amendment, then the citation should not refer to other unrelated portions. If, however, the amendment might reflect an important change in the statute, without superseding the earlier version, it is unwise to omit references to the amendment. The advocate should cite the amendment so that the reference is in its current context. Hence, in discussing the present version of a law, cite:

> 28 U.S.C.A. § 2201(b)(Supp. 1977), <u>amending</u>
> 28 U.S.C.A. § 2201 (1964).

But, if discussing the former version of a statute, cite:

> 28 U.S.C.A. § 2201 (1964), <u>as amended</u>, 28
> U.S.C.A. § 2201(b)(Supp. 1977).

Current statutes that are not yet codified, are cited by the title of the Act, the public law number (which indicates the enacting congress "95-142" means "95th Congress"), the section number, the statutes-at-large reference, and the date.

> Medicare-Medicaid Anti-fraud and abuse
> Amendments, Pub. L. No. 95-142, § 4, 91
> Stat. 1180 (1977).

b. Rules of procedure. The Federal Rules of Civil and Criminal Procedure, and the Federal Rules of Evidence are cited in a manner similar to statutes. For example:

> Fed. R. Civ. P. 52.
>
> Fed. R. Crim. P. 49.
>
> Fed. R. Evid. 410.

No section sign, date, or other signal appears before or with the citation of a federal rule. If amended, however, the date of amendment may become a relevant portion of the citation.

2. State Statutes

When citing state statutes, refer to the current official code. If the statute is not in the current official code, cite the preferred unofficial code, or the session laws.

Codifications may be organized in one general multivolume code (*e. g.*, Nev.Rev.Stat. § x (19xx)), in separate subject-matter codes, or both. In citing separate subject-matter codes, include the subject matter as part of the name of the code. Cal.Bus. & Prof.Code § 650 (Deering Supp.1978); N.Y.Bank.Law § 121 (McKinney 1954). A list of the state codifications that should be cited are as follows:

Alabama	Ala. Code Tit. x, § x (19xx).
Alaska	AS x (19xx). (Note, there is no section sign.)
Arizona	Ariz. Rev. Stat. § x (19xx).
California	Cal. [subject] Code § x (West 19xx) or Cal. [subject] Code § x (Deering 19xx).
Colorado	Colo. Rev. Stat. § x (19xx).
Connecticut	Conn. Gen. Stat. § x (19xx) or Conn. Gen. Stat. Ann. § x (West 19xx).
Delaware	Del. Code tit. x, § x (19xx).
District of Columbia	D.C. Code § x (19xx) or D.C. Code Encycl. § x (West 19xx).
Florida	Fla. Stat. § x (19xx) or Fla. Stat. Ann. § x (West 19xx).
Georgia	Ga. Code § x (19xx) or Ga. Code Ann. § x (19xx).
Hawaii	Haw. Rev. Stat. § x (19xx).
Idaho	Idaho Code § x (19xx).

Illinois	Ill. Rev. Stat. ch. x, § x (19xx) or Ill. Ann. Stat. ch. x, § x (Smith-Hurd 19xx).
Indiana	Ind. Code § x (19xx) or Ind. Code Ann. § x (Burns 19xx).
Iowa	Iowa Code § x (19xx) or Iowa Code Ann. § x (West 19xx).
Kansas	Kan. Stat. § x (19xx); Kan. U.C.C. Ann. § x (Vernon 19xx); Kan. Civ. Pro. Stat. Ann. § x (Vernon 19xx); Kan. Crim. Code & Code of Crim. Proc. § x (Vernon 19xx).
Kentucky	Ky. Rev. Stat. Ann. § x (19xx) or Ky. Rev. Stat. Ann. § x (Baldwin 19xx).
Louisiana	La. Rev. Stat. Ann. § x (West 19xx); La. Civ. Code Ann. art. x (West 19xx); La. Code Civ. Pro. Ann. art. x (West 19xx); La. Code Crim. Pro. Ann. art. x (West 19xx).
Maine	Me. Rev. Stat. tit. x, § x (19xx).
Maryland	Md. [subject] Code Ann. § x (19xx), if therein, otherwise cite Md. Ann. Code art. x, § x (19xx).
Massachusetts	Mass. Gen. Laws Ann. ch. x, § x (West 19xx) or Mass. Ann. Laws ch. x, § x (Michie/Law. Co-op 19xx).
Michigan	Mich. Comp. Laws § x (19xx) or Mich. Comp. Laws Ann. § x (19xx).
Minnesota	Minn. Stat. § x (19xx) or Minn. Stat. Ann. § x (West 19xx).
Mississippi	Miss. Code Ann. § x (19xx).
Missouri	Mo. Rev. Stat. § x (19xx) or Mo. Ann. Stat. § x (Vernon 19xx).

Montana	Mont. Rev. Codes Ann. § x (19xx).
Nebraska	Neb. Rev. Stat. § x (19xx).
Nevada	Nev. Rev. Stat. § x (19xx).
New Hampshire	N.H. Rev. Stat. Ann. § x (19xx).
New Jersey	N.J. Rev. Stat. § x (19xx) or N.J. Stat. Ann. § x (West 19xx).
New Mexico	N.M. Stat. Ann. § x (19xx).
New York	N.Y. [subject] Law (McKinney 19xx) or N.Y. [subject] Law (Consol. 19xx).
North Carolina	N.C. Gen. Stat. § x (19xx).
North Dakota	N.D. Cent. Code § x (19xx).
Ohio	Ohio Rev. Code Ann. § x (Page 19xx); Ohio Rev. Code Ann. § x (Baldwin 19xx); Ohio Rev. Code Ann. § x (Anderson 19xx).
Oklahoma	Okla. Stat. tit. x, § x (19xx) or Okla. Stat. Ann. tit. x, § x (West 19xx).
Oregon	Or. Rev. Stat. § x (19xx).
Pennsylvania	Pa. Cons. Stat. § x (19xx) or Pa. Cons. Stat. Ann. § x (Purdon 19xx), if therein, otherwise cite Pa. Stat. Ann. tit. x, § x (Purdon 19xx).
Rhode Island	R.I. Gen. Laws § x (19xx).
South Carolina	S.C. Code § x (19xx).
South Dakota	S.D. Compiled Laws Ann. § x (19xx) or S.D. Uniform Prob. Code § x (19xx).
Tennessee	Tenn. Code Ann. § x (19xx).

Texas	Tex. [subject] Code Ann. tit. x, § x (Vernon 19xx), if therein, otherwise cite to one of the following codifications: Tex. Stat. Ann. § x (19xx); Tex. Rev. Civ. Stat. Ann. art. x, § x (Vernon 19xx); Tex. Bus. Corp. Act Ann. art. x, § x (Vernon 19xx); Tex. Code Crim. Proc. Ann. art. x, § x (Vernon 19xx); Tex. Elec. Code Ann. art. c, § x (Vernon 19xx); Tex. Ins. Code Ann. art. x, § x (Vernon 19xx); Tex. Prob. Code Ann. art. x, § x (Vernon 19xx); or Tex. Tax-Gen. Ann. art. x, § x (Vernon 19xx).
Utah	Utah Code Ann. § x (19xx).
Vermont	Vt. Stat. Ann. tit. x, § x (19xx).
Virginia	Va. Code § x (19xx).
Washington	Wash. Rev. Code § x (19xx) or Wash. Rev. Code Ann. § x (19xx).
West Virginia	W. Va. Code § x (19xx).
Wisconsin	Wis. Stat. § x (19xx) or Wis. Stat. Ann. § x (West 19xx).
Wyoming	Wyo. Stat. § x (19xx).

When citing to one of the above codifications, cite to the first one listed for each state; otherwise cite to one of the subsequently listed codifications. The name of the publisher or reporter is given in parentheses whenever the state itself is not the publisher. As indicated on the above list, certain states require such information as part of the citation to the statute.

Codifications are ordinarily updated by means of annual supplements, bound separately or intended for insertion as pocket parts, which should be cited in the same manner as the main volumes they supplement, but with "Supp." and the year of the supplement in parenthesis following the citation. This information is necessary so that the court can locate the same version of the provision cited in the brief.

The date given in a statutory citation is that of the year appearing on the spine of the volume, the title page, or of the latest copyright year. If other dates (such as the date on which an act or amendment became effective) would be useful, they may be added parenthetically after the parenthetical containing the volume reference date. If the date of the volume or supplement spans more than one year, give all years covered. Hence:

29 U.S.C. § 160(j)(1970)

If the codification is in looseleaf form, the date on the page on which the material is printed should be used rather than the date of the volume as a whole.

3. Uniform Acts

Uniform acts cited as the law or source of the law of a particular state should be cited as a state statute.

Cal. U. Comm. Code § 2316 (1970)

This statute is the same as U.C.C. § 2–316, which may be cited in addition to the state act. This draws a connection between the analysis and interpretation of the uniform act and the similarly worded state statute. Uniform acts are cited without a date, unless the act or section has been revised. Uniform acts, other than the U.C.C., are cited by their full title rather than in abbreviated form.

Uniform Limited Partnership Act § 11.

4. Constitutions

When citing or listing both statutes and constitutional provisions, the constitutional provision should precede the statute. Citation of a constitutional provision is similar to the citation of any other code.

Cal. Const. art. VI, § 11, cl. 3; Cal. Const. art. VI, § 13.

Note that this citation does not contain the date or a reference to the publisher.

The United States Constitution is cited as follows:

U.S. Const. art. I, § 8; U.S. Const. amend. XIV, § 2.

Note, unlike case law citations, statutes and constitutional provisions are not underscored.

5. Legislative Materials

In addition to statutes, the legislative process generates bills and resolutions, committee hearings, reports, documents and committee prints, floor debates, and, occasionally, separately bound legislative histories. When citing any United States legislative material, except debates, identify the house, the number of the Congress, the session, and the year of publication.

```
S. Rep. No. 105, 80th Cong., 1st Sess. 27
(1947).
```

If this information may be found in some widely available source, that source should be cited whenever possible. For example, the *Statutes at Large*, the *Congressional Record*, the *United States Code Congressional and Administrative News*, or a separately bound legislative history might be cited in the following manner:

```
I NLRB, Legislative History of the Labor
Management Relations Act, 1947 (1948).
```

6. Federal and State Administrative Regulations

Federal regulations are cited to the *Code of Federal Regulations* (C.F.R.), if included there. Regulations that have not yet been published in C.F.R. should be cited to the *Federal Register* (Fed. Reg.).

The *Federal Register* and the *Code of Federal Regulations* are prima facie evidence of the original regulations and are required by federal statute to be judicially noticed. *Federal Register* regulations, if not revoked or if not of short duration, are subsequently published in the C.F.R. (C.F.R. regulations must be general, permanent, and in force). *Code of Federal Regulations* and the daily *Federal Registers* are arranged under 50 functional titles, alphabetically grouped, except for the first three titles. These titles are subdivided into chapters, subchapters, parts, and sections. The *Code of Federal Regulations* and *Federal Register* are cited by section numbers which embody the numerical designations of the superior divisions. A single title is generally contained in a separate C.F.R. volume, whereas the *Federal Register* will usually contain references to more than one title. The decisions rendered pursuant to these regulations are discussed in the section on citation of cases.

Some regulations and decisions of state agencies are variously published by the states; but, notwithstanding such publication, they often are not readily accessible. In about 15 states, administrative rules are officially codified and kept up to date by supplements or releases. The decisions of some state agencies, such as public utilities, workmen's compensation, and unemployment insurance commissions, are often published. Some state administrative rulings are privately published by looseleaf reporters or services.

If a state has an administrative code, consult it for the rules of an administrative body. In the absence of a code, inquiry should be directed to the pertinent agency for its regulations. A few state administrative law topics, such as public utilities and taxation, are covered by looseleaf services and reporters. These services should be freely consulted.

The availability of a state agency's decisions may also be determined by inquiry. Some decisions are officially published (*e. g.*, Wisconsin Employment Relations Board Decisions) and a few areas are covered by looseleaf reporters (*e. g.*, Unemployment Insurance Reports (CCH) (Michigan)).

C. Citation to Secondary Authority

1. Restatements

Publications of the American Law Institute should be cited as follows:

> Restatement Torts § x (1936);
> Restatement (Second) of Conflict of Laws § x (1958);
> Restatement of Trusts § x, comment x (1935);
> Restatement of Contracts § x (Tent. Draft No. x, 1929);
> Restatement of Agency Neb. Ann. § x (1934), 7 A.L.I. Proceedings 256 (1930).

These sources should not be relied on as primary authority. Nevertheless, they may provide useful background information and analysis.

2. Treatises

Citations to treatises should include the following elements: volume number, name of the author, title of the individual volume, page or section number, edition, and year.

These elements are discussed in detail below.

    a. Volume Number. The volume number of a multiple volume work precedes the name of the author.

    b. Name of the author. The name is cited with the first initial and last name, unless more would be necessary for identification.

When there is an institutional author (or editor) the name of the institution or organization promulgating the treatise should appear in place of the author's name.

In special cases where individual volumes of a multivolume treatise are written or edited by different people, this is indicated in parentheses as:

American Law of Property § x (Casner ed. 1952).

c. Title of the individual volume. If the volumes of a set have different titles, the name of the set is given first (underscored) followed by a comma and the title or subject title of the volume. If there is no single author or editor of the set, the name of the author or editor of the particular volume should be included in parentheses.

Federal Practice and Procedure § x (Wright & Miller ed. 19xx).

Even if the individual volumes do not have separate titles, if the work is sub-divided into independently identified subject areas, the subject areas of the material cited follow the citation to the title of the set in a similar manner as when referring to separate volume titles.

4 B.E. Witkin, Summary California Procedure Judgments 3235 (2d ed. 1971).

Note, when the subpart does not constitute a separate independently paginated volume there is no comma separating the title of the set from the title of the subpart.

d. Page or section number. When giving a page number, do not use "at" or "p." or a comma before the page or section number.

4 B.E. Witkin, Summary California Procedure Judgments § 127 (2d ed. 1971--Supp. 1977).

If the section or paragraph numbers are not consecutively numbered throughout the work, be sure to identify the subpart title containing the particular section cited. In the above example, the supplement is cross-referenced by section rather than page number. Thus, citation is to the section in which the relevant material appears rather than to the page. In the Table of Authorities, omit any page or section reference.

e. Edition and year. The edition and year of the volume should be contained in parentheses. When citing the first edition of the treatise, only the year is indicated. This date, alone, indicates that the treatise is in its first edition.

2 J. Gilson, <u>Trademark Protection and Practice</u> § 10.02 [6] (1977).

Each volume of a set may be in a different edition or year of publication. The year and edition of each volume cited should be checked independently. Sometimes editions are described by other than numbers, such as revised editions (rev. ed.) or permanent editions (perm. ed.). This should be indicated where applicable. Always cite to the most recent edition of a work which provides the material.

3. Law Review Articles and Notes

The abbreviation of the name of a law review is usually given in the front of the law review volume itself. A partial list of common abbreviations for law reviews is provided in *A Uniform System of Citation* (12th ed.) It is preferable to obtain the abbreviation from the law review, because certain law review abbreviations differ from the standard abbreviations used for the terms in its title. For example: Columbia is Colum., California is Calif., and Texas is not abbreviated at all.

Citations to law review articles should give the following information in the following order:

a. Author (last name only), followed by a comma;

b. Title of the article (underlined), followed by a comma;

c. Volume; if the periodical has no volume number, use the year of the publication (*e. g.*, Ellsworth, <u>Disgorgement in Securities Fraud Actions Brought by the SEC</u>, 1977 Duke L.J. 641.);

d. Name of the review;

e. Page number on which the article begins; and

f. Date (in parentheses).

Hence:

Siegel, <u>Section 10(j) of the National Labor Relations Act: Suggested Reforms for Expanded Use</u>, 13 B.C. Indus. & Com. L. Rev. 457 (1972).

Student contributions to law reviews, other than short commentaries, are cited by the designation used in the publishing review (*i. e.*, note or comment). The name of the student author is never given, but the title is always included.

Note, The 10(j) Labor Injunction: An Exercise in Statutory Construction, 42 Wash. L. Rev. 1117 (1967).

Notice that, in a brief, only the title of the article is underscored. The identification of the law review is in regular type, even when the brief is printed. The citations in a brief are in the text and use of any lettering other than that used in the text would unnecessarily highlight this reference. This is true of all citations which might otherwise be printed in a different type form.

Short commentaries, such as "Recent Decisions" and "Case Notes," are cited to the law review without any additional identification. Thus, these sources should only be cited in close proximity to the material or case which is the subject of the review, and with a logical nexus to the discussion of that subject or case. Recent case write-ups are cited in the following manner:

28 Colum. L. Rev. 130 (1928).

When used with the citation to the case itself, cite:

Beale v. Williston, 71 F.2d 334 (2d Cir. 1934), reviewed by 43 Yale L.J. 881.

If the date of the write-up differs from the date of the case, give both dates:

Jones v. York, 310 Mass. 613, 8 N.E.2d 790 (1939), reviewed by 53 Harv. L. Rev. 806 (1940).

4. Annotations

As a general rule, do not give A.L.R. references for the decisions you choose to cite. A.L.R. annotations may, however, be used for an additional unofficial citation where the cited case is reported there and is the subject of an annotation which provides additional support for the proposition asserted. Indicate the page upon which the case report, not the annotation, begins. When citing the annotation alone, indicate the page upon which the annotation begins, and the date of publication of the volume.

```
Annot., 12 A.L.R.2d 221 (19xx).
```

5. Citation to Briefs

The citation to an opponent's brief or an earlier brief in the same litigation (*e. g.*, citation to an appellant's opening brief in a reply brief) need only identify the brief and the page number. For example:

```
Brief for Appellee at 10.
```

If a brief in another case is cited, the case itself must also be clearly identified. For example:

```
Brief for Appellant at 26, Burka v. Cogan,
248 F.2d 60 (D.C. Cir. 1974).
```

III.   INDICATION OF PURPOSE AND WEIGHT

The proper citation of any authority includes an indication of why the particular authority was cited and what relationship the authority bears to the proposition advanced. This is done through the use of introductory signals.

The precedential value of a case or statute will be indicated by the citation. In addition, the citation may be supplemented by parentheticals identifying the relationship of the language cited in the brief to the case cited as its source (*e. g.*, holding, dictum, or concurring opinion) or other explanatory statements.

```
Kennedy v. Telecomputing Corp., 43 Lab.
Cas. ¶ 17,297 (S.D. Cal. 1961)(injunction
issued against an employer who paid union
scale wages after unilaterally renouncing
the union's representation).
```

Citation sentences or clauses are usually introduced by a signal (for example, "accord," "see", "cf.") followed by the relevant authorities. Such citation "sentences" may contain more than one introductory signal when the authorities cited relate differently to the proposition in the text. When more than one signal and its connected authorities are used within one citation sentence, a semicolon immediately precedes the succeeding signal and its connected authorities.

E.g., NLRB v. Dixie Terminal Co., 210 F.2d 538 (6th Cir. 1954); accord, United States v. Morton Salt Co., 338 U.S. 632 (1949).

Citation sentences should contain exclusively supporting citations, contrary citations, or background citations. That is, these categories of citations should not be mixed together within any one citation "sentence."

All signals must be underscored. This highlights the authorities cited and differentiates the use of the term as a signal from its common use. For example, "accord" and "accord", or "see" and "see".

When citing multiple authorities in support of a proposition, the citations are set forth in citation phrases or sentences with each individual authority set off by semicolons. When the citations are set forth as a citation sentence a period should follow the last authority cited.

Bodle, Fogel, Julber, Reinhardt and Rothschild, 206 N.L.R.B. 512 (1973); Evans and Kunz, Ltd., 194 N.L.R.B. 1216 (1972).

When the citations are included within the textual sentence they are incorporated as follows:

Thus, even though the NLRB declined to exercise jurisdiction over law firms in the first two cases to raise this issue, Bodle, Fogel, Julber, Reinhardt and Rothschild, supra; and Evans and Kunz, Ltd., supra, the Board was able to exercise jurisdiction in the more recent cases concerning law practices, Camden Regional Legal Services, supra; Legal Services for Northwestern Pennsylvania, 230 N.L.R.B. No. 103, Lab. L. Rep. (CCH) ¶ 18,334 (1977); Foley, Hoag, and Elliot, supra.

A. Signals Indicating Support

Whenever a point of law or proposition is asserted, some authority should be cited as the source of such proposition or as supporting the advocate's argument. The nature of the relationship between the cited authority and the proposition, or the degree to which the authorities cited support the proposition, are indicated by using the following signals.

1. [No Signal]

When the proposition asserted in the brief is directly quoted from, directly paraphrased from, or is a direct holding of the authority cited, no introductory signal is used. The absence of a signal indicates this relationship to the court.

```
The National Labor Relations Act provides
that the National Labor Relations Board has
the necessary jurisdiction "to prevent any
person from engaging in unfair labor prac-
tices . . . affecting commerce." 29 U.S.C.
§ 160(a) (1970).
```

In this example, "[no signal]" was used because the quotation in the immediately preceding sentence was from the authority cited. This should be the most common signal used in a brief.

2. "E. g."

When the authority cited is merely a sampling of a general pool of authorities supporting the same proposition use "e. g.,". This signal indicates to the court that there are additional cases directly supporting the proposition in the text but citation to them would not be helpful. "E. g., may, however, be used in combination with other signals, the combination indicating a somewhat different relationship. For example, "see e. g.," would indicate that the proposition asserted will be suggested by an examination of the authority cited, which is but part of a pool of similar authorities. On the other hand, "but see, e. g.," indicates that the authority cited is part of a pool of authorities casting doubt upon the proposition discussed. The signal "e. g.," should always be followed by a comma, and, when it is used in combination with other signals, it should also be preceded by a comma.

```
Furthermore, the NLRB has recently held
that labor disputes affecting federally
funded community legal service offices
affect commerce sufficiently to invoke
the Board's jurisdiction. E.g., Camden
Regional Services, Inc., 231 N.L.R.B. No.
47, Lab. L. Rep. (CCH) ¶ 18,430 (1977);
Legal Services of Northwestern Pennsylva-
nia, 230 N.L.R.B. No. 103, Lab. L. Rep.
```

> (CCH) ¶ 18,334 (1972). The NLRB, however, confines the exercise of its powers of jurisdiction to controversies which substantially affect interstate commerce and infringe upon the rights of employees. See, e.g., NLRB v. Denver Building and Construction Trades Council, 341 U.S. 675 (1951). The labor dispute at Smith & Jones is such a case.

In this example, "see, e. g.," was used because the statement in the immediately preceding sentence was not taken directly from the authority cited, but would be suggested by a reading of the cited authority and other similar cases. Likewise, "E. g.," was used in the example because these cases are two of the cases which would support the general proposition made in the immediately preceding sentence that such labor disputes affect commerce sufficiently for the Board to assert jurisdiction. It would also have been appropriate to use "[no signal]" because this citation identifies certain NLRB decisions referred to in the text. The advocate must decide for which purpose the authorities are being cited and then use the appropriate signal to indicate this purpose.

3. "Accord"

The weight signal "accord," is commonly used to introduce a string of authorities which are on point, but which do not state the quotation directly. Hence, and "accord," citation usually follows citation to an authority which is the direct source of the proposition. By reworking the example previously used, the difference between this signal and those previously discussed will become more apparent.

> Furthermore, the NLRB has recently held that labor disputes affecting federally funded community legal service offices affect commerce sufficiently to invoke the Board's jurisdiction. Camden Regional Services, Inc., 231 N.L.R.B. No. 47, Lab. L. Rep. (CCH) ¶ 18,430 (1977); accord, Legal Services of Northwestern Pennsylvania, 230 N.L.R.B. No. 108, Lab. L. Rep. (CCH) ¶ 18,334 (1977); Wayne County Neighborhood Legal Services, Inc., 229 N.L.R.B. No. 171, Lab. L. Rep. (CCH) ¶ 18,229 (1977).

In this example there is "[no signal]" before the first citation because the advocate is using *Camden* to identify specifically the case referred to in the text. "Accord," is used to introduce the other cases because they were not directly referred to in the text nor were they the advocate's direct source for the proposition asserted. Nevertheless, they directly support the proposition that such legal service offices affect commerce sufficiently for the Board to assert jurisdiction. Thus, the relevance of these other cases is worth bringing to the attention of the court.

Similarly, the law of one jurisdiction may be cited as in "accord," with that of another. This is often used when the jurisdiction in which the case is on appeal has very little case law interpretation of the relevant statute. The advocate would first cite the statute at issue and follow this with "accord," and citation to several similar statutes in other jurisdictions in which there has been greater case law development. References to other jurisdictions are made relevant to the reviewing appellate court by this transitional connection.

4. "See"

The signal "see" indicates that the authorities which follow the signal constitute the basic source material which supports the proposition asserted in the text. "See" is used instead of "[no signal]" when the proposition is not specifically set out by the cited authority but rather follows logically from it. This is also the difference between the use of "accord," and "see".

> The courts have recognized that public interests other than the interest in collective bargaining must be borne in mind. See Siegel, Section 10(j) of the National Labor Relations Act: Suggested Reforms for an Expanded Use, 13 B.C. Indus. & Com. L. Rev. 457 (1972).

In this example, "see" is used because the proposition asserted was not taken directly from the article, but the article would lend support to this statement. Notice that "see" is not followed by a comma unless used in combination with "e. g.,".

The word "see" is not always used as a weight signal. It can be used as an ordinary non-signal term, and incorporated in a textual phrase as an easy and fluid way to introduce an authority. "See" in its non-signal sense could be used as follows:

> For a discussion on the public recognition courts have given the public interest involved in such labor disputes, see Siegel, Section 10(j) of the National Labor Relations Act: Suggested Reforms for an Expanded Use, 13 B.C. Indus. & Com. L. Rev. 457 (1972).

A non-italicized or non-underscored "see" is used to introduce an authority which discusses a point not directly dealt with in the brief, but which relates tangentially to the general subject matter. This is considered a non-signal similar in use to signals indicating general background material.

5. "Cf."

When the cited authority supports a proposition different from that asserted but sufficiently analogous to lend support, the weight signal "cf." is used. Literally, "cf." means compare. In addition, "cf." should not be used without a parenthetical explaining the analogy. The advocate could have used "cf." in connection with the following excerpt:

> In this respect the Firm's decision is distinguishable from those of several employers who have been found by lower courts to have no statutory duty to bargain about terminating or relocating parts of their ongoing businesses, because "no amount of collective bargaining could erase the economic factors that give rise to the [employer's] decision . . . ." NLRB v. Thompson Transport Co., 496 F.2d 698, 703 (10th Cir. 1969); cf., NLRB v. Royal Plating and Polishing Co., 350 F.2d 191 (3rd Cir. 1965) (where the employer was charged with an unfair labor practice after he accepted a "take it or litigate it" offer from a housing authority which had condemned the property on which one of his plants was located).

In this example, "cf." was used because the authority following that signal was not cited as supporting the proposition stated in quotations, but for the comparative value of its factual circumstances. The advocate should remember that it is the use the advocate makes of the particular authority that determines which signal should be used, not the nature or relationship of the authority as a whole to the statement or case on appeal. Thus, this same authority may later be cited as the direct source for a statement very similar to the one mentioned.

B. Signals That Suggest a Profitable Comparison

When the comparison of one authority to another will suggest or illustrate the statement or proposition asserted, this is indicated as follows: Compare . . . [and] . . . with . . . [and] . . . .

For example, the following could have been used in Petitioner's brief in *Peggy v. Smith & Jones*:

> Even though the Board has often recognized that it had statutory jurisdiction, it was not until the more recent cases that the Board was able to assert jurisdiction. Compare Bodle, Fogel, Julber, Reinhardt and Rothschild, 206 N.L.R.B. 512 (1973) and Evans and Kunz, Ltd., 194 N.L.R.B. 1216 (1972) with Foley, Hoag and Elliot, 228 N.L.R.B. No. 180, Lab. L. Rep. (CCH) ¶ 18,116 (1977).

In this example, the authorities cited illustrate the change in the Board's decision to assert jurisdiction over law firms. Usually a more direct citation is preferable.

The advocate guides the court to the differences between two different lines of authority instead of distinguishing the cases in the text of the brief. This method is used because the authorities distinguished are not central to the issue on appeal but their general propositions of law may have some general bearing on the case. This signal differs from "cf." in that "cf." invites a comparison between the cited authority and the textual statement whereas, "Compare . . . with . . . ." indicates that a comparison of the two cited authorities would suggest or illustrate the proposition asserted.

C. Signals Which Indicate That an Authority Supports a Contrary Position

An advocate has a duty to inform the court of authority directly adverse to his case. A contrary signal may be useful as a transition from a discussion of adverse authority to the main theme of the advocate's case. When introducing contrary authority, the signal indicating this purpose should start a new sentence.

1. "Contra"

When the authority cited directly supports a proposition contrary to that in the immediately preceding discussion the signal "Contra," is used just as "[no signal]" is used to indicate supporting authority. By way of example, the advocate could have used "Contra," in the sample brief in the following way:

> The decision to reorganize a partnership is based upon considerations which are partic-

ularly suitable for discussion at the bargaining table. See Fibreboard Paper Products Corp. v. NLRB, 379 U.S. 203 (1964).
Contra, NLRB v. Thompson Transport Co., 406
F.2d 698 (10th Cir. 1969), where the employer's decision to close was caused by
economic factors beyond the control of the
parties and for which collective bargaining
could have no solution.

In this example, "Contra," is used to introduce a case which the advocate feels must be distinguished. Use of contrary signals avoids
unnecessarily extending the introduction and discussion of such
authority.

2. "But see" and "but cf."

When the authority cited would suggest a conclusion contrary to
that set forth, use "but see". The term "but see" is the counterpart of
"see". It is used to introduce authority which inferentially rejects the
statement in the text:

In no event would the Board's assertion of
jurisdiction require a breach of the con-
fidential attorney-client relationship.
See Camden Regional Legal Services, Inc.,
231 N.L.R.B. No. 47, Lab. L. Rep. (CCH)
¶ 18,430 (1977). But see Evans & Kunz,
Ltd., 194 N.L.R.B. 1216 (1972).

In this example, "but see" is used to introduce an authority which
discusses an apparently contrary statement.

When the authority cited supports a proposition analogous to a
proposition contrary to that set forth in the text, use "but cf.".
This signal should always be used with an explanatory parenthetical.

Respondent asserts that it is reorganizing
for managerial reasons, and as such, does
not have to discuss such a decision with
its employees at the bargaining table. See
N.L.R.B. v. Thompson Transport Co., 406
F.2d 698 (10th Cir. 1969). But cf. Fibreboard Paper Products Corp. v. N.L.R.B., 379
U.S. 203 (1964)(The employer's contracting
out of services previously performed by em-

ployees resulted in a termination of several of those employees. This was held to be
a subject for collective bargaining.).

The difference between "but see" and "but cf." is often just the emphasis the advocate wants to place on the authority cited. In these
examples, "but see" introduced legal principles which could serve as a
basic source, but the factual circumstances of that case were only
analogous and thus "but cf." could have been used to compare the
factual determinations.

When either one of these signals follows a similarly contrary signal
and authority, the "but" is dropped from the signal introducing the
subsequent authority.

But see Ozark Trailers, Inc., 161 N.L.R.B.
561 (1966); cf. Fibreboard Paper Products
Corp., 379 U.S. 204 (1964)(where the employer's contracting out of services previously
performed by employees resulted in a termination of several of those employees--this
was held to be a subject for collective bargaining).

In the above example, "cf." is really "but cf.". Signals that introduce
contrary authority should not be used in the same sentence as signals
introducing authorities which support the textual proposition. Note
that neither "but see" nor "but cf." is followed by a comma.

**D. Signals Indicating Background Material: "See generally" and
"See also"**

Neither "See generally" nor "see also" is followed by a comma.
Both of these signals should only be used to begin a new citation
sentence, not as part of a citation sentence or phrase which in addition
contains either supporting or contrary authority.

Since the brief is used as a persuasive tool, citation to background
information should be limited. It is most profitable to inform the
court through the use of supporting authority directly related to the
proposition asserted, or distinguishing authority which deals directly
with the relevant cases. General background signals are most often
used to introduce secondary authorities.

The signal "See generally", is used when the authority cited does
not provide support for the specific proposition stated, but provides the
reader with a source for obtaining a general background on the subject
matter or proposition discussed in the text immediately preceding the

citation.   Authorities introduced in this manner are merely informative.   Generally, they are neither supportive nor adverse to the proposition asserted.   The signal "See generally" should not be used when a more affirmative signal such as "see" would also be appropriate.

> From years of experience with temporary injunctions, the NLRB has developed criteria by which the regional director's request for injunctions are reviewed. Casehandling Manual (Part 1), Unfair Labor Practice Proceedings § 10310.2 (April 1975). The general counsel applies these standards to every request for a temporary injunction from the regional directors. The district court receives petitions for injunctions only after the general counsel is satisfied that injunctive relief is essential. See generally Note, Temporary Injunctions under Section 10(j) of the Taft-Hartley Act, 44 N.Y.U.L. Rev. 181 (1969).

In this example, "See generally" is used because, although the Casehandling Manual is the direct source of the material in the text, the Note provides further background material specifically on the point discussed in the text.

The signal "see also" is used when the authority cited provides background to a question analogous to the proposition stated and a comparison would provide an additional background perspective.   This signal differs from "cf." and "but cf." since it is not cited as supporting or contrasting authority.   Rather, it is used to introduce an authority which provides background information on a point analogous to the proposition.   This does not mean, however, that the same authority may not be used at another point in the brief as direct authority for the same proposition or a different one:

> Thus, in 1970 the general counsel received 191 requests for injunctive relief from the regional directors, but only 17 petitions for injunctive relief were filed with the district courts. NLRB Annual Report 196 (1970). See also Siegel, Section 10(j) of the National Labor Relations Act: Suggested Reforms for an Expanded Use, 13 B.C. Indus. & Com. L. Rev. 457 (1972).

In this example, "see also" is used because the central point in the preceding text provides general historical facts about the Board's treatment of requests for injunctive relief. Although this information may also be contained in the article cited, the advocate introduces the article as providing general information on a different but related point. This information neither supports nor opposes the historical statement, nor is it cited as background material on the historical application of section 10(j). Remember, if an authority is introduced by the signal "see also" for one citation, it does not necessarily mean that the same weight signal must be used in any other citation to that authority. *Thus*:

> In addition to requiring a showing of reasonable cause to believe that an unfair labor practice has occured, many courts also require a showing that the injunction will further the purpose of the Act and its enforcement. See Siegel, Section 10(j) of the National Labor Relations Act: Suggested Reforms for an Expanded Use, 13 B.C. Indus. & Com. L. Rev. 457 (1972). This second requirement has been defined and developed by the courts in a case-by-case approach. Various circuit courts have singled out different specific circumstances warranting injunctive relief. Siegel, supra at 475.

In this example the same authority previously introduced by "see also" is cited as the basic source of the statement in the text.

Thus, a signal is used more to describe the advocate's use of the authority than the information contained in that authority. The signal should be used to guide the court to those sources the advocate wants the court to review. The more the advocate wants the court to review its authorities, the more direct the signal should be. Generally, direct citations will include the page which the advocate wants the court to examine, whereas general background citations will usually be to the authority as a whole.

E.   Order of Presentation

When more than one authority is cited in connection with a single proposition, these authorities should be presented in the most persuasive order. One way this is accomplished is by indicating the order of importance by placing the most direct signals first. The other is by placing the authorities following each introductory signal into a reverse chronological order, giving priority to decisions rendered by the higher courts, however, for example, a United States Supreme Court decision would precede a federal circuit court case regardless of the years of decision.

Authorities are usually listed in citation sentences or phrases and preceded by an introductory signal or [no signal]. Citation sentences are treated like any textual sentence which must be concluded by the appropriate punctuation—a period.

> Ozark Trailers, Inc., 161 N.L.R.B. 561, 566 (1966).

When multiple authorities are cited, a semicolon is used between individual authorities to separate them.

> See, e.g., United States v. Morton Salt Co., 338 U.S. 632 (1949); NLRB v. Dixie Terminal Co., 210 F.2d 538 (6th Cir. 1954).

More than one signal can be used in a citation sentence or phrase to indicate how each of the authorities relates to the immediately preceding statement in the text. Nevertheless, authorities which support the text should not be placed in the same sentence with authorities which are contrary to the text or with authorities which merely provide background information. Each of these categories, when cited in relation to the same statement, should be in separate sentences unless appearing within a citation clause within a textual sentence. This avoids undue confusion. *Thus*:

> Fibreboard Paper Products Corp. v. NLRB, 379 U.S. 203 (1964). But see NLRB v. Thompson Transport Co., 406 F.2d 698 (10th Cir. 1969). See also NLRB v. Transmarine Navigation Corp., 380 F.2d 933 (9th Cir. 1967).

But:

> Although the NLRB has exercised its jurisdiction over law firms, Camden Regional Legal Services, Inc., supra; but see Bodle, Fogel, Julber, Reinhardt & Rothschild, supra, this Court has not yet held that this exercise of Board power is appropriate under the Act.

F. Order of Signals

When more than one signal is used in connection with a single statement, the signals (together with the authorities they introduce) should appear in the order in which they were presented in the preceding material and as follows: [1] [no signal]; [2] "e. g.,"; [3] "accord,"; [4] "see" ("see, e. g.,"); [5] "c.f.". [6] "Compare . . . with . . . ." [7] "Contra,"; [8] "[but] see," ("[but] see, e. g.,"); [9] "[but] cf.". [10] "See generally"; [11] "see also".

The non-signal "see", since it is not a signal, may be placed anywhere in the order of citations, but as a practical matter it always appears separately as part of an introductory textual phrase.

> For a discussion on the recognition courts have given the public interest involved in such labor disputes, see Siegel, Section 10 (j) of the National Labor Relations Act: Suggested Reforms for an Expanded Use, 13 B.C. Indus. & Com. L. Rev. 457 (1972).

A signal should only appear once in connection with any one statement. That is, every authority cited as being in "accord" should appear with every other authority bearing the same weight and relationship to the statement.

G. Order of Citations Within a Signal

The authorities cited following a single weight signal are given in this order: cases, statutes, and secondary authority. This order places the most persuasive authorities first. Case authority should appear before statutory authority because the cases are usually interpretations of the more general statutes. This, however, is only the general rule. Should a particular proposition call for a different order as being more persuasive, that order should be used. Consistency itself can help maintain a persuasive flow; variation from the general rule should be avoided unless the variation naturally follows.

> A Section 10(j) injunction should be exercised to prevent irreparable harm. See Angle v. Sacks, 382 F.2d 655, 660 (10th Cir. 1967); 29 U.S.C. § 160(j) (1970); House Subcomm. on Education and Labor, 87th Cong., 1st Sess., Administration of the Labor-Management Relations Act by the NLRB 52 (Comm. Print 1961).

Within each sub-group of cases, statutes, or secondary authority, there are also general rules prescribing the order of the citations.

1. Case Law

Decisions emanating from a higher court in the same jurisdiction are more persuasive. Thus, it is most persuasive to present these cases first. In arranging the cases by their respective courts of decision, all United States courts of appeal are treated as one court. Nevertheless, the circumstances may require the advocate to differentiate among the circuit court opinions by placing cases decided within the circuit hearing the appeal first. Furthermore, when an appeal is taken within the state system, the most persuasive order of presentation may not be the same as if the case were before a federal court.

Cases decided by the same court are listed in reverse chronological order (the most recent decisions first). In a federal appeal, cases cited in connection with a single weight signal should appear in the following order:

Federal
Sources: (1) United States Supreme Court decisions;
(2) United States courts of appeal;
(3) district courts;
(4) administrative agencies (in alphabetical order);

State
Sources: (5) state court decisions (in alphabetical order by state, then by rank of the court within each state);
(6) state agencies (in alphabetical order by state, then alphabetically within each state).

In the United States Supreme Court, for example, the following cases would be cited in this order if all were advanced for the same proposition.

See Fibreboard Paper Products Corp. v. NLRB, 379 U.S. 203 (1964); NLRB v. Thompson Transport Co., 406 F.2d 698 (10th Cir. 1969); NLRB v. Transmarine Navigation Corp., 380 F.2d 933 (9th Cir. 1967); NLRB v. Royal Plating and Polishing Co., 350 F.2d 191 (3d Cir. 1965); Hoban v. Connecticut Foundry Co., 53 Lab. Cas. ¶ 11,255 (D. C. Conn. 1966); Ozark Trailers Inc., 161 N.L.R.B. 561 (1966).

This is not to recommend that the advocate should string citations together. No more authorities should be cited than are absolutely necessary to support the advocate's point. The citation of too many cases interrupts the flow of the argument. It is better to analyze thoroughly a few closely related cases than to waste the space on needless citation.

2. Statutes

Just as with cases, the strongest and most applicable statutes should be cited first following each weight signal. Next, statutes generally applicable to the proposition should be listed, usually following background signals. The order in which statutory authorities should generally appear is as follows:

- a. Constitutions (United States Constitution first and then state constitutions in alphabetical order by state).
- b. Federal statutes:
  —currently in force and in U.S.C. or U.S.C.A. (by progressive order of U.S.C. title number);
  —currently in force but not in U.S.C. or U.S.C.A. (most recently adopted first and thereafter in reverse chronological order);
  —repealed (by order of date of repeal, the most recently repealed first and thereafter in reverse chronological order).
- c. Rules, regulations, and administrative materials should follow the pattern generally applicable to statutes.

3. Secondary Materials

Within each of the following categories, citations are listed in reverse chronological order, and within any one time period, by alphabetical order according to the author's last name or, if the author is unknown, by title. Secondary material should be presented in the following order:

- a. Legislative history;
- b. Treatises (by date of the particular volume or supplement);
- c. Books;
- d. Articles;
- e. Student-written law review material (listed alphabetically by the name of the periodical);
- f. Informal materials such as lectures or seminars. (Because the court may not have access to such information the pertinent parts should be attached to the appendix with a description of the nature of the presentation and the organization or individual making the presentation.)

This is a general ordering based on the weight the court may give to an authority within any one of these categories. This order should be changed if a particular secondary authority would be more persuasive than another.

H. Citation Parentheticals

Parentheticals may be used following a citation to provide the reader with additional facts explaining why the particular authority was cited. Like introductory signals, parentheticals used for different purposes are separated. It is possible to have more than one parenthetical following a citation. In such a case, the parentheticals should be presented in the following order:

(1) Parentheticals indicating weight;

(2) Explanatory parentheticals;

(3) Informative parentheticals.

Each of these parentheticals is described below:

1. Parentheticals Indicating Weight

Parenthetical comment is another tool which can be used to indicate the persuasiveness of the authorities cited. When the statement in the text represents something other than the majority holding of a case cited in connection with that statement, this must be indicated in parentheses immediately following the citation. Among the most common terms indicating weight are:

(1) "(dictum)"

(2) "(concurring opinion)"

(3) "(dissenting opinion)"

(4) [points decided by implication] "(by implication)" or "(alternative holding)"

(5) [points on which the holding of the court is not clear] "(semble)".

For example, if the advocate wanted to cite the concurring opinion in *Fibreboard Paper Products Corp. v. NLRB*, 379 U.S. 203 (1964), as providing the basic source material for a statement in the text, the citation might appear as follows:

```
See Fibreboard Paper Products Corp. v.
NLRB, 379 U.S. 203, 217 (1964)(concurring
opinion).
```

In this example, "see" ties the statement in the text to this case as a basic source for this line of reasoning. The parenthetical is necessary, however, to show that the basic source material supporting the statement is in the concurring rather than the majority opinion.

2. Explanatory Parentheticals

All parentheticals are generally explanatory. The purpose of the various types of parentheticals varies, however, when several parentheticals are used following a single citation. The second parenthetical may be used to further describe the context in which the proposition relates to the authority cited. Thus, the information contained in a parenthetical indicating weight may also serve as the basis for an explanatory parenthetical at another point in the brief.

```
See Fibreboard Paper Products Corp. v.
NLRB, 379 U.S. 203 (1964)(dictum)(concur-
ring opinion).
```

This example indicates that the proposition in the text is supported by both the dicta of the majority opinion and the holding of the concurring opinion. This technique may be used when a point is raised tangentially by the majority opinion but is further discussed in the concurrence.

Explanatory parentheticals are used to provide certain additional information about the opinion. For example: "([Judge's name])" "(4-3 decision)" "(per curiam)" "(memorandum opinion)". Because explanatory parentheticals provide additional information to supplement the authority cited or the preceding parenthetical, there is no limit to the number of parentheticals that may be used following a single citation.

```
See Fibreboard Paper Products Corp. v.
NLRB, supra (concurring opinion)(Stewart,
J.)(Douglas and Harlan, JJ., joining)(5-
Justice majority)(Goldberg, J., took no
part).
```

Whenever this many parentheticals are necessary, the case should be discussed more fully in the text.

3. Informative Parentheticals

This category of parenthetical is used to provide the reader with a short statement about the case, or to include a comment on the case which helps explain the citation.

```
NLRB v. Jones and Laughlin Steel Corp.,
301 U.S. 1 (1937)(steel production that is
completely intrastate affects the nation's
commerce).
```

In this example, a parenthetical is used to describe a situation similar to the one in *Peggy v. Smith & Jones.* Although the factual similarities help support the point asserted by the advocate, further analysis in the limited context of the brief would not be beneficial.

4. Citing Material from One Authority Which Originated in Another

This type of parenthetical is very similar in context to a parenthetical in the regular text of the brief, and is the type of parenthetical that should be used with authorities following the "cf." or "but cf." introductory signals.

The informative parenthetical follows the parenthetical indicating weight and the explanatory parenthetical, but the informative parenthetical may also be used without the other forms of parentheticals. There should only be one informative parenthetical per citation. If further description is required, perhaps the case should be more fully discussed in the text.

I. Related Authority

Phrases identifying related authorities are also appended to a citation to provide the reader with further information about the case or statute cited in the text. These other authorities are related to the cited authority in such a manner as to refer the reader to another work which: (1) conveniently reprints the cited authority, (2) provides the prior or subsequent history of a case, (3) discusses or quotes the cited authority, or (4) is quoted or discussed in the cited authority.

References to related authority references are generally introduced by an underscored explanatory phrase which follows the citation and immediately precedes the related authority. The explanatory phrase describes the relationship between the cited authority and the related authority. For example, if a statute has been reprinted in a book, and the advocate wishes to draw this to the attention of the court, the advocate might cite the authority as follows:

```
H.R. 3020, 80th Cong., 1st Sess. § 301
(1947), reprinted in I NLRB, Legislative
History of the Labor Management Relations
Act 1947, at 92-94 (1948).
```

Note, no comma follows the explanatory phrase in the above example. When introducing the subsequent history of a case, however, a comma will usually follow the explanatory phrase.

Darlington Manufacturing Co. v. NLRB, 397
F.2d 760 (4th Cir. 1968), cert. denied, 393
U.S. 1023 (1969).

If more than one type of related authority is used, these additional
authorities should be presented in the following order: reprinted authorities, relevant history, authorities discussing the cited authority,
and authorities discussed by the cited authority.

In only one instance should the explanatory phrase not be underlined. Where the related authority is discussed or quoted in the cited
authority, the relationship between the two authorities is introduced
and explained as a parenthetical:

Fibreboard Paper Products Corp. v. NLRB,
379 U.S. 203, 211 (1964)(construing 29
U.S.C. § 158(d)(1970).

The above example should be distinguished from situations in which
the cited authority is discussed in (rather than discusses) the related
authority:

29 U.S.C. § 158(d)(1970), construed in
Fibreboard Paper Products Corp. v. NLRB,
379 U.S. 203, 211 (1964).

Other common explanatory phrases which describe the relationship between authorities are: "noted in", "quoted in", "reviewed by", "questioned in", "(noting)", "(quoting)", "cert. granted," "vacated," "appeal
denied," "enforcement denied," and "modified".

Chapter Four

THE ORAL ARGUMENT

Oral argument affords the advocate an additional chance to convince the court of the propriety of the client's position. In oral argument, the advocate is able to answer the court's questions and assuage any concerns the court may have. When the advocate determines that oral argument may advance his client's interests and when the court agrees to hear oral argument, the advocate must be well prepared.

I. DESCRIPTION OF A HEARING

In order to understand how to prepare and present an oral argument, it is first necessary to understand what actually occurs during the appellate hearing. For descriptive purposes, the hearing will be broken down into the general procedure and the specific elements of a presentation.

A. General Procedure

The hearing is conducted before a tribunal usually composed of three judges. The advocate faces the bench from behind a lectern or podium. The petitioner is entitled to make the first presentation and may also reserve time for rebuttal. After counsel for petitioner has spoken, but before he delivers a rebuttal, counsel for the responding party is offered the opportunity to address the court. During these presentations, the court will frequently interject comments or queries, requesting the advocate to address specific concerns of the court. Following these arguments, the court indicates it will take the matter under submission or recesses to reach a decision.

Regulations governing attire, where counsel should sit, time allotted for argument, and other procedural aspects of the appellate hearing may be found in the local court rules. The Moot Court Rules at the University of California at Los Angeles, for example, require that each party to the litigation be represented by two advocates, each of whom is permitted to speak for up to fifteen minutes. The advocate presenting the rebuttal may reserve up to five minutes of his time for rebuttal, but this must be done at the beginning of his initial speech.

B. Elements of a Presentation

The oral argument contains the following elements: introduction, prepared argument, answers to questions from the tribunal, transitions back to the argument, summary of uncovered materials, and conclusion. While all of these elements might not occur in a single presentation, it is important that the advocate be familiar with their purpose and use.

An introduction is an opening statement to the court which informs the court of purely formal matters, such as identifying the advocate and his client, delineating the issues to be discussed by the advocate, and reserving rebuttal time. Since the court will be familiar with the general fact pattern of the case from the briefs, further information need not be provided in the introduction. Rather, the introductory portion should capsulize the central idea the advocate wishes the court to keep in mind.

After the introduction, the advocate will begin to present the substance of his argument to the court. This is normally a prepared argument consisting of two parts: a summary of the main contentions and the argument of individual points. In summarizing the contentions, the advocate should enumerate the various arguments and subpoints which make the contentions compelling. After this enumeration, the most important and persuasive subpoints are asserted.

At various points throughout the argument, the advocate will be interrupted by questions from the bench. The advocate must answer these questions in the most responsive, complete, and persuasive way possible, and then return to his prepared argument by use of an appropriate transition sentence.

II.   OUTLINING THE ARGUMENT

The first step in preparing a presentation is to construct an outline. An outline should be prepared even if the advocate plans on using different notes, or no notes, during the hearing. Mere preparation of the outline will help the advocate to understand better the substance, supporting materials, and organization of the argument.

A. Building the Outline

Building a skeletal outline of the argument is a relatively simple process. The advocate should list in the outline the contentions, points of analysis which support those contentions, and the factual or legal authority used as the basis for such analysis in the brief. In addition, the advocate should include unfavorable legal authorities and ways in which they can be distinguished from the case on appeal. In most cases, the outline prepared for the hearing will closely resemble the outline of the brief. In preparing the outline, the advocate must attempt to determine what the court will view as the legal issues crucial to a decision in the case. These issues should then be treated in greater detail in the outline. While the level of specificity in the

outline will vary with each advocate, it is recommended that this
outline be no longer than one or two pages so that it can be used for
quick reference at the hearing. The "jurisdiction" portion of Petitioner's outline in *Peggy v. Smith & Jones* might be structured in the
following way:

The Board has jurisdiction over the labor
dispute at S. & J.:

A. Law firms, as a class, affect commerce:

GOLDFARB: law practice=commerce.

FAINBLATT: There's an effect even if
enterprise is intrastate.

FOLEY: Board held law firms affect
commerce. Overruled prior
Board decisions that law
firms do not affect commerce
(i.e., EVANS and BODLE,
FOGEL).

B. Law firm satisfies jurisdictional
standards set by Board.

CAMDEN: $250,000 gross receipts an-
nually.

FOLEY: Board asserted jurisdiction
over law firms.

Board intends to assert jurisdiction
as evidenced by complaint: HOFFMAN
says this should be dispositive.
Jurisdiction need not be proven.

SEIMONS MAILING: $50,000 inflow/out-
flow. This is a
guideline, not a
congressional man-
date. Thus, is not
dispositive per
CHAUFFEURS.

C. Associate Lawyers are employees.

> LUMBERMAN'S: S.Ct. held attys=em-
> ployees
>
> WAYNE CO.:   Board held attys=employ-
> ees
>
> Prof'l employees within act, per
> congressional intent: H.Rep. 1947.
>
> Attorney-client confidentiality:
> Not a viable exception. Attys at S.
> & J. do not represent competing
> unions. Other confidential infor-
> mation available to attys doesn't
> necessarily mean duty of confiden-
> tiality will be violated:
>
> > HAMESTER: trade secrets
> >
> > BELL: Military secrets
>
> Managerial exception - Per BELL
> AEROSPACE. Not a viable exception,
> because Rufus Smith does all manage-
> rial decision-making (R. 20).

B. Purposes of the Outline

The outline serves three purposes: it provides a convenient reference for understanding the organization of the argument and its supporting materials, it organizes the materials from which an extemporaneous
speech can be delivered, and it enables the advocate adeptly to handle
questions from the bench.

First, this outline structures the materials for the advocate and,
ultimately, for the court. By articulating to the court at the outset of
his argument the contentions listed in the outline, the advocate provides the court with an idea of what he deems the critical elements to
be discussed.

Second, the proposed outline serves to guide the advocate in the
presentation of his argument. By following the outline and discussing
the points of analysis in support of his contentions, the advocate presents an oral argument which is both persuasive and logical. Note that
the argument of individual points is presented through the use of facts

in conjunction with legal precedents and public policy. These most specific elements of the outline aid the advocate in proving his contentions and demonstrating why his client should prevail.

Third, the outline aids the advocate in responding to questions posed by the court. Since the outline will be an organized analysis of all the major issues in the case, with references to legal authority, case facts, and equitable policy considerations, the advocate need merely look to the outline to find the subject of the court's question. He can then use the organized analysis in the outline both to respond to the query and to continue his argument of the contentions.

III. PRESENTING THE ORAL ARGUMENT

Like the written brief, the oral argument has its own requisite elements. The effectiveness of the oral argument depends in large part upon the advocate's mastery of these elements: introduction, prepared argument, responses to questions from the court, transitions, summary and conclusion.

To prepare effectively for the various contingencies in the oral hearing, the advocate should first prepare the outline. The outline should then be reviewed carefully to anticipate possible questions and formulate responses. The final step is to prepare an introduction and conclusion to the oral argument.

A. Introduction

The introduction should set the tone of the argument. The advocate must capitalize on the court's initial attention by couching both the facts and issues in an accurate but persuasive manner. This can easily be done through the use of a thesis statement expressing the central idea which the advocate wants the court to remember throughout the argument. The thesis is a one-sentence affirmative capsulization of the most persuasive theme in the advocate's argument. The thesis may be based on the policy considerations, case law, or the equities in the case. Although the thesis statement should be composed in advance, the advocate should be sensitive to the court's concerns and be prepared to modify his thesis accordingly. Thus, counsel for Petitioner in *Peggy v. Smith & Jones* might introduce her argument as follows:

```
Your Honors:  I am Kathy Rohwer, counsel
for Petitioner, John L. Peggy, Regional
Director of the National Labor Relations
Board.  Your Honors, the National Labor Re-
lations Board requests this Court to sus-
```

```
tain the 10(j) injunction issued by the
District Court of Erewhon.  This injunction
is essential to preserve the law firm of
Smith & Jones so that after the Board has
demonstrated the Firm's discriminatory
practices and refusals to bargain, the
Board can effect a remedy.  For the next
fifteen minutes, I will indicate that the
injunction is warranted because there is
reasonable cause to believe the Firm has
violated Sections 8(a)(3), (5), and (1) of
the National Labor Relations Act.  My co-
counsel, Gwen Whitson, will then establish
that the Board has jurisdiction and that
the Court acted properly in issuing the
injunction to preserve the Firm.  We would
like to reserve 5 minutes of my co-coun-
sel's time for rebuttal.
```

This introduction not only provides the court with the essential factual information within the context of the issues involved, but it does so in a way which is designed to evoke a favorable response to the advocate's position—it is clearly part of her argument. Note, the advocate may wish to use the more formal salutation, "May it please the Court," in lieu of "Your Honors."

B. Prepared Argument

After the introduction, the advocate will begin to present the substance of his argument. This argument will be drawn from the contentions and analysis prepared in the outline.

1. Selection of Arguments

It is not necessary that the advocate orally argue every point listed in the outline; in fact, it is generally a mistake to repeat all of the arguments of the brief. Unnecessary repetition of arguments presented in the brief will bore the court and waste its time. No argument is waived merely because it is not developed in oral argument. The advocate should utilize his limited time by selecting only his most crucial arguments for oral presentation. Likewise, it is not wise to select only the strongest argument of the case if it is clear that the advocate must prevail on a weaker argument if he is to win. Evasion of vital weaknesses is never persuasive. On the other hand, he should avoid subjecting his weakest arguments to the cross-examination of the bench if possible.

In selecting the arguments to be presented at the oral hearing, the advocate should keep in mind a few basic rules. First, the selection of arguments is at least somewhat dependent upon the side being represented. For example, the advocate representing the appellant or petitioner should select as his arguments those which show that reversible error was committed by the lower court; counsel for respondent or appellee, on the other hand, should select arguments which show that the trial court either applied the correct legal standard or properly exercised its discretion. In addition, the order in which the advocates present their respective cases has a bearing on the selection of arguments. The advocate who argues first has the disadvantage of not really knowing what issues the court perceives to be crucial to a determination of the case; as a result, he must rely on his own sense of the case, trends in the law, and his knowledge of the court and its members in selecting the arguments to be presented. The advocate arguing second, on the other hand, can discern the court's concerns by listening to the questions posed to his opponent, and modify his selected arguments accordingly. Above all, the advocate must know his legal arguments and be flexible enough in his approach to add or delete arguments to meet the court's concerns.

The number of separate arguments made in oral arguments should be kept to a minimum. The advocate should concentrate his efforts rather than scatter them among all the arguments presented in the brief. If, upon reviewing the briefs, relevant case law, and the record, in preparation for oral argument, the advocate discovers that some point helpful to his case was not sufficiently emphasized in his brief, he may use oral argument to provide that emphasis. Ideally, oral argument should supplement, not repeat, the briefs. Thus, for example, Petitioner in *Peggy* might have decided to underscore during argument the fact that upon reorganization an attorney-associate who chose not to join the union was retained while all the attorney-associates who joined the union were no longer employed.

Similarly, the advocate should beware of excessively arguing in the alternative. It is probably a by-product of law school training that the lawyer argues in the alternative more often than necessary. Such arguments tend to make the presentation overly intricate. Moreover, they reflect an equivocal stance by the advocate which indicates a vulnerable case.

Finally, the advocate should bear in mind that these techniques of oral persuasion are not ends in themselves; the goal of oral argument is to persuade the court. The advocate should not insist on pursuing a line of reasoning which is unacceptable to the court when other arguments are available. There may be many reasons why a court does not want to base its decision on certain grounds, and the advocate should be perceptive enough to discover the road of least resistance that will lead to the desired result.   Since all the relevant arguments are covered in the written brief, the advocate need not fear that the court is unaware of his position.   Flexibility does not imply surrender. When an argument is crucial to the favorable disposition of the case, however, it should be made with vigor and tenacity regardless of the court's predisposition against it.   The effective advocate can readily discern the times when he should follow the court and those times when he should lead it.

2.   Use of Authority

When orally arguing his contentions, the advocate should be wary of citing too many cases to the court.   Most briefs are well peppered with case authority.   Of course case authority is necessary in the written brief to substantiate all points that are made.   But this technique does not work well in the oral presentation of an appeal.   Only very important cases should be cited.   The court will not be able to follow or remember too many cases.   Consequently, authority must be selected with care.   The advocate should present only those cases most directly on point and relating to the most important arguments.

Although it is usually safe to assume that the judges have read the brief, counsel cannot assume that they remember the facts of all the cases that were cited.   Thus, whenever the court's attention is drawn to a case, a full discussion of the facts should be given as well as a discussion of the legal doctrine.   Without a factual context, most cases are useless as authority.

The "rule" given above is not to be followed universally.   Occasions arise where the case cited does not need factual elaboration.   If the case is particularly well-known or was recently decided by the same court, reference by name only is appropriate.   If the case is cited in the brief, it is usually sufficient in oral argument to identify the case by name, jurisdiction, and date alone.   If, on the other hand, the case is not cited in the brief, the court should be informed of this and provided with a full citation to the case.   The advocate must not assume, however, that the court shares his detailed familiarity with the cases.

Statutes and decisions should be quoted only when the language significantly adds to the clarity or persuasiveness of the oral argument. Hearing is a poor mechanism for catching verbal refinements, so quotations should generally be limited to presentation in a brief.   The advocate should not attempt to direct the court to the precise arrangement of words or the phrasing of a quotation.   Rather, he should direct the court to the underlying meaning of the material by paraphrasing the quotation.

There are times, however, when quotation is necessary.   These occasions arise with particular frequency when statutory construction or definitional meaning is involved. In these cases, the precise language may determine the disposition of the case. An effective method of assisting the court in these instances is to invite the court's attention to the particular page of the brief on which the quotation appears. This permits the court to follow the words and, by combining both visual and aural perception, to grasp the significance of the quoted language.

There is a serious drawback, however, in citing to the brief—a disadvantage common to most visual aids. Whenever such aids are employed, there is often added difficulty in redirecting the court's attention to an issue other than that which was the subject of the visual material. In the pressure of time, it is imperative that the court follow the presentation of the advocate at the pace which the advocate is setting; when visual material is introduced, the judge can become so involved that he momentarily stops listening and lets his mind linger instead upon what he is seeing. Keeping in mind the potential drawbacks of references to the brief, the advocate should be extremely selective in choosing only the most vital language to lay before the court.

If a statute is important enough to form the body of an argument on oral presentation, it is important enough to be set forth in the brief. Thus, there should be no problem in calling the court's attention to the relevant pages of the brief before making a statutory argument. It is generally a mistake, however, to assume that the court knows the statute well enough to understand an intricate argument based upon it without the aid of the written word. Often the advocate has so thoroughly researched the language that his intimacy with the statute makes him insensitive to the difficulty of its construction. Since the advocate's primary objective is to communicate, he must employ devices which will assist him in his presentation. These observations lead not only to the conclusion that the advocate should cite to the brief, but also that arguments on statutory construction should be kept as simple as possible.

3. Repeating Arguments

The advocate should not hesitate to pursue his cause by repetition of his contentions throughout the argument. Obviously the advocate should not sound like a broken record; the reiteration of contentions should be made within the context of the responses to questions, the transitions from one issue to another, and the conclusions.

The need for repetition is particularly great when the court is actively engaged in questioning the advocate. Often some members of the panel are thinking about their next question while the advocate is answering a question from another member of the bench. It is the advocate's obligation to make sure that all of the judges have heard and understood his main points. It would be a rare case indeed, where one simple statement of the details of the argument could accomplish this goal.

4. Handling Opponent's Arguments

In the oral argument the advocate must answer the relevant contentions advanced by opposing counsel. These answers can be effectively presented within the framework of the outline, as an affirmative posture is more persuasive than a point-by-point refutation of contentions raised by the opposition. The advocate should not debate specific legal principles with opposing counsel; instead, he should couch his responses within the analysis of his own contentions.

C. Responding to Questions

Many an appeal is determined by how well the advocate responds to questions from the bench. Questions not only evince an interest in the on-going oral presentation, but also reveal the thoughts and concerns of the deciding tribunal. Accordingly, questions should be welcomed by the advocate and answered with care.

The advocate should not evade or postpone a question no matter how embarrassing the question may be or how much it interrupts the organization of the argument. The court has the right to expect and receive prompt replies to its questions. If he is well-prepared and has a sound position, the advocate should have no trouble responding to the court.

Likewise, it is generally a poor practice to defer a question either to a later time in the advocate's argument or to a co-counsel. Although the tribunal's questions may interrupt the logical order of the advocate's outline, he should never defer the question to a later time in his argument. To delay responding to its concerns only increases the court's apprehension regarding the subject matter of the question, and leaves the impression that the advocate cannot effectively respond to the concern.

The advocate should expect that the court will interrupt his structured argument, and design the outline so that an immediate shift can be executed smoothly. Many arguments, in fact, are composed almost entirely of questions from the bench and the advocates' responses. Consequently, the advocate must be prepared to answer questions. The advocate should also have a brief summation of the main point he wants the court to remember in the event he is allowed only two to three minutes to summarize his case after rigorous questioning.

1. Types of Questions

While the court may question the advocate on any subject relevant to the case, questions will usually fall within three main areas: legal authorities, policy considerations, and factual information.

    a. Authority. Questions concerning the legal authorities which affect the advocate's contentions require that he be able to interpret and distinguish statutes and prior court opinions. The court may want to know how a particular authority supports the advocate's contention, or why a conflicting authority should not govern the court's decision in the case. Sometimes the court merely wishes to discover whether the advocate has any legal authority upon which he bases his analysis. To a court bound by principles of *stare decisis*, answers to these questions are very important in persuading the tribunal that it may rule in favor of the advocate. For example, counsel for Petitioner in *Peggy v. Smith & Jones* might respond to the following question in this manner:

```
Q:  Counselor, what does "just and proper,"
    as used in the statute, mean if not sat-
    isfying the traditional equitable stand-
    ards?  What have the courts said?

A:  Your Honor, this Court in the case of
    Hecht v. Bowles indicated that in issu-
    ing statutory injunctions courts may ap-
    ply different standards than the tradi-
    tional standards for equitable injunc-
    tions.  This Court has not yet indicated
    what should be considered by a court con-
    fronted with a petition for a 10(j) in-
    junction.  The statute only provides that
    the issuance of the injunction be "just
    and proper."  In interpreting this lan-
    guage several circuit courts have reach-
    ed different conclusions.  Petitioners
    urge your Honors to clarify this unset-
    tled area of law by holding that a 10(j)
    injunction is "just and proper" if it
    would promote the goals of the NLRB, and
    prevent irremediable violations of the
    Act.
```

Judges may also wish to question the advocate concerning the ramifications of principles enunciated by the cited legal authorities. Judges are especially interested in the potential limits of the principles applied by the advocate. In responding to questions regarding the scope and limits of legal principles, the advocate must be prepared to establish the practicable boundaries to which these principles should apply. Judges concerned with extending principles beyond all reasonable limits must be reassured by the advocate that the principle under discussion will be not applied in an overbroad manner. Thus, the advocate may respond to a question reflecting a concern that the 10(j) injunction will be overused as follows:

Q: According to your definition of "just
    and proper" Ms. Whitson, is there a
    time when an alleged refusal to bargain
    would not warrant the issuance of a 10(j)
    injunction?

A: Yes, your Honor, there is. For example,
    if a businessman completely cease his
    business operation because he lost all
    of his goods in a fire, and no amount of
    bargaining could mitigate the total loss
    of stock, then the businessman would be
    justified in closing his business without
    bargaining and a 10(j) injunction would
    not be justified.

b. Policy ramifications and equitable considerations.

Questions concerning policy ramifications and equitable considerations of the case require the advocate to look beyond a favorable decision in the instant case to discern its effect upon the judicial process and society as a whole. Questions relating to policy considerations involve determining whether the legal principles advanced by the advocate would promote or hinder desired public policies. These questions are vitally important to the court because of the impact this particular decision might have upon society and its institutions. The following example demonstrates the concern judges have in aligning their decision with desired public policies, and how an adept advocate can assuage their concerns:

Q: Counselor, how can this Court infringe
    upon the prerogatives of the partners to
    hire and fire whomever they wish?

A: Your Honor, the injunction does not in-
    fringe upon the partners' rights to fire

any of the associates. It merely retains
the operational structure of the firm
Smith & Jones. Under the injunction, the
partners could terminate the employment
of all unionized employees. If it was
subsequently found that this constituted
an additional unfair labor practice then
the law firm of Smith & Jones still exists and can be subject to the Board's
order to remedy its practice.

When a judge poses questions regarding the equities of the case,
the advocate should understand that the court is concerned whether
simple justice between the parties requires a particular result. These
questions are important because the court will want to base its decision
not only on case law and policy considerations, but also on broader,
more discretionary principles. The advocate should already have determined which actions by both parties constitute just or unjust conduct, in order to reassure the court that a decision favoring the advocate's client is also the just determination of the case:

Q: But Counsel, it sounds like you're ask-
     ing the Court to step in and prevent
     these partners of Smith & Jones from
     exercising their right to bail out of a
     sinking operation. Why should we force
     the partners to continue a business
     which might well go bankrupt?

A: Your Honor, the record is, at best, am-
     biguous as to the present financial
     position of the Firm. The partners of
     Smith & Jones have offered no evidence
     to show that they are at present losing
     money. But with all due respect, your
     Honor, this issue cannot be determined
     merely by examining the balance sheets.
     The Firm is attempting to undercut the
     right of the associates to unionize and
     bargain collectively. The associates
     have the right to band together to bar-
     gain collectively with their employer,
     without being forced to choose between
     having a union or having a job. To
     permit the partners of Smith & Jones to

```
close up shop to avoid bargaining with
the union would wipe out these rights.
These rights of the associates and the
national policy favoring unionization
must be protected.  That is why the
Section 10(j) injunction is crucial.
```

c. Information. Finally, the court may question the advocate merely to seek factual information regarding the case on appeal. Answers to these questions typically involve clarifying the court's understanding of the procedural posture of the case itself, or the actions which resulted in litigation between the parties. The way in which the advocate responds to these questions is important because the court's decision will be based in large part upon what it perceives to be the crucial facts involved in the case. The advocate must be prepared to argue persuasively even the facts of the case, as the following example demonstrates:

```
Q:   In relation to the alleged 8(a)(5) vio-
     lation, Ms. Rohwer, didn't Respondent
     offer to hand over to Mr. Wind of Wind
     & Zephyr the associates' resumes, so
     that he could consider hiring some or
     all the associates?

A:   The affidavit of Mr. Rufus Smith indi-
     cates that he did deliver these resumes
     to Mr. Wind.  But, your Honor, the fact
     remains that only one associate--a non-
     union nephew of Mr. Smith--was offered
     employment at Wind & Zephyr.  Petition-
     er suspects that this may be more than
     just coincidental.  And it should be
     kept in mind, your Honor, that the
     8(a)(5) standard articulated in Fibre-
     board requires the employer to bargain
     over not only the effects of the deci-
     sion, but also the decision itself.
```

Notice, the advocate has answered the request for information and provided additional facts from the record and cited authorities which help her case.

2. Preparing for Questions

Preparation for the oral argument involves more than merely refreshing one's memory as to the research embodied in the brief. The well-prepared advocate must not only completely master his own arguments and the cases he has cited to support them, but he must acquire an equal mastery over the arguments and authorities of his opponent. The advocate must understand the sophisticated distinctions involved in his case so that he can make them clear to the court in the short time allotted for his presentation.

Preparation is essential if the advocate is to be able to answer questions from the tribunal. To prepare for the court's questions, the advocate should re-read the record on appeal, examining and analyzing every relevant fact of the case so that he will be able to use these facts when responding to queries. The advocate should familiarize himself with the facts and holding of each case cited in the written brief, as judges often will ask him to explain how cited authorities support the contentions being advanced.

When preparing for policy oriented questions, the advocate should examine every contention in the outline to determine the legal principle enunciated, and attempt to define its limits. Even when the advocate does not propose a new principle, but merely the application of an established doctrine to a new factual situation, this different application of the principle will still raise questions concerning its scope in future cases before the tribunal. Thus, the advocate will want to establish limits to the principle which are reasonable and acceptable to the court.

Equitable considerations raised by the facts must also be analyzed. The advocate should prepare for questions regarding the equities in the case by examining the facts and law applicable to each contention, and discovering the most persuasive way to explain their consequences in light of the court's predilections.

One effective method of preparing for questions from the bench is to work with an attorney familiar with the case who can test the advocate's ability to respond to potential questions. The questioner should pursue every conceivable fact, legal principle, policy ramification, and equitable consideration raised by the contentions in the written brief, working with the advocate to create the most persuasive answers possible to these questions. Questions regarding the procedural posture of the case and the remedies requested in the brief should also be considered so that these issues can be handled adroitly if they are raised at the oral hearing.

3. Effective Responses

Once the advocate is prepared to respond to questions, the queries posed by the tribunal will aid his presentation of his case. These inquiries provide the basis for the advocate's affirmative arguments and reveal the court's approach to the various issues raised by both sides. The issues that intrigue the court when petitioner is speaking are likely to be the same issues that will be important when respondent argues his case. Either respondent should stress these points if they are in his favor, or he should prepare himself for interrogation by the court.

By listening carefully to the judges' questions the advocate may discover which judges are persuaded by public policy considerations and which members of the court are concerned with conceptual refinements. This should cue the perceptive advocate to modify his arguments accordingly. Furthermore, listening to the questions is important to the responsiveness of the advocate. It is not unusual for an advocate to read more into a question than was intended. No question should be answered until it is fully understood. Asking the court to repeat a question is less damaging than giving an unsolicited and unresponsive answer.

The advocate must not assume that all questions coming from the tribunal are meant to challenge his position. Sometimes questions are designed to draw out a particular line of reasoning which the court finds especially appealing, or to redirect the advocate's attention to the dispositive issues of his case. Each question should be evaluated before it is answered so that friendly questions are not rejected. The advocate should pause to consider the question asked, if such a pause would be helpful. There is no premium on speedy response, inasmuch as judges are persuaded by the content of responses and not by immediacy or glibness.

Above all the advocate must maintain his composure while defending his position. In particular, it is essential that proper deference to the court be shown regardless of the advocate's personal opinion of the question or members of the panel. The advocate must answer every question with a view toward his client's interest and an awareness that his responses and demeanor affect those interests.

4. Problematic and Unanswerable Questions

Notwithstanding the advocate's thorough preparation, the appellate court may often pose questions which the advocate cannot easily answer. Perhaps the appellate court's question is couched in confusing terms or addresses points of law which the advocate failed to consider. On the other hand, the advocate may simply be caught not knowing the precise answer to an obvious and clear question. When faced with these predicaments the advocate has several alternatives.

a. Confusing questions. When a question is phrased in confusing terms the advocate should explain to the judge that he is perplexed by the question and would appreciate a clarification.

In the following example, counsel for Petitioner in *Peggy* must politely correct a member of the court who incorrectly believes that the

Supreme Court decided *Goldfarb* prior to the National Labor Relations Board's ruling in *Bodle, Fogel*:

> Q: Counsel, didn't the NLRB itself back down from the holding we established in Goldfarb when the Board subsequently decided Bodle, Fogel and Foley, Hoag?
>
> A: Excuse me, your Honor, I'm somewhat confused. Would you please rephrase the question?
>
> Q: Certainly, Ms. Whitson. Oh, I'm sorry; the Board decided Bodle, Fogel before our Goldfarb decision, didn't it?
>
> A: I believe so, your Honor. Goldfarb was decided in 1975 and the Board ruled on Bodle in 1973.
>
> Q: That would make Foley, Hoag consistent with Goldfarb?
>
> A: Yes, your Honor. Foley, Hoag came after Goldfarb and follows the Goldfarb holding that the practice of law is indeed a type of commerce. In doing so, it overruled the Bodle determination.
>
> Q: Thank you Ms. Whitson. You may proceed.

Obviously, such a request for clarification would not be appropriate when it might antagonize the court; for example, the advocate should not request clarification when such a request has previously been made.

b. Irrelevant questions. When a question delves into points of law which the advocate considers tangential, the advocate should attempt to respond to the court's concern while indicating why that concern—although appealing—is not dispositive of the case. For instance:

> Q: Counsel, I don't see how we can let an injunction issue when we have no conclu-

sive showing in the record that there was
a Section 8(a)(3) violation.

A: Your Honor, the record at this stage of
     the proceeding is admittedly incomplete.
     But at this point in the proceeding, all
     the Board must do is show reasonable
     cause to believe unfair labor practices
     have occurred. The Board does not need
     to establish actual violation to obtain
     the injunction. The proof of the actual
     violations will be provided at the Board's
     hearing on the merits of the Complaint.

Note that in responses of this sort, the advocate must be careful to
maintain a deferential attitude.

   c. Unanswerable Questions. Clearly the most damaging questions
are those which are clear, cogent, pertinent, and a surprise to the
advocate. When confronted with this problem, the advocate should
seek to minimize the impact of his apparent ignorance. This is occasionally accomplished when the advocate politely and simply acknowl-
edges that he is unable to answer the question. Thus, the advocate
might react to the following question in this way:

Q: But Counsel, you're asking us to place
     Messrs. Smith, Jones, and Barkley in
     limbo until the NLRB concludes its in-
     vestigation. That could be a consider-
     able period of time. Ms. Whitson, do you
     know off-hand how long this NLRB proce-
     dure is going to take before we have the
     Board's decision?

A: No, your Honor, I'm afraid I don't.

An alternative remedy is to offer to provide a supplemental brief on
the issue. Of course, this alternative is feasible only if supplemental
briefs are allowed by the local court rules.

   The advocate may occasionally elicit assistance from the court in
responding to troubling questions. For example, if the court asks an
advocate to distinguish a case and the advocate cannot remember the

precise facts of the case, the advocate might respond in the following way:

> Q: Counsel, concerning this duty to bargain--aren't the facts of this case closer to NLRB v. William Burns Detective than they are to Fibreboard?
>
> A: I'm sorry, your Honor; I can't seem to recall the facts of the Burns Detective case. Perhaps, if you would refresh my memory . . . ?
>
> Q: Certainly. In Burns, the Eighth Circuit Court of Appeals determined no violation of Section 8(a)(5) when the respondent detective agency failed to bargain over the closing of an uneconomical branch operation.
>
> A: Thank you, your Honor. I believe the facts in Burns are distinguishable from the case at bar. In Burns, as in Morrison Cafeteria and Royal Plating, the court concluded that the employer's closing of a single, separate, and autonomous branch of its business is not a subject of mandatory bargaining. Here, your Honor, the law firm of Smith & Jones is not composed of a number of branch offices. The Firm's sole office, its entire operation, is being moved to Wind & Zephyr. As indicated by this Court in Fibreboard, a case involving this type of apparent subcontracting requires mandatory bargaining.

In this example, the advocate candidly admits her ignorance of the facts of the precedent in question. But when provided with a factual summary of *Burns*, she persuasively distinguishes it from *Fibreboard*, and demonstrates why the court should follow the *Fibreboard* holding in deciding this case.

Only as a last resort should the advocate give an answer that is somewhat non-responsive to the question. This type of dodge should generally be avoided because it raises questions about the advocate's ethics and credibility.

d. Questions within Co-counsel's Expertise. While the advocate should be familiar with any contentions to be argued by his co-counsel, he may, on occasion, be confronted with questions exceeding his expertise. If this occurs, the advocate should attempt to give the court some information in response to the question, while politely informing the tribunal that the question can be answered better by co-counsel. For example, in response to a question regarding the existence of jurisdiction the advocate arguing the existence of unfair labor practices in *Peggy v. Smith & Jones* might respond as follows:

A: Your Honor, Ms. Whitson, who will be discussing the existence of jurisdiction is more familiar with this issue than I. However, inasmuch as the Board's exercise of jurisdiction is constitutional given this Court's decision in Goldfarb and inasmuch as this case meets the $250,000 jurisdictional limitation of Camden, jurisdiction surely exists. I'm sure my co-counsel will be happy to elaborate on this in her presentation.

If the Court continues to ask questions on the same issue, each succeeding answer might reveal less and less information and defer more and more to co-counsel. For example:

Q: Just because it's constitutional for the Board to exercise jurisdiction, and just because this case falls within a nonbinding and non-statutory jurisdictional guideline, it's not certain that the Board will exercise its jurisdiction. How can we be sure the Board will decide to apply its jurisdiction to this case?

A: Briefly, your Honor, we can be fairly sure the Board will exercise this jurisdiction because the case falls within the applicable guidelines promulgated by the Board. My co-counsel can elaborate on this in her presentation.

Finally, when the advocate cannot answer the question, she should defer entirely to her co-counsel:

> Q: But, Counselor, there is no showing in this case that the Firm satisfies the Board's inflow-outflow standard. Doesn't that conclusively refute the existence of jurisdiction?
>
> A: No, your Honor, it doesn't; I'll have to defer to my co-counsel to explain why that is not fatal to jurisdiction.

Responding to the first question in this manner, the advocate politely but firmly defers to her co-counsel, while nonetheless giving a superficial response.

There are, however, situations in which the advocate will not follow this type of response pattern. If the advocate is well versed in co-counsel's arguments, or feels comfortable enough to fully argue them, he should answer the questions directly without any qualifications. On the other hand, if the advocate knows something about co-counsel's arguments but is afraid that the answer might cause problems, he should immediately defer to co-counsel without revealing any information. And, if co-counsel has already spoken and will not speak again, but the court demands an answer, the advocate must give the best possible response in light of his knowledge.

The advocate must attempt to maintain his organization in the face of questions from the bench. Even the most inquisitive panels may permit the advocate to adhere to his basic organization if he can relate his answers to the contentions he is advancing. If the advocate permits the court to do the leading, he gives up his initiative, which may result in his inability to develop fully his arguments.

5. Transitions

After answering the question, the advocate will then return to the prepared outline of his prepared extemporaneous argument. The transition should serve to direct the court's attention to the next point in the outline, while showing its relationship to the immediately preceding response. In the context of *Peggy v. Smith & Jones*, an advocate wishing to move from a question calling for the advocate to distinguish the facts in *Darlington* and *Lees Shopping Center* to a discussion of whether the dissolution of Smith & Jones constituted a complete termination might say:

> A: Your Honor, <u>Darlington</u> involved the closing of a plant wholly owned and controlled by a parent corporation. Darlington Corporation was, in effect, in an alter-ego relationship with the parent firm. In <u>Lees</u>, Mr. Lees had a controlling interest in each of the three technically autonomous businesses in the shopping center. As such, <u>Lees</u> involved a horizontally integrated single employer enterprise. In both <u>Lees</u> and <u>Darlington</u>, a single employer enterprise was ultimately found; and in each case, the closing of part of this enterprise violated the three-part test articulated by this Court in <u>Darlington</u>.
>
>   In <u>Darlington</u>, however, this Court established two standards--one for businesses which close completely, and one for partial closings of businesses. Petitioner submits that the purported closing of Smith & Jones is not a complete closing. Smith & Jones will continue to practice law under the umbrella of Wind & Zephyr. Many of the same clients will be served from the same offices with the same library and the same secretaries. Although the Firm name will change, the business of Smith & Jones will continue.

D.   Summary and Conclusion

Toward the end of his argument, the advocate will usually discover that there are some contentions which have not been fully covered either by his prepared presentation or in his responses to questions from the tribunal. At this point, the advocate will want to bring these issues to the court's attention by quickly summarizing them and inviting the court to their discussion in the written brief. And, if a relatively minor point has been subjected to lengthy inquiry, the advocate should place that point in its proper perspective.

Finally, the advocate will conclude his presentation. The conclusion will normally repeat the thesis statement of the argument and then ask the court to grant the relief requested in the written brief. However, the theme should change if the hearing reveals concerns of the court that could be more important in deciding the case. Petitioner in *Peggy v. Smith & Jones* might conclude her oral argument in the following manner:

```
If it please the Court, I'd like to take a
moment to conclude.  As my co-counsel and I
have explained, the labor dispute at Smith
& Jones is within the jurisdiction of the
NLRB.  Moreover, there is reasonable cause
to believe that the labor dispute at Smith
& Jones resulted from the Firm's discrimi-
natory practices and refusals to bargain.
Finally, in this situation the issuance of
a 10(j) injunction is just and proper in
that it serves the purpose of the National
Labor Relations Act to promote collective
bargaining and preserves the Firm's opera-
tional structure so that the Union will be
able to bargain with Smith & Jones.

     If no injunction issues, Smith & Jones
will go out of business; the Firm will have
avoided its statutory duty to bargain.  If
this Court allows Smith & Jones to close,
this evasive tactic will be condoned.  Pro-
fessional firms everywhere will be encour-
aged to evade their obligations by dissolv-
ing instead of bargaining.  For these rea-
sons, we urge this court to overrule the
decision of the Twelfth Circuit and rein-
state the injunction.
```

E. Rebuttal

Generally, it is wise for the advocate for the moving party to reserve a short amount of time for rebuttal. Rebuttal provides the advocate with the opportunity to reinforce his arguments and leave a favorable last impression with the court by rebutting the arguments made by opposing counsel.

The rebuttal speech is short, and thus is limited to an attack on a few key points raised by the opposition. The rebuttal is actually prepared at the oral hearing, and is designed as a response to all that has previously occurred at the hearing, including the presentations of both sides, the judges' questions, and the advocate's answers.

The rebuttal should be focused, but the focus of each rebuttal must evolve from the dynamics of the particular hearing. The advocate may touch on those of his arguments which the court found appealing, but he should concentrate on opposing counsel's strong points or on glaring weaknesses in his own previous presentation. The rebuttal should conclude with a summary of the advocate's contentions, an affirmative reiteration of the dispositive issues, and a prayer for relief.

IV. SPEAKING STYLE

Perhaps the most difficult element of oral argument to prepare is one's personal speaking style, inasmuch as this aspect of the advocate's oral argument develops only after lengthy practice and speaking experience. Nonetheless, there are certain components of presentation which, if perfected, will increase the persuasiveness of that presentation. In particular, the advocate should cultivate poise, persuasive use of voice and language, and a proper attitude.

A poised advocate exudes a confident, professional demeanor. Appropriate grooming and attire aid immeasurably in creating this impression. The best interests of the client will not be served if the advocate distracts the court with a sloppy personal appearance and casual dress. Likewise, the advocate's demeanor is reflected in his mannerisms in the courtroom. Certain affectations should always be avoided: pounding on the lectern, slouching, pacing, and pointing at the judges distract substantially from the advocate's presentation.

On the other hand, certain mannerisms aid the advocate in persuading the court. The advocate should strive to develop a personal link with each of the judges through eye contact. Appropriate, natural gestures complement the oral presentation. And, as a courtesy both to the court and to opposing counsel, the advocate should remain quiet, attentive, and respectful while not at the podium.

Persuasive use of voice and language will also aid the advocate in orally presenting his contentions. Certain fundamentals of public speaking should be followed unhesitatingly. The voice should never sound forced, but the words should be clearly articulated. The flow of sentences should be emphasized by voice inflection and variation in pace and volume.

The appellate tribunal is not immune from boredom, and it is most difficult for judges to give unflagging attention to every legal contention presented. In order to arouse the court's interest, the advocate should make every effort to use an interesting vocabulary when addressing the court. At the same time, however, the advocate should avoid using terms in the vernacular; the court is a forum deserving of a formal oral presentation. The advocate should make an effort to use proper legal terms when appropriate, in order to explain precisely the points to be made.

It may be worth noting that there is a distinction between the Moot Court situation and an actual appellate hearing. Moot Court is designed to evaluate the ability of the advocate, while a real hearing is an adjudication of the merits of the case. It does not necessarily follow, however, that the two situations should be approached differently. Although the attention of the tribunal is, on the one hand, drawn to the individual advocate, and on the other to the position of his client, it is likely that excellence in both situations will ensue from precisely the same techniques. These include preparation, organization, good speaking skills and an awareness of the court's concerns.

Finally, an oral presentation is most persuasive when the advocate is at once assertive and deferential. Just as an obsequious advocate may fail to convince the court, so too, an overly aggressive advocate may alienate the tribunal. The advocate should therefore guard against erring in these two extremes.

R. D.

M. Q.

*

Appendix A

BRIEF FOR PETITIONER FILED IN THE CASE OF
PEGGY v. SMITH & JONES

IN THE

SUPREME COURT OF THE UNITED STATES

OCTOBER TERM 1977

No. 77-1182

JOHN F. PEGGY, DIRECTOR OF REGION 007
OF THE NATIONAL LABOR RELATIONS BOARD,
FOR AND ON BEHALF OF THE NATIONAL
LABOR RELATIONS BOARD,

                              Petitioner,

        - AGAINST -

SMITH & JONES, A PARTNERSHIP,

                              Respondent.

ON WRIT OF CERTIORARI
TO THE UNITED STATES COURT OF APPEALS
FOR THE TWELFTH CIRCUIT

BRIEF FOR THE PETITIONER

Gwen Whitson
Kathy Rohwer
Counsel for Petitioner
  UCLA School of Law
  Los Angeles, California
  (213) 825-1128

*

TOPICAL INDEX

TABLE OF AUTHORITIES

<u>CONSTITUTION</u>

<u>STATUTES</u>

LEGISLATIVE HISTORY

SECONDARY AUTHORITIES

IN THE

SUPREME COURT OF THE UNITED STATES

OCTOBER TERM 1977

No. 77-1128

JOHN F. PEGGY, DIRECTOR OF REGION 007
OF THE NATIONAL LABOR RELATIONS BOARD,
FOR AND ON BEHALF OF THE NATIONAL
LABOR RELATIONS BOARD,

Petitioner,

- AGAINST -

SMITH & JONES, A PARTNERSHIP,

Respondent.

ON WRIT OF CERTIORARI
TO THE UNITED STATES COURT OF APPEALS
FOR THE TWELFTH CIRCUIT

BRIEF FOR THE PETITIONER

OPINIONS BELOW

The order of the United States District Court for
the Southern District of Erewhon is unreported, and contained
in the Transcript of Record (R. 29-32). The opinion of the
United States Court of Appeals for the Twelfth Circuit is
unreported, and contained in the Transcript of Record (R.33-35).

JURISDICTION

A formal statement of jurisdiction has been waived by Rule 4(c), 1977 Rules of the National Moot Court Competition.

CONSTITUTIONAL PROVISIONS AND STATUTES INVOLVED

The text of the following constitutional provisions and statutes relevant to the determination of the present case are set forth in appendices: U.S. Const. art. I, § 8; National Labor Relations Act §§ 8 (d), 2(7), 8(a)(3), 8 (a)(5), 29 U.S.C. §§ 158(d), 158(a)(5), 158(a)(3), 152(7)(1970); Labor Management Relations Act §§ 10(j), 10(a), 14(c)(1), 29 U.S.C. §§ 160(j), 160(a), 164(c)(1)(1907).

QUESTIONS PRESENTED

I. Whether the District Court, pursuant to section 10(j) of the National Labor Relations Act, as amended, properly issued a temporary injunction restraining Smith & Jones from changing its operational structure.

II. Whether the National Labor Relations Board has established that there is reasonable cause to believe that this labor dispute is within the jurisdiction of the Board.

III. Whether the National Labor Relations Board has established that there is reasonable cause to believe that Smith & Jones is engaging in labor practices that are prohibited by sections 8(a)(5) and 8(a)(3) of the National Labor Relations Act.

[2]

IV. Whether, under the circumstances involved in this case, issuance of a temporary injunction, pursuant to section 10(j) of the National Labor Relations Act, as amended, promotes the purposes of the National Labor Relations Act.

STATEMENT OF THE CASE

Petitioner in this case is John L. Peggy, Regional Director of the National Labor Relations Board (hereinafter referred to as "the Board" or "the NLRB"). Acting on the basis of an unfair labor practice charge filed on July 28, 1977, by Local 1 of the American Association of Law Firm Associates (hereinafter referred to as "the Union"), the Board has investigated the labor practices of Smith & Jones (R. 9). Mr. Peggy has concluded that Smith & Jones is engaging in certain unfair labor practices affecting commerce within the meaning of sections 2(6) and (7) of the National Labor Relations Act (hereinafter referred to as "the Act")(R. 3-7).

Smith & Jones (hereinafter referred to as the "the Firm"), Respondent in this case, is a law partnership which has engaged in the general practice of law in the State of Erewhon for over twenty-five years. The Firm specializes in real estate matters and annually provides legal services valued in excess of $250,000 (R. 11). The Firm presently consists of three partners who employ ten lawyer-associates and fifteen clerical personnel (R. 23-24). Most of the Smith & Jones associates also donate time to the Neighborhood Legal Office, a federally funded program designed to provide legal services to indigent persons (R. 20). Smith & Jones currently has a close business and personal relationship with the firm of Wind & Zephyr. The offices of the two firms are located in the same

[3]

building; the firms share library facilities, they have clients in common, and their respective managing partners meet regularly to advise each other on business decisions (R. 24, 25).

When the associates at Smith & Jones first discussed the possibility of unionization, managing partner Rufus Smith told the employees he was "shocked" by their interest in union representation (R. 15, 22). Mr. Smith further stated that the lawyer-associates were "privileged" to work for his firm and that employees have "no rights" (R. 21, 22).

On June 20, 1977, the Union was certified by the Board as the collective bargaining representative of the lawyer-associates at Smith & Jones. Four days later, and before any negotiations had been scheduled between the Firm and the Union, the partners at Smith & Jones decided to reorganize the partnership due to allegedly unfavorable business projections (R. 26, 27). Under the terms of the reorganization agreement, the partnership would be dissolved on August 31, 1977. After that date, the partners and their secretaries would join the law firm of Wind & Zephyr, and the lawyer-associates who are members of the Union would be unemployed. After the reorganization, the partners of Smith & Jones will render legal services to clients of Wind & Zephyr as well as to their present clients. Furthermore, the lawyer-associates of Wind & Zephyr who are not represented by a union will begin to perform the work formerly performed by unionized Smith & Jones associates (R. 27).

Following the union certification, Mr. Smith indicated some willingness to discuss the consequences of the reorganization plan. Nevertheless, he refused to consult with unionized associates concerning possible alternatives to the planned reorganization. Mr. Ludley, the Union's representative, offered to negotiate temporary pay reductions and to assist in

[4]

bringing in additional clients. These offers to negotiate were
rejected by Mr. Smith (R. 28).

The NLRB General Counsel has issued a Complaint pursuant
to section 10(b) of the Act, alleging that Smith & Jones'
refusal to bargain about the decision to reorganize the partnership violates section 8(a)(5) of the Act and that this reorganization of the firm would result in a violation of sections
8(a)(1) and 8(a)(3) of the Act (R. 10-14). On August 8, 1977, the
Board requested the District Court to issue an injunction
pursuant to section 10(j) of the Act, enjoining the reorganization of Smith & Jones pending final disposition of the proceedings
on the Complaint which are now pending before the Board (R.
3-7). The District Court issued the temporary injunction on
August 18, 1977, after finding that the Board has jurisdiction
over the Firm and that the partners of Smith & Jones have a duty
to bargain with the associates concerning the pending reorganization (R. 32).

An appeal, pursuant to 28 U.S.C. §§ 1291 and 1292(a)(1),
was taken from the order of the District Court (R. 33). On
September 15, 1977, the Court of Appeal decided that the
issuancé of the injunction was erroneous. The majority concluded
that the proposed dissolution of Smith & Jones was a complete
termination of the business of the Firm, obviating any duty to
bargain over the decision to close. The concurring opinion,
after considering other issues, concluded that the Board has no
jurisdiction over this labor dispute and that section 10(j) of
the Act could not apply to this dispute because no "public
interest" is involved. Pending appeal to this Court, the Court
of Appeals has entered a temporary stay of its order dissolving
the injunction (R. 33-35).

[5]

On October 6, 1977, this Court granted a writ of certiorari
to the Court of Appeals in order that all of the questions
raised by the record could be considered (R.36).

SUMMARY OF ARGUMENT

The fundamental question presented by this litigation
is whether the District Court of Erewhon erred in issuing a
Section 10(j) injunction, temporarily restraining the
contemplated dissolution and reorganization of the Smith &
Jones law partnership.

Section 10(j) injunctions were designed to prevent frustration of the National Labor Relations Act pending the National
Labor Relation Board's adjudicatory proceedings. These temporary
injunctions can be granted by the District Court upon a petition
by the National Labor Relations Board when the Board establishes
reasonable cause to believe that an employer is engaging in an
unfair labor practice, and further indicates that the issuance
of the injunction will promote the goals of the Act. A showing
of reasonable cause requires both an indication that the
controversy is within the jurisdiction of the Board and, in
addition, a showing of facts which if undisputed would
constitute unfair labor practices. Thus, Petitioner need
not conclusively prove the existence of the Board's jurisdiction and the liability of Smith & Jones for unfair labor
practices. Those determinations should be made in the first
instance by the NLRB in their upcoming hearings to be held
on the unfair labor practice charges. Nevertheless, in
order to explain fully why the temporary injuction is
essential, Petitioner begins by establishing the case
against Smith & Jones.

[6]

The Board has jurisdiction over all labor disputes that affect commerce. Because the practice of law affects commerce, Petitioner contends that law firms fall within the statutory jurisdiction of the NLRB. Furthermore, the law practice of Smith & Jones, with gross annual revenues of $250,000, falls within the narrow guidelines employed by the Board to limit its exercise of jurisdiction. This showing, plus the Regional Director's issuance of a complaint in this matter indicates that the NLRB will exercise its jurisdiction over the dispute at Smith & Jones. This court is therefore urged to find that sufficient jurisdiction exists for the NLRB to petition the court for an injunction.

There is reasonable cause to believe that Smith & Jones is engaging in a labor practice that is prohibited by section 8(a)(5) of the Act. Smith & Jones has refused and continues to refuse to bargain about its decision to dissolve and reorganize the partnership. Such a decision is a mandatory subject for bargaining within the meaning of section 8(d) of the Act.

Furthermore, there is also reasonable cause to believe that Smith & Jones is engaging in a labor practice that is prohibited by Section 8(a)(3) of the Act. Smith & Jones is terminating the employment associates who have recently unionized so that the Firm may replace them with non-union employees. Smith & Jones may reasonably foresee that the proposed reorganization of the Firm will discourage further unionization of its employees. To discourage this unionization Smith & Jones has decided to dissolve and reorganize the partnership.

The showing that the Board has jurisdiction and will likely exercise it, and the evidence that Smith & Jones is

[7]

reorganizing the operational structure of its law practice
without bargaining about that decision constitute a showing of
reasonable cause to believe that unfair labor practices are
occurring. This showing of reasonable cause, coupled with
considerations of public policy and equity, require that a
temporary injunction be issued to promote the goals of the
Act.

ARGUMENT

I

THE UNFAIR LABOR PRACTICES OF
SMITH & JONES ARE WITHIN THE
JURISDICTION ASSERTED BY THE
NATIONAL LABOR RELATIONS BOARD.

The National Labor Relations Act provides that the
National Labor Relations Board has the necessary jurisdiction "to prevent any person from engaging in unfair labor
practices . . . affecting commerce." 29 U.S.C. § 160(a)
(1970). Only the Commerce Clause, U.S. Const., art. I, § 8,
limits this grant of broad jurisdictional power. See, e.g.,
NLRB v. Reliance Fuel Oil Corp., 371 U.S. 224, 226 (1963).
The NLRB, however, confines the exercise of its powers of
jurisdiction to controversies which substantially affect
interstate commerce and infringe upon the rights of employees.
See, e.g., NLRB v. Denver Building and Construction Trades
Council, 341 U.S. 675 (1951). The labor dispute at Smith &
Jones is such a case. It satisfies the selective jurisdictional criteria delineated by the Board, as well as the
single statutory requirement.

[8]

A. THE BOARD IS EMPOWERED TO ASSERT ITS JURIS-
    DICTION OVER SMITH & JONES BECAUSE THE FIRM'S
    UNFAIR LABOR PRACTICES AFFECT COMMERCE.

The sole statutory limitation upon the Board's jurisdiction
is that the Board may prevent those unfair labor practices
which affect commerce. As defined by the Act, "affecting
commerce" can mean either engaging in commerce or "burdening,
or obstructing commerce or the free flow of commerce . . .."
29 U.S.C. § 152(7)(1970). This Court recently concluded in
Goldfarb v. Virginia State Bar, 421 U.S. 773 (1975) that the
practice of law affects interstate commerce. In Goldfarb, the
Court held that the Sherman Act applies to attorneys because
the title searches performed by attorneys incident to the sale
of property are crucial to commercial activities. Thus, the
minimum fee schedule for title searches, suggested by the bar
association, was illegal because it restrained competition
among attorneys. Similarly, the National Labor Relations Act
applies to Smith & Jones because the firm's legal services,
especially those relating to real estate transactions, are
essential to certain commercial activities of its clients.

Notwithstanding this, Respondent contends that because the
effects of the labor dspute will be felt predominantly in
Erewhon, the NLRB lacks jurisdiction to hear the complaint.
This contention fails for several reasons. The Firm has a
potential for a large interstate practice as indicated by the
fact that one of the nation's five hundred largest industrial
companies is considering retaining Smith & Jones for all of
their real estate work (R. 18). In addition, it is clear that
the Firm can affect commerce regardless of the locations of its
clients. The writing of a lease for a local apartment house,
for example, may affect many commercial variables: the housing

[9]

market, the economy, and the relocations of our mobile population. Finally, this Court has repeatedly recognized that local transactions can have nationwide commercial implications. In NLRB v. Jones and Laughlin Steel Corp., 301 U.S. 1 (1937) this Court held that steel production that is completely intrastate affects the nation's commerce. Likewise, in NLRB v. Fainblatt, 306 U.S. 601 (1939) this Court held that one small sewing shop engaged in stitching together pre-cut fabric for a larger manufacturer affects commerce. Similarly, in Polish National Alliance v. NLRB, 322 U.S. 643 (1944) this Court concluded that labor dispute in an intra-state business affects commerce if it is representative of other similar disputes nationwide.

Although the specific question of whether a labor dispute at a private law firm affects commerce has not been presented to this Court, the NLRB has considered this issue on three occasions. In every instance the NLRB concluded that the operations of the law firm affected commerce within the meaning of the Act. In two of these cases, the Board acknowledged the statutory jurisdiction but declined to assert that jurisdiction. Bodle, Fogel, Julber, Reinhardt and Rothschild, 206 N.L.R.B. 512 (1973); Evans v. Kunz, Ltd., 194 N.L.R.B. 1216 (1972). In the most recent decision, however, the Board partially reversed its earlier decisions by acknowledging its statutory jurisdiction and asserting it.[1] Foley, Hoag and Eliot, 229 N.L.R.B. No. 80, Lab. L. Rep. (CCH) ¶ 18,116 (1977).

---

1. The Board has never questioned that lawyers can be employees. See Lumberman's Mutual Casualty Co. of Chicago, 75 N.L.R.B. 1132 (1948). Their status as professionals as defined by 2(12) of the Act, 29 U.S.C. § 152 (12) (1970) does not exclude them from the Act's protections. Rather, professionals are distinguished from other employees only insofar as they may not be included in a bargaining unit of non-professional employees.

[10]

Furthermore the NLRB has recently held that labor
disputes affecting federally funded community legal service
offices affect commerce sufficiently to invoke the Board's
jurisdiction. Camden Regional Services, Inc., 231 N.L.R.B.
No. 47, Lab. L. Rep. (CCH) ¶ 18,430 (1977; Legal Services of
Northwestern Pennsylvania, 230 N.L.R.B. No. 103, Lab. L.
Rep. (CCH) ¶ 18,334 (1977); Wayne County Neighborhood Legal
Services, Inc., 229 N.L.R.B. No. 171, Lab. L. Rep. (CCH)
¶ 18,229 (1977). Inasmuch as the labor dispute at Smith & Jones
affects both a private law practice and the services rendered
at a federally funded community legal center (R. 20), the
dispute is within the NLRB's statutory jurisdiction. Any
other conclusion would be contrary to all of the NLRB's
decisions on point. Moreover, a denial of the existence of
statutory jurisdiction in this case would be a contradiction
of the definition of "affecting commerce" developed by the
Supreme Court over the last forty years.

    B.   THE COURT SHOULD ALLOW THE NLRB TO EXERCISE ITS
         DISCRETION TO HEAR THIS CASE, INASMUCH AS THIS
         CASE FALLS SQUARELY WITHIN THE NARROW JURISDIC-
         TIONAL LIMITATIONS PROMULGATED BY THE BOARD.

Because the NLRB's exercise of its jurisdiction is discretionary, all cases falling within its statutory jurisdiction
are not heard by the Board. In this instance, however, there
are significant indications that the Board will exercise its
jurisdiction--the NLRB recently asserted jurisdiction over
law firms as a class; the Board has promulgated jurisdictional
standards for law firms; and in this particular matter, the
Regional Director of the NLRB has issued a complaint (R. 10-14).

[11]

Given these indications, the district court was correct to defer to the NLRB's judgment and allow the Board to assert its jurisdiction.

    1.   <u>The Board's exercise of jurisdiction</u>
            <u>is discretionary.</u>

The discretionary powers of the NLRB are expressly set out in 29 U.S.C. § 164(c)(1)(1970): "The Board, in its discretion, may . . . decline to assert jurisdiction over any labor dispute . . .." If, however, the Board declines to assert its jurisdiction over a particular type of dispute, it is not foreclosed from later asserting that jurisdiction. <u>See</u>, <u>United States v. Morton Salt Co.</u>, 338 U.S. 632 (1949).; <u>NLRB v. Dixie Terminal Co.</u>, 210 F.2d 538 (6th Cir. 1954). Thus, even though the NLRB declined to exercise jurisdiction over law firms in the first two matters, <u>Bodle, Fogel, Julber, Reinhardt and Rothschild</u>, <u>supra</u>; and <u>Evans and Kunz, Ltd.</u>, <u>supra</u>, the Board decided to exercise jurisdiction in the more recent cases concerning law firm practices, <u>Camden Regional Legal Services</u>, <u>supra</u>; <u>Legal Services for Northwestern Pennsylvania</u>, 230 N.L.R.B. No. 103, Lab. L. Rep. (CCH) ¶ 18,334 (1977); <u>Wayne County Neighborhood Legal Services</u>, <u>supra</u>; and <u>Foley, Hoag, and Eliot</u>, <u>supra</u>. Likewise, the Board still has the discretion to grant jurisdiction over the Smith & Jones labor dispute. This Court should once again affirm this discretionary power by allowing the NLRB to assert jurisdiction in this matter.

    2.   <u>The NLRB has indicated that labor dis-</u>
            <u>putes at law offices, in general, and the</u>
            <u>controversy at Smith & Jones, in particular,</u>
            <u>should be brought before the Board.</u>

The NLRB's intent to exercise jurisdiction over this labor dispute is evident from the Regional Director's issuance of a complaint. In <u>Hoffman v. Retail Clerk's Union, Local 648</u>, 422

F.2d 793 (9th Cir. 1970) the court of appeals held that the
district court erred in denying a temporary injunction because
the NLRB had failed to prove its jurisdiction over a labor
dispute at a retail store. The Ninth Circuit Court of Appeals
stated that the district court should assume that the NLRB
regional director "proceeds on a knowledgeable determination
that the Board is likely to assert its jurisdiction." 422 F.2d
at 795. In effect, the issuance of a complaint establishes
sufficient reasonable cause to believe that the NLRB will
assert its jurisdiction.

The NLRB's recent decision in Foley, Hoag and Eliot is a
further indication that the Board will assert its jurisdiction
over the labor dispute at Smith & Jones. In that case, the
Board overruled its previous holding in Bodle, Fogel, Julber,
Reinhardt and Rothschild. In Bodle, the Board had refused to
assert its jurisdiction because it concluded that the practice
of law was not a type of commerce. The subsequent Supreme
Court holding in the Goldfarb case contradicted this. In
Goldfarb, this Court wrote:

> [T]he exchange of such a service for money is
> "commerce" in the most common usage of that word.
> It is no disparagement of the practice of law
> as a profession to acknowledge that it has this
> business aspect. 421 U.S. at 787.

As a consequence of this holding the Board in Foley announced
that it would assert its jurisdiction over law firms as a
class.

3. The law practice of Smith & Jones
   satisfies the monetary jurisdictional
   guidelines promulgated by the Board.

The NLRB promulgated the jurisdictional standard to be
applied to law firms in Camden Regional Services, Inc.
The employer in Camden was a non-profit legal corporation with

[13]

a gross annual revenue of $900,000. In deciding to assert its jurisdiction, the Board stated:

> We have examined the most recent empirical data collected by the Bureau of the Census and the American Bar Foundation and are of the opinion and find that it will effectuate the policies of the Act to limit our assertion of jurisdiction over law firms in general and legal assistance programs such as is involved herein to those that receive at least $250,000 in gross annual revenues. Camden Regional Services, Inc., supra, 231 N.L.R.B. No. 47 at ¶30, 615.

The record indicates that Smith & Jones' gross annual revenues exceed $250,000 (R. 15). Therefore, Smith & Jones satisfies the Board's jurisdictional standard.

Although the NLRB has not imposed any other specific jurisdictional standards for law firms, it has on occasion considered the total amount of money coming into the firm from out-of-state (inflow) or the total amount of money the firm pays to out-of-state concerns (outflow), when determining if jurisdiction should be asserted. E.g., Camden Regional Legal Services, supra; Bodle, Fogel, Julber, Reinhardt and Rothschild, supra; and Evans & Kunz, Ltd., supra. This inflow-outflow standard was used by the NLRB in Siemons Mailing Service, 122 N.L.R.B. 81 (1958). In that matter, the Board decided to assert jurisdiction over a California corporation engaging in processing, addressing and mailing materials submitted to it by customers. The Board explained the application of the standard in this manner:

> [J]urisdiction is asserted over all nonretail enterprises which have an outflow or inflow across State lines of at least $50,000, whether such outflow or inflow be regarded as direct or indirect . . . . In applying this standard, the Board will adhere to its past practice of adding direct and indirect outflow, or direct and indirect inflow. It will not add outflow and inflow. Siemons Mailing Service, supra, 122 N.L.R.B. at 85 (emphasis in original).

[14]

The NLRB has never declined jurisdiction over a law firm because the firm failed to meet these inflow-outflow standards. Moreover, in Camden, even though the legal service program satisfied the outflow standard, the Board did not expressly condition their grant of jurisdiction on that finding.

Assuming, arguendo, that the inflow-outflow standard applies to law offices, it is probable that Smith & Jones can satisfy that standard, as well as the $250,000 minimum. In the absence of evidence in the record substantiating the $50,000 of outflow or inflow, the Court should nonetheless grant jurisdiction. This would allow the Board to determine if the inflow-outflow standard applies to law firms in addition to the flat $250,000 jurisdictional standard. Furthermore, the Board could accumulate the necessary evidence to establish that Smith & Jones satisfies the inflow-outflow standard.

4. The Board can assert jurisdiction even if the monetary guidelines are not satisfied.

If it is the case that the inflow-outflow standard applies to law firms and Smith & Jones does not satisfy that standard, the NLRB can nevertheless assert its jurisdiction. As the court noted in NLRB v. Chauffeurs, Teamsters, and Helpers, Local 364, 274 F.2d 19 (7th Cir. 1960), the jurisdictional standards imposed by the NLRB do not implement specific statutory requirements. The Board's standards are guidelines. When, in the interest of enforcing the Act, the NLRB wants to assert jurisdiction, it can, even when the dispute fails to satisfy the monetary standards used by the Board as a guideline. Thus, in the Chauffeurs case, the court allowed the Board to assert jurisdiction and obtain an injunction against a secondary boycott even though the statutory minimum was not

[15]

clearly satisfied. Likewise, the NLRB should be allowed to assert its jurisdiction, even if the satisfaction of the jurisdictional minimums is disputed.

In summary, the Smith & Jones labor dispute satisfies all the statutory and discretional jurisdictional requirements imposed by the Act. Public policy requires such a holding; unless the Board is allowed to exercise its jurisdiction, the merits of the unfair labor practice will never be determined.

II

THE DECISION TO DISSOLVE AND REORGANIZE THE PARTNERSHIP IS A MANDATORY SUBJECT FOR BARGAINING WITHIN THE MEANING OF SECTION 8(d) OF THE ACT.

Section 8(d) of the Act defines "collective bargaining" as "the performance of the mutual obligation of the employer and the representative of the employees to meet at reasonable times and confer in good faith with respect to wages, hours, and other terms and conditions of employment." 29 U.S.C. § 158(d) (1970). The employer's statutory duty to bargain about terms of employment has been limited by this Court to those terms which are suitable for discussion within the collective bargaining framework, lie outside the core of entrepreneurial control, and directly and vitally affect the interests of employees. Fibreboard Paper Products Corp. v. NLRB, 379 U.S. 203 (1964). Section 8(a)(5) of the Act makes it an unfair labor practice for an employer to refuse to "bargain collectively with the representatives of his employees" with respect to decisions which affect such terms of employment. 29 U.S.C. § 158(a)(5).(1970).

The Firm's decision to terminate all union employees pursuant to a plan for reorganization of the partnership falls

[16]

within the literal meaning of section 8(d) of the Act and within the limitations placed on this section by the Fibreboard decision. Therefore, the Firm's refusal to bargain about this decision constitutes a violation of section 8(a)(5) of the Act.

A. THE DECISION DIRECTLY AND VITALLY AFFECTS THE INTERESTS OF EMPLOYEES IN THE BARGAINING UNIT.

This Court recognized in Fibreboard that an employer's decision to terminate all employees in a bargaining unit vitally affects the interests of employees. In Fibreboard it was a decision to contract out maintenance work previously performed by employees in the bargaining unit which resulted in their termination. Upon these facts this Court concluded that the subject of contracting out was well within the meaning of section 8(d) with respect to terms and conditions of employment. Specifically, this Court held that inclusion of this subject within the meaning of section 8(d) "would promote the fundamental purpose of the Act by bringing a problem of vital concern to labor and management within the framework established by Congress as most conducive to industrial peace." Fibreboard Paper Products Corp. v. NLRB, supra, 379 U.S. at 211.

The profound significance of this issue as a mandatory subject for bargaining is recognized by the Board. In explaining its approach to section 8(d) problems the Board has stated:

> [J]ust as the employer's interest in the protection
> of his capital investment is entitled to consideration
> in our interpretation of the Act, so too is the
> employee's interest in the protection of his livelihood.
>
> For, just as the employer has invested capital
> in the business, so the employee has invested
> years of his working life, accumulating seniority,

[17]

accruing pension rights, and developing skills that may or may not be salable to another employer. <u>Ozark Trailers Inc.</u>, 161 N.L.R.B. 561, 566 (1966).

The associates at Smith & Jones have invested years of their lives specializing in the real estate matters handled by the Firm. One of the associates, for example, has been with the Firm for eight years (R. 21). Whether their special skills are salable in the present market is unclear. It is clear, however, that the Firm's decision to reorganize the partnership directly threatens their livelihoods and thus vitally affects their interests. Thus, the Firm has a duty under sections 8(d) and 8(a)(5) of the Act to bargain with the representative of the associates.

B. THE DECISION IS A SUITABLE SUBJECT FOR DISCUSSION AT THE BARGAINING TABLE.

The facts of the present case demonstrate that the decision to reorganize the partnership is based upon considerations which are particularly suitable for discussion at the bargaining table. The Firm maintains that the decision is based upon a number of factors: the decline in revenues, which resulted from the loss of an important client to another firm and the loss of a number of other clients; projections for future declines in revenues; and failure to attract a new client of substantial size (R. 25, 26).

These economic difficulties could potentially be resolved through discussions with the associates' representative. Indeed, their representative has already advised the Firm that one of them may be able to bring in a substantial new client. The Firm has also been advised that the associates are willing to consider other ways to alleviate the Firm's financial stress, including a cut in pay (R. 18).

[18]

Moreover, the fact that agreement on these issues may not not be reached by the Firm and the representative of the associates is not determinative of whether such subjects are suitable for discussion within the collective bargaining framework.

As this Court ponted out in Fibreboard:

> [T]hough it is not possible to say whether a satisfactory solution could be reached, national labor policy is founded upon the congressional determination that the chances are good enough to warrant subjecting such issues to the process of collective negotiation. 379 U.S. at 214.

Certainly the opportunity for resolution of the problems involved in the present case is as good as, if not better than, the chances for resolution of the problems as they existed in Fibreboard. In that case, high labor costs were the primary factor in the employer's decision to contract out the maintenance work. This Court concluded that matters which relate to fringe benefits, over-time payments, and other labor costs were peculiarly suitable for resolution by collective bargaining. 379 U.S. at 213. Bargaining about these matters in the present case could substantially change the Firm's financial situation, thus eliminating the reasons given by the Firm for reorganization.

Furthermore, the Firm's decision to reorganize is not based upon considerations which would tend to make bargaining meaningless. In this respect the Firm's decision is distinguishable from those of several employers who have been found by lower courts to have no statutory duty to bargain about terminating or relocating parts of their ongoing businesses, because "[n]o amount of collective bargaining could erase the economic facts that gave rise to the [employer's] decision . . .." NLRB v. Thompson Transport Co., 406 F.2d 698, 703 (10th Cir. 1969).

[19]

In <u>Thompson Transport</u> the employer decided to close one of his
two oil terminals after losing the major part of his business in
the town where one of them was located. <u>See also</u>, <u>NLRB v.
Transmarine Navigation Corp.</u>, 380 F.2d 933 (9th Cir. 1967)
(where, in order to avoid losing his principal customer due to
the physical inadequacies of his shipyard facilities, the
employer decided to close his Los Angeles shipyard and to enter
into a joint venture to provide expanded facilities in the Long
Beach Harbor); <u>NLRB v. Royal Plating and Polishing Co.</u>, 350 F.2d
191 (3d Cir. 1965) (where the employer was charged with an unfair
labor practice after he accepted a "take it or litigate it" offer
from a housing authority which had condemned the property on
which one of his plants was located).

There is no evidence in the present case that collective
bargaining could not erase the economic facts giving rise to the
Firm's decision to reorganize. For this reason, and because the
considerations involved here are particularly suitable for
discussion at the bargaining table, the decision to reorganize
the partnership is subject to the collective bargaining requirements of the Act.

    C. THE DECISION DOES NOT INVOLVE A MAJOR
        CHANGE IN THE NATURE OF THE BUSINESS.

In <u>Fibreboard Paper Products Corp. v. NLRB</u>, 379 U.S. 203
(1964), this Court concluded that section 8(d) does not require
an employer to bargain about every business decision which
results in termination of employees or which is suitable for
discussion at the bargaining table. As Justice Stewart explained
in his concurring opinion in <u>Fibreboard</u>, some decisions are so
basic to the scope and direction of the employer's enterprise
that to require bargaining about them would interfere with the

[20]

"prerogatives of private business management." 379 U.S. at 223.
As an illustration of such a decision, Justice Stewart noted
that section 8(d) does not require an employer to bargain about
a decision to liquidate its assets and go out of business.
379 U.S. at 223.

In the present case the Firm's decision to reorganize the
partnership will result neither in a dissolution, nor a partial
liquidation of assets. Rather, upon termination of the
existing partnership agreement, the partners of Smith &
Jones will simultaneously enter into a new partnership agree
ment with the partners of Wind & Zephyr (R. 26, 27).
Thereafter, the partners will continue to carry on their
business "as usual" (R. 27). Notably, they will continue to
work in the same building, use the
same law library, serve the same clients, and specialize in the
same area of the law (R. 26, 27). The only significant change
in operations will be the assistance of associates who are not
represented by a union (R. 13). In this respect the situation
in the present case is remarkably similar to that in Fibreboard.
Here, as in Fibreboard, the decision to reorganize will not
result in a major change in the nature and direction of the
employer's business: "[T]he same work will be done at the same
location under similar conditions of employment." 379 U.S. at 21

In short, the Firm has refused and continues to refuse to
bargain about a decision which, for all practical purposes,
involves a simple reorganization of its business operations. As
the facts indicate, the partners of Smith & Jones have no
intention of discontinuing their practice of law or liquidating
the assets of the Firm. Certainly the mere fact that a partnership will be dissolved as one step in this reorganization does
[21]

not place the decision to reorganize outside the scope of the court's holding in Fibreboard. Therefore, because the decision to reorganize vitally affects the interests of employees in the bargaining unit, and because it is a suitable topic for discussion at the bargaining table, Smith & Jones is required by sections 8(d) and 8(a)(5) of the Act to bargain with the employees concerning its decision to dissolve and to reorganize the partnership.

III

THE DECISION TO REORGANIZE THE OPERATION OF SMITH & JONES, IF EFFECTUATED, WILL RESULT IN A VIOLATION OF SECTION 8(a)(3) OF THE ACT.

Section 8(a)(3) of the Act provides that it shall be an unfair labor practice for an employer "by discrimination in regard to hire or tenure of employment . . . to encourage or discourage membership in any labor organization." 29 U.S.C. § 158(a)(3)(1970). In Textile Workers Union of America v. Darlington Mfg. Co., 380 U.S. 263 (1965), this Court held that section 8(a)(3) is violated when an employer may reasonably foresee that discrimination in regard to tenure of employment will discourage union membership and discriminates between union and non-union employees for that purpose.

The plan to reorganize the operations of the Firm discriminates between union and non-union employees in terms of tenure of employment. Petitioner submits that the Firm may reasonably foresee that the plan will have a chilling effect upon unionization and that the Firm's purpose in dissolving the partnership and executing a new partnership agreement is to discourage further unionization of its employees. The Firm's purpose in dissolving the partnership and in executing a new partnership agreement is to discourage further unionization of its employees.

[22]

A. THE DECISION IS DISCRIMINATORY BECAUSE IT WILL
   NOT RESULT IN A COMPLETE LIQUIDATION OF THE BUSINESS.

The discriminatory impact of the decision to reorganize the operations of Smith & Jones is clear. Associates who are members of the Union will be discharged and replaced by associates of Wind & Zephyr who are not represented by a union (R. 13, 18). In contrast, secretaries who are unrepresented and at least one of the associates who has refused to pay Union dues will not be discharged (R. 17, 18).

In Darlington this Court observed that "one of the purposes of the Labor Relations Act is to prohibit the discriminatory use of economic weapons in an effort to obtain future benefits." 380 U.S. at 271. Given this purpose, this Court concluded that section 8(a)(3) does not apply to an employer who for the sole purpose of discouraging unionization completely liquidates his business. This Court came to this conclusion because the permanence of the employer's action to liquidate completely deprives him of any future economic benefit. Conversely, if the employer does not liquidate his business completely, section 8(a)(3) does apply because the employer's discriminatory actions may enable him to reap future benefits.

In the present case there is evidence that Smith & Jones does not intend to liquidate its business completely. The assets of the partnership will not be liquidated, and the partners will not be left without a business. Rather, there already exists a proposed partnership agreement pursuant to which the partners of Smith & Jones will merge with Wind & Zephyr. Thus, it is evident that Smith & Jones is using the device of "dissolve and merge" as an economic weapon against the associates who have joined the Union and that such device is being used in an

effort to obtain future economic benefits. These benefits
include the lower cost of labor resulting from the elimination
of union employees and a continued chilling effect upon future
unionization.

B. THE PURPOSE OF THE DECISION IS TO DISCOURAGE UNIONIZATION OF THE FIRM'S UNREPRESENTED EMPLOYEES.

In Darlington this Court decided that one of the prerequi-
sites to the establishment of a violation of section 8(a)(3)
is a finding that the employer's purpose in discriminating was
to discourage unionization in a business in which he has an
interest. In its supplemental decision on remand from that
decision, the Board observed that in cases of this kind, direct
evidence is rarely available to prove the employer's purpose.
Darlington Mfg. Co., 165 N.L.R.B. 1074 (1967). Therefore, the
Board concluded that the employer's motive may be proved by
looking at all the facts and circumstances of the case. The
Board's position was subsequently approved by the circuit court
of appeals in Darlington Mfg. Co. v. NLRB, 397 F.2d 760 (4th Cir.
1968), cert. denied, 393 U.S. 1023 (1969).

The Board found in the Darlington case that one of the
facts which demonstrated the employer's anti-union motive was
the timing of his decision to terminate certain union employees.
One day after being notified of unionization of employees in one
of his plants, the employer recommended to his company's board
of directors that the plant be closed; within three months of the
union's victory the plant was no longer in operation. In the
present case, the Firm's decision to reorganize its operations
immediately followed notice of union certification. The Firm
has stated that its decision was "based upon the decline in

[24]

revenues, the projections for future declines and our failure
to attract a new client of substantial size . . .." (R. 26).
However, the Firm's revenues have been declining since 1975.
The Firm was informed of the loss of an important client on
April 30, 1977, and received the results of its annual audit in
the first week of June, 1977 (R. 25, 26). It was only after
the Union was certified on June 20, 1977, as the representative
of the associates, that the partners of Smith & Jones met
on June 24, 1977, and decided to dissolve the partnership upon
August 31, 1977 (R. 16, 26).

Further evidence of the Firm's anti-union motive is found
in the record. First, during the years prior to certification
of the Union, the Firm refused to accept any suggestions by
the associates that changes be made in the terms and conditions
of employment offered by the Firm (R. 21). Second, the Firm
objected to the union election (R. 16). Third, all of the
associates who have paid their union dues will be terminated.
Finally, at least one of the associates who has refused to pay
dues to the Union will not be terminated (R. 18).

Considering all of these facts and the circumstances
involved in the present case, Petitioner submits that these facts
demonstrate that the Firm's purpose in reorganizing the partnership is to discourage unionization of its unrepresented
employees.

    C. IT IS REASONABLY FORESEEABLE THAT THE DECISION
       WILL HAVE A CHILLING EFFECT ON THE SECTION 7
       RIGHTS OF THE FIRM'S EMPLOYEES.

In its supplemental decison on remand from this Court's
decision in Darlington, the Board concluded that foreseeability

[25]

of a chilling effect is established if the following criteria
are met:

(1) it was foreseeable that news of the employer's
decision to terminate union employees would be communicated to his non-union employees;

(2) it was foreseeable that the employer's non-union
employees would be aware of the connection between the
business operation in which the union members were
employed and the business operation in which the non-
union employees are employed; and

(3) it was foreseeable that the circumstances surrounding termination of the union employees would cause the
employer's non-union employees to fear that they also
would be terminated if they unionized.

Darlington Mfg. Co., 165 N.L.R.B. 1074, 1084-86 (1967). These
criteria were approved by the circuit court of appeals in
Darlington Mfg. Co. v. NLRB, 397 F.2d 760, 772 (4th Cir. 1968).

Each of these criteria is met in the present case. First,
Smith & Jones called a special meeting of all of its employees
in order to announce that the Firm was being reorganized (R. 16).
Since this meeting the Firm has made no effort to conceal the
fact that Smith & Jones, minus the associates who are Union
members, plans to merge with Wind & Zephyr (R. 18). Second, the
Firm's employees all work in the same building, share the same
offices, and report to the same partners. Therefore, all of the
employees must realize that they are working for a firm that is
terminating the associates who recently unionized in order to
replace them with non-union employees.

Finally, it is foreseeable that, given the timing of the
Firm's decision to reorganize, the employees who remain will fear

[26]

that they also would be terminated if they unionized. Respondent may argue that under the terms of the proposed partnership agreement with Wind & Zephyr the partners of Smith & Jones will have no formal control over personnel matters (R. 27). However, even if the partners have no formal control, the employees will still fear that their views will be reflected in the policies of the reorganized firm because there already exist close personal and working relationships between members of the respective firms (R. 26). More important, if the Firm's "dissolve and reorganize" tactics enable it to discriminate against union employees with impunity, it is foreseeable that the employees will fear that if they unionized, the partners would immediately call for another "dissolution and reorganization," which this time would result in their termination.

Thus, the foreseeable effect of the Firm's decision to reorganize is exactly the same as the Firm's purpose in reorganizing--to discourage unionization of its unrepresented employees. For this reason, and because the discriminatory impact of the decision to reorganize is clear, Petitioner contends that there is reasonable cause to believe that Smith & Jones is engaging in a labor practice that is prohibited by section 8(a)(3) of the Act.

IV

THE DISTRICT COURT PROPERLY ENJOINED THE
REORGANIZATION OF SMITH & JONES.

The National Labor Relations Act, as amended by the Labor Management Relations Act, specifically allows the NLRB to petition the appropriate United States district court for a

[27]

temporary injunction against unfair labor practices. The Act
provides:

> The Board shall have power, upon issuance of a
> complaint . . . charging that any person has
> engaged in or is engaging in an unfair labor
> practice, to petition any United States district
> court, . . . for appropriate temporary relief or
> restraining order. Upon the filing of any such
> petition the court . . . shall have jurisdiction
> to grant to the Board such temporary relief or
> restraining order as it deems just and proper.
> 29 U.S.C. § 160(j)(1970).

Because this Court has not previously considered the issue of
when a Section 10(j) injunction is appropriate, the requirements
imposed by this provision have not been clearly delineated.
See Note, The 10(j) Labor Injunction: An Exercise in Statutory
Construction, 42 Wash. L. Rev. 1117 (1967). A review of the
lower court's decisions, however, reveals that two criteria
are generally applied: the NLRB must show that there is
reasonable cause to believe that unfair labor practices have
occurred, and the injunction must be necessary to protect the
goals of the Act. Because the NLRB has satisfied both of these
criteria, a Section 10(j) injunction should be issued.

A. THE NLRB HAS ESTABLISHED REASONABLE CAUSE TO
BELIEVE THAT SMITH & JONES IS ENGAGING IN
UNFAIR LABOR PRACTICES.

The federal courts agree that for the NLRB to obtain a
Section 10(j) injunction, it must demonstrate reasonable cause
to believe that an unfair labor practice has occurred. See,
e.g., Eisenberg v. Hartz Mountain Corp., 519 F.2d 138 (3rd Cir.
1974); Boire v. International Brotherhood of Teamsters, 479 F.2d
778 (5th Cir. 1973); Angle v. Sacks, 382 F.2d 655 (10th Cir. 1967).
Several courts have issued Section 10(j) injunctions on this

[28]

showing alone; e.g., MacLeod v. General Electric Co., 257 F. Supp.
690 (S.D.N.Y.), rev'd 366 F.2d 847 (2d Cir. 1966), cert. granted
on this issue but remanded, 385 U.S. 533 (1967); Johnston v.
Evans, 223 F. Supp. 722 (E.D.N.C. 1963). Few courts, however,
have been as thorough as the court in Douds v. International
Brotherhood of Teamsters, Local 294, 75 F. Supp. 414 (E.D.N.Y.
1948) in discussing what constitutes a showing of reasonable
cause. In Douds, the NLRB director sought a temporary injunction
restraining a union and its agents from violating section 8(b)
of the Act. The court issued the injunction because the NLRB
established a prima facie case that the union was violating
the Act. The court explained the precise requirements for the
issuance of a Section 10(j) injunction in this manner:

> The requirements of a prima facie case are met
> when the factual jurisdictional requirements are
> shown, and credible evidence is presented which,
> if uncontradicted would warrant the granting of
> the requested relief . . .. Douds v. Interna-
> tional Brotherhood of Teamsters, Local 294, supra,
> 75 F. Supp. at 418.

The opinion further emphasized that the court should not be
concerned with finding ultimate facts, since the actual adjudication of the charges is the exclusive domain of the Board
itself. Douds, supra; accord, National Licorice Co. v. NLRB,
309 U.S. 350 (1940).

Measured by the criteria set forth in Douds, the NLRB
has clearly met its burden of proof. The NLRB has shown that
all the jurisdictional requirements have been met. Credible
evidence has been presented in the hearings and affidavits to
prove both discrimination against union members and the intent
to effect a retaliatory partial closing through an altered
partnership agreement.

B. A TEMPORARY INJUNCTION AGAINST THE REORGANIZATION
OF SMITH & JONES IS ESSENTIAL TO PROMOTE THE GOALS
OF THE ACT

In addition to requiring a showing of reasonable cause
to believe that an unfair labor practice has occurred, many
courts also require a showing that the injunction will further
the purpose of the Act and its enforcement. See generally
Siegel, Section 10(j) of the National Labor Relations Act:
Suggested Reforms for an Expanded Use, 13 B.C. Indus. & Com. L.
Rev. 457 (1972). This second requirement has been defined and
developed by the courts in a case-by-case approach. Various
circuit courts have singled out different specific circumstances
warranting injunctive relief. Siegel, supra, 13 B.C. Indus. &
Com. L. Rev. at 475. Nonetheless, the cases in which injunctions
have been issued share a common thread: the issuance of the
injunction in each circumstance was required to promote the
goals of the Act. In the interest of harmonizing the various
formulations, Petitioner urges this Court to adopt this criterion
 as the second requirement of the standard by which injunctions
are issued. This standard would be both easy to apply and
appropriately selective. Moreover, the considerations indicated
below (which have in the past persuaded the appellate courts to
allow injunctions to stand) are the same considerations which
the court should apply to determine if the purpose of the Act
would be promoted by the issuance of an injunction.

1. A temporary injunction would serve
    the public interest.

The Senate report that accompanied the Taft-Hartley
Act stated that one of the goals of the act was to protect the
public interest. The committee declared:

> [W]e have provided that the Board acting in the
> public interest and not in vindication of purely
> private rights, may seek injunctive relief in the
> cases of all types of unfair labor practices. S.
> Rep. No. 105, 80th Cong., 1st Sess. 27 (1947).

The court in Eisenberg v. Hartz Mountain Corp., 519
F.2d 138 (3d Cir. 1974), used this distinction as a standard by
which to judge the application for a Section 10(j) injunction.
In Eisenberg, a minority union sought a temporary injunction
against representation by the employer-favored majority union
pending the outcome of a dispute concerning which union was to
represent the employees. The court held that the public
interest in ongoing collective bargaining--one of the cornerstones of the National Labor Relations Act--and the predom-
inating interest of the majority of workers who favored the
currently certified representative militated against issuance
of an injunction.

In a number of cases the same considerations of protecting
the membership of a particular union have caused the courts
to issue injunctions. E.g., Sachs v. Davis and Hemphill,
Inc., 60 Lab Cas. ¶ 10,068 (4th Cir. 1969) (court issued an
injunction requiring the employer to bargain to avoid the
"frustration of the purposes of the Act which § 10(j) was meant
to prevent"); Brown v. Pacific Telephone and Telegraph Co., 218
F.2d 542 (9th Cir. 1954) (an injunction issued, requiring the
employer to bargain with the designated representative to
prevent the union members from "drifting away" from the union);
Hoban v. Connecticut Foundry Co., 53 Lab. Cas. ¶ 11,255 (D.C.

[31]

Conn. 1966) (an injunction was issued requiring the employer to bargain with an elected representative notwithstanding pre-election irregularities because the court felt that the union's majority position would be endangered by the employer's refusal to bargain.) Moreover, the courts often issue temporary injunctions to protect unions from loss of members even though the activity of the employer being enjoined provides immediate benefits to the employed members of the union. See, e.g., American Gypsum Co. v. Pine, 81 Lab. Cas. ¶ 13,147 (10th Cir. 1977) (injunction preventing an employer from giving non-negotiable raises in pay to certain employees pending the adjudication of refusal-to bargain charges); Brooks v. Square Tube Corp., 50 Lab. Cas. ¶ 19,155 (E.D. Mich. 1964) (injunction issued to prevent employer from giving a non-negotiable raise to all unionized employees); Kennedy v. Telecomputing Corp., 43 Lab. Cas. ¶ 17,297 (S.D. Cal. 1961) (injunction issued against an employer who paid union scale wages after unilaterally renouncing the union's representation).

Frank McCulloch, past chairman of the National Labor Relations Board advocates more extensive use of the Section 10(j) injunction to guarantee additional protection to fledgling unions. McCulloch, New Problems in the Administration of the Labor-Management Relations Act: The Taft-Hartley Injunction, 16 S.W.L.J. 82 (1962). McCulloch singled out cases of refusals to bargain, refusals to discuss certain matters, and refusals to furnish required information as particularly amenable to the remedy of a Section 10(j) injunction. He explains his position by stating:

> [W]e . . . seek to enjoin an employer from
> threatening to close a plant because the
> employees vote for a union, for this type of

[32]

> threat and action effectively kills freedom
> of self-organization and collective bargain-
> ing beyond hope of resurrection. McCulloch,
> *supra*, 16 S.W.L.J. at 99.

McCulloch describes precisely why a Section 10(j) injunction

should be issued to protect the nascent organization efforts

of the Smith & Jones employees. If the injunction does not issue,

the partners will reorganize and terminate the employment of

all those associates who support the Union. These acts would

effectively abolish the Union local and undermine the announced

public interest in collective bargaining.

The courts have recognized that public interest other than

the interest in collective bargaining must be considered.

See Siegel, Section 10(j) of the National Labor relations Act:

Suggested Reforms for an Expanded Use, 13 B.C. Indus. & Com.

L. Rev. 457 (1972). For example, in Boire v. International

Brotherhood of Teamsters, 479 F.2d 778 (5th Cir. 1973), the

court held that the decline in public services caused by the

labor dispute at one of the employer's freight terminals was

one of the major reasons for issuing a Section 10(j) injunction.

Similarly, the advancement of public services dictate that

an injunction should be issued in the Smith & Jones labor

dispute. The public interest in adequate, affordable legal

services is served by the efficient operations of community

legal centers. The Neighborhood Legal Office will not be

able to function effectively if the associates of Smith &

Jones who donate their spare time to the center--forty

percent of the staff--are caught up in a fight to keep their

jobs, or if they are required to search for other gainful

employment (R. 20). If a temporary injunction is issued,

the public interest in the availability of this public

[33]

service would be served pending the resolution of the dispute.

In short, the public's interest in generally available legal services, as well as the public's interest in fostering collective bargaining supports the issuance of an injunction in this case.

2. A temporary injunction will prevent irremediable violations of the Act.

The issuance of an injunction would protect a second of the stated goals of the Act--it would prevent the employer from accomplishing an illegal objective pending the resolution of the charges. In the Senate Report on the Taft-Hartley Act, the Committee expressed concern that on occasion violators of the Act would accomplish their unlawful objectives prior to the Board's decision on the merits of a case. See S. Rep. No. 105, 80th Cong., 1st Sess. 8, 27 (1947). This fear was echoed by the 1961 Pucinski Committee. That Committee remarked:

> [F]ailure to utilize the 10(j) discretionary injunction sometimes results in irreparable injury. This subcommittee therefore recommends that the Labor Board give careful consideration to greater utilization of the 10(j) injunction in situations when unfair labor practice charges are filed and the Board finds reasonable cause to believe that such unfair labor practice is continuing and will be continued unless restrained and will cause irreparable . . . injury . . . . Illustrative are . . . the situations where employers . . . flagrantly refuse to bargain in good faith, and the situations wherein the employer threatens to intimidate his employees by closing the plant or shifting work to affiliated factories. House Subcomm. on National Labor Relations Board of the Comm. on Education and Labor, 87th Cong., 1st Sess.; Administration of the Labor-Management Relations Act by the NLRB 52 (Comm. Print 1961) (emphasis added).

Congress has thus expressed its intent that the Section 10(j) injunction be used in situations identical to the Smith & Jones labor dispute. Their policy is clear: the full panoply of statutory remedies must be used to prevent irreparable harm.

[34]

Of the various remedies available, the temporary relief afforded by section 10(j) is perhaps the most important. As explained by the court in Angle v. Sachs, 382 F.2d 655, 660 (10th Cir. 1967):

> [W]hen the circumstances of a case create a reasonable apprehension that the efficacy of the Board's final order may be nullified, or the administrative procedures will be rendered meaningless, temporary relief may be granted under Section 10(j). Preservation and restoration of the status quo are then appropriate considerations in granting temporary relief pending determination of the issues by the Board.

Bearing these considerations in mind, the court in Angle issued an injunction restraining the employer from interrogating or coercing his employees, inasmuch as there existed a probability that the purpose of the Act would be frustrated unless temporary relief was granted. Angle v. Sachs, supra; accord, Davis v. Huttig Sash and Door Co., 288 F. Supp. 82 (W.D. Okla. 1968).

If the test of the Angle case is applied to the Smith & Jones labor dispute, a Section 10(j) injunction must be issued. Should the NLRB decide that Smith & Jones committed unfair labor practices, and order that the unionized employees be reinstated, that final order will be nugatory unless a Section 10(j) injunction is used to prevent the Firm's dissolution. Thus, a temporary injunction is necessary in the Smith & Jones labor dispute both to insure that no unlawful purpose is accomplished pending adjudication, and to guarantee that any relief to which the employees may eventually be entitled will be more than a hollow victory. By insuring these objectives, the Section 10(j) injunction will accomplish the express goals of the National Labor Relations Act.

C. THE COURT SHOULD HEED THE EXPERTISE OF THE BOARD
   IN DETERMINING THE PROPRIETY OF AN INJUNCTION.

Even though temporary injunctions further the remedial
goals of the Act, some courts have issued injunctions infrequently.
While it is true that courts are to exercise their discretion
in issuing temporary injunctions, it is well to remember that
the courts should defer to the judgment of the NLRB personnel.
See Boire v. International Brotherhood of Teamsters, 479 F.2d
781 (5th Cir. 1973). It is they who have the expertise and
experience necessary to evaluate the need for injunctions.
From years of experience with temporary injunctions, the NLRB
has developed criteria by which the regional director's request
for injunctions are reviewed. Casehandling Manual (Part 1),
Unfair Labor Practice Proceedings § 10310.2 (April 1975). The
general counsel applies these standards to every request for a
temporary injunction from the regional directors. The district
court receives petitions for injunctions only after the general
counsel is satisfied that injunctive relief is essential. See
generally Note, Temporary Injunctions under Section 10(j) of the
Taft-Hartley Act, 44 N.Y.U.L. Rev. 181 (1969). Thus, in 1970
the general counsel received 292 requests for injunctive relief
from the regional directors, but only 17 petitions for injunctive
relief were filed with the district courts. NLRB Annual Report
196; see Siegel, Section 10(j) of the National Labor Relations
Act: Suggested Reforms for an Extended Use, 13 B.C. Indus. &
Com. L. Rev. 457 (1972). This careful scrutiny by the general
counsel, who is an expert in labor law matters, insures that
the temporary injunction will not be abused by the NLRB. The
courts therefore should heed the Board's recommendation.

[36]

V

BECAUSE THE ISSUANCE OF THE TEMPORARY INJUNCTION
WAS JUST AND PROPER, THE COURT OF APPEALS ERRED
IN DISSOLVING THAT INJUNCTION.

When presented with the legal theories and facts discussed
in the foregoing sections, the United States District Court for
the Southern District of Erewhon granted the NLRB's petition
for a Section 10(j) injunction. This injunction was dissolved
because the Court of Appeals for the Twelfth Circuit was
persuaded that "the issuance of the injunction was erroneous"
(R. 34). Petitioner contends that the court of appeals erred
in dissolving the injunction because the court of appeals applied
an improper standard of appellate review. According to Minnesota
Mining and Manufacturing Co. v. Meter, 385 F.2d 265 (8th Cir.
1967) (and cases cited therein), a Section 10(j) injunction is
reviewable only to the extent that the district court made
findings of fact that were clearly erroneous, or abused its
discretion by issuing the injunction. In this case, the
appellate court does not disagree with any of the district court's
findings of fact (R. 33). Thus, the Court of Appeals must have
overruled the district court for abusing its discretion. Inasmuch
as the Board established the existence of jurisdiction and
reasonable cause to believe that unfair labor practices occurred,
and inasmuch as the injunction would further the goals of the
Act, the issuance of the injunction was just and proper. This
is all that the Act requires. Therefore, surely the issuance
of an injunction was well within the court's discretion.

[37]

CONCLUSION

For the reasons set forth above Petitioner respectfully requests that the judgment of the United States Court of Appeals for the Twelfth Circuit be reversed, and that Smith & Jones be enjoined from changing its operational structure pending final disposition of the matters involved herein present before the Board.

Respectfully submitted,

Gwen H. Whitson

Kathy Rohwer
Attorneys for Petitioner

APPENDIX A

United States Constitutional Provisions:

article 1, § 8, cl. 3:

> [Congress shall have the power to] regulate Commerce
> with foreign Nations, and among the several States,
> and with the Indian Tribes.

APPENDIX B

National Labor Relations Act:

§ 2(7), 29 U.S.C. § 152(7)(1970):

>   The term "affecting commerce" means in commerce,
>   or burdening or obstructing commerce or the free
>   flow of commerce, or having led or tending to
>   lead to a labor dispute burdening or obstructing
>   commerce or the free flow of commerce.

§§ 8(a)(3) and 8(a)(5), 29 U.S.C. §§ 158(a)(3) and 158(a)(5)

(1970) provide in relevant part:

>   (a)   It shall be an unfair labor practice for an
>   employer
>
>   . . . .
>
>   (3)   by discrimination in regard to hire or
>   tenure of employment or any term or
>   condition of employment to enc ourage or
>   discourage membership in any labor
>   organization . . . .
>
>   . . . .
>
>   (5)   to refuse to bargain collectively with the
>   representatives of his employees, subject
>   to the provisions of section 159(a) of
>   this title.

§ 8(d), 29 U.S.C. § 158(d)(1970) provides in relevant part:

>   For the purposes of this section, to bargain col-
>   lectively is the performance of the mutual
>   obligation of the employer and the representative
>   of the employees to meet at reasonable times and
>   confer in good faith with respect to wages, hours,
>   and other terms and conditions of employment or
>   any question arising thereunder, and the execution
>   of a written contract incorporating any agreement
>   reached if requested by either party, but such
>   obligation does not compel either party to agree
>   to a proposal or require the making of a con-
>   cession . . . .

APPENDIX C

Labor Management Relations Act:

§ 10(a) , 29 U.S.C. § 160(a)(1970) provides in relevant part:

> The Board is empowered, as hereinafter provided, to
> prevent any person from engaging in any unfair
> labor practice (listed in section 158 of this
> title) affecting commerce. This power shall not be
> affected by any other means of adjustment or preven-
> tion that has been or may be established by agreement,
> law, or otherwise. . .

§ 10(j), 29 U.S.C. § 160(j)(1970):

> The Board shall have power, upon issuance of a
> complaint as provided in subsection (b) of this
> section charging that any person has engaged in or is
> engaging in an unfair labor practice, to petition
> any United States district court, within any dis-
> trict wherein the unfair labor practice in question
> is alleged to have occurred or wherein such person
> resides or transacts business, for appropriate
> temporary relief or restraining order. Upon the
> filing of any such petition the court shall cause
> notice thereof to be served upon such person, and
> thereupon shall have jurisdiction to grant to the
> Board such temporary relief or restraining order as
> it deems just and proper.

§ 14(c)(1), 29 U.S.C. § 164(c)(1)(1970):
> The Board, in its discretion, may, by rule of
> decision or by published rules adopted pursuant
> to the Administrative Procedure Act, decline to
> assert jurisdiction over any labor dispute involv-
> ing any class or category of employers, where, in
> the opinion of the Board, the effect of such labor
> dispute on commerce is not sufficiently substantial
> to warrant the exercise of its jurisdiction:
> Provided, That the Board shall not decline to
> assert jurisdiction over any labor dispute over
> which it would assert jurisdiction under the standards
> prevailing upon August 1, 1959 (emphasis in original).

*

TRANSCRIPT OF PETITIONER'S ORAL ARGUMENT IN PEGGY v. SMITH & JONES

May it please the court, I am Jeffrey Masters,
Counsel for Petitioner. As my co-counsel,
Mr. Edmundson, noted, I will be addressing my
analysis this afternoon first to the scope of
Board jurisdiction - reasonable cause to
believe that jurisdiction exists here; and
secondly, to the larger issue of the equities,
of whether or not the District Court properly
enjoined the dissolution of Smith and Jones;
whether the injunction was just and proper.
Before proceeding with those questions,
Your Honors, I would extend Mr. Edmundson's
analysis in this sense about the equities;
they are substantial here, Your Honors. If
the injunction does not issue, the Board's
remedial capacity will essentially be crippled.
While the Board will go ahead on full record
and make some determination in this case,
the entity of Smith and Jones, the bargaining
relationship, the employment structure, all
will pass out of existence.

Q: Well, isn't there a successor employer here?
Why is it impossible to go after the other
firm?

[39]

A: Wind & Zephyr.

Q: If it turns out at the end of the proceedings
            that there was this ploy?

A: That's a problematic question, Your
            Honor, because it's not clear to what extent
            Wind & Zephyr would be a successor. There
            is some good authority from this Court that
            is useful here in such cases as Wiley and
            Howard Johnson. But, just very briefly,
            it appears that because of the very small
            percentage of associates and attorneys that
            Smith and Jones will provide Wind & Zepher,
            the successor relationship is probably unlikely
            here, so it appears unlikely that Wind &
            Zephyr itself will be liable.

Q: And, wouldn't there be a personal obligation
            on the partners of Smith and Jones for any
            back pay?

A: There would, indeed, Your Honor.

Q: And, why isn't that enough of an adequate
            remedy in this unusual situation in which
            you're asking for unusual relief?

A: Backpay is . . . Well, it's very interesting
            to break this down. The backpay cases -

[40]

there's a great run of them - say that when
you consider an 8(a)(3) violation and an
8(a)(5) violation together, often reinstatement
and backpay are used. The very damning evidence
comes when you consider an 8(a)(5) violation
alone. There too, backpay alone is utilized,
which indicates that there really is no
discrete, significant money remedy or damages
for failure to collectively bargain. So,
while money damages may be utilized, they
are, as ex-Board Chairman Frank McCulloch
referred to them, a kind of license to union
hunt. The damages may be paid, but the
damage to the Act, to the employees, to the
bargaining relationship, is already done.
It's not a very satisfactory course, Your Honor.

Q: The theme is that this is an application for a
temporary restraining order or preliminary
injunction and under familiar principles. But,
before you can get this kind of relief, you
must show that you have a probability of
success on the merits which would mean, of
course, before the Board, and also, that you
would suffer irreparable damage. And, in
some instances, it's necessary to balance
the irreparability of the damage against the
other side's similar problem. Now, what
have you done in this case to show that you
will ride on the merits?

A: Well, to answer
your first question, Your Honor, it involves
the reasonable cause question that Mr. Edmundson's
already introduced. And because the District
Court has made undisputed findings of fact
that there is at least reasonable cause to
believe that an unfair labor practice has
occurred, that seems to give some credence
to the belief that we would prevail at the
Board level. Secondly, regarding the equities,
again we can utilize a weighing process here,
although initially, I would think that that
really shouldn't be applied because with a
statutory injunction as this Court made clear
in Hecht v. Bowles, construing the emergency
Price Control Act of 1942, a statutory injunction that is built into the statute, such as
this one, should be weighed not so much by the
private litigation standards of weighing
irreparable harms, as by public standards.
And, here the public standards involve the
public interest in collective bargaining, the
primary purpose of the Act. So that's
really the weighing that should be done.
I would also note, parenthetically, that
Congress has really already performed this
weighing process before by providing the
statutory remedy.

Q: So, under certain conditions.

[42]

A: Right, Your Honor, and I will posit here
that this is precisely the condition that
Congress intended. On page 40 of our brief
we utilize useful legislative history from
1961, which pinpoints the very
situation we're confronting here where an
employer intimidates or terminates employees
by threats of closing the plant or shifting
work to an affiliated factory. That's a
pretty apt characterization of Smith and Jones'
actions.

Q: Of course, to the extent you say that the
trial judge is not required to do this
weighing, that Congress has already weighed
it, then it's a matter of law and we're
not bound by its findings.

A: Well, to the extent that a reasonable cause is determined a legal term which
arguably it may be, it is a term of art
here. It's completely supported and completely
made up and comprised of factual findings.
And, that's really the rub here.
Because all the factual findings are
undisputed. Well, in a
sense I would agree, there may have been
error there, but it was error in a sense
that now favors petitioner. They exceeded -
fulfilled a higher standard is what I'm trying

[43]

to say. They found not only reasonable cause;
the District Court there very strongly implied
that there was a proven violation of 8(a)(5).

Q: Isn't there a very serious question of jurisdiction here which we haven't talked about?
Before this case, has the Board ever taken
jurisdiction over a case involving simply
lawyers as distinguished from employees of
law firms, other than lawyers?

A: Not on the particular facts here, but by
utilizing the previous Board decisions,
for example, in Wayne County which focused
specifically on attorneys, and Foley, Hoag and
Elliot, which focused on the law firm itself,
what we have here is a picture of the Board
moving in the direction of classifying law
firms as a regulated class. And, that is
really the upshot of the Board decisions in
their relying on the good authority of this
Court in Goldfarb as well for that decision.

Q: Yes, but this is an unusual situation in
which the Board has decided that it wants to
get preliminary injunctive relief from a
District Court before the Board itself ever
has had a chance to really go through the
record and find out if they should continue
to exercise jurisdiction over this case and

[44]

whether there was an unfair labor practice.
So, I go back to my question, in such an
unusual case where the Board has rarely, if
ever, taken jurisdiction over a case involving
just lawyers, why should we allow jurisdiction
to be taken in this unusual 10j situation?
Why shouldn't we say to the Board, Go
through your normal procedures? - Don't come
to the District Court first.

A: Yes.

Q: Why shouldn't we say that?

A: That's the crucial question of this case.

Q: I know.

A: We cannot say that.   (Laughter)
        That's just a preface.

        We cannot allow that to happen because in
        this unusual professional setting by a very
        painless, swift and ruthless action, Smith
        and Jones can evade their responsibilities
        under the Act. That is unlike any other case
        the Board has had to decide. It's much
        different, as Mr. Edmundson pointed out, from
        Darlington, where you   had movement
        of capital and plant and equipment and

[45]

facilities. Smith and Jones are taking the
painless step to avoid, to evade, bargaining.
And, that is why this is such a crucial instance,
and,   that this Court make it clear that
this is not a course that can be followed.

If Smith and Jones are allowed to dissolve,
that evasion will occur. And, that is
precisely why in this specific factual setting
we need the injunction. Petitioner
never asks for a conclusive finding on the
merits or any final determination. All that
is sought is an injunction to preseve the
status quo, to preserve the bargaining
relationship, to preserve issues of fact of law,
to allow the Board to make its eventual determination.

Q: Of course, there was jurisdiction involved
            in Darlington, where all the companies,
            the textile companies, were really controlled
            by the same entity. That's not true here.

A: Well, not so directly, Your Honor. But,
            I think that a good argument can be made for
            a different proposition, that because law
            firms are so uniquely situated in their
            management responsibilities, perhaps the
            Darlington standard might not be as applicable
            as it would appear at first glance.

[46]

Q:	They are uniquely situated because they
	have a personal service contract with one
	another. Isn't that what you're trying
	to enforce here?

A:	Well, I'm not sure if that's directly it. The
	point that I was making was the fact that
	there's a little autonomy in each attorney's
	practice and in a sense, to use a homely
	example, they take their factory with them.
	So the <u>Darlington</u> analysis is extremely
	useful as this Court has used it.

Q:	 Don't these attorneys have a personal
	service contract each with the other under
	the terms of the partnership laws. Isn't
	there a policy of the law that we do not
	enforce a personal service contract?

A:	That's true.

Q:	Isn't that what we're doing here?

A:	No, I think we're not, Your Honor. That's
	perhaps a too narrow view of what would be
	happening here. The autonomy of the attorneys
	really is unquestioned within the law firms.
	It's an idiosyncratic feature of different
	law firms. And, for that reason, I don't
	think the same management/control analysis

[47]

could be utilized as profitably as
it would in an industrial setting, for example.

Q: Now, you've indicated that this 10(j) remedy
is a very unusual remedies, not often provided.
Yet, you come into court - you came into the
District Court, anyway - with a case where
the jurisdiction was seriously
questioned. And, that was only your first
hurdle. You have then to get to the question
of the merits, assuming there was jurisdiction.
Yet, you've done that in an area where, uh,
this particular statute has not been often
used. And, yet, you've only used it in a case
where you have very, very difficult burdens
to overcome.

A: Let me address those jurisdictional hurdles now,
Your Honor. They're not, perhaps, as insurmountable as they seem. After this Court's
decision in <u>Goldfarb</u>, which classified the
practice of law itself as trade or commerce,
that essentially opened the door of Board
jurisdiction over law firms as labor disputes
affecting commerce.
After weighing it, it becomes clear that the
threads come together that attorneys themselves
are subject to the provisions of the Act.
On jurisdiction, moreover, there's a discretionary basis of jurisdiction aside from the
statutory basis of affecting commerce and

[48]

that can be summed up in one word, which is
Camden. That was the Board's
decision limiting its jurisdiction under the
commerce clause to those law firms of gross
annual revenues over $250,000.

Q: But, that isn't the only thing the Board
considers, is it? Is it automatic that the
Board will assume jurisdiction if there is
over $250,000 revenues?

A: They could still decline jurisdiction but
every indication in the present case is that
they will assert it, Your Honor.

Q: But on what basis is there an effect here
on interstate commerce?

A: Well, just as . . .

Q: On the gross revenues, is that it?

A: No, actually there's much more, while that
is an important indication. Utilizing the
Goldfarb analysis, which is the effect of
a real estate practice on interstate commerce,
I think it's clear that the real estate
practice here will also have a significant
impact on commerce and I would make this
differentiation - our facts may be stronger.
Goldfarb dealt with a residential

[49]

real estate practice, whereas ours is
commercial. In taking judicial notice of the
existing real estate market all over the
country, a practice that affects apartment
houses and commercial properties can have
a very substantial **effect** on interstate
migration, interstate economic and marketing
conditions. There's a very significant
impact on commerce here. Moreover, if you
look at Smith and Jones itself, there's
potential for interstate commerce in the Fortune
500 client that may be attracted and in the
general notion of their real estate practice.
So, for all these reasons, jurisdiction is
very likely to be asserted by the Board.

So, looking into the crucial area of the
equities on the 10j, there's somewhat of
a split of opinion here as to what constitutes a "just and proper" 10(j) injunction
with the best reasoned authority being that which
indicates the following, something like as
follows: Reasonable cause as demonstrated
above, plus the fact that the injunction
is necessary to prevent frustration of the
Act's purposes. Note that that is precisely
what is occuring in the instant case.
Collective bargaining is the keystone of
the National Labor Relations Act. What

[50]

has happened here, by allowing Smith and
Jones to dissolve and failing to enjoin
the dissolution, collective bargaining
will be meaningless. A Board order, a
decision to bargain in the future will
really be impotent because the bargaining
relationship . . .

A: Doesn't that mean any refusal bargain situa-
        tion you would feel justified, or the Board
        would feel justified, in going for a 10(j)?

Q: Well, that would be a consideration.   I
        can't speak . . .

A: That can't be the law, can it?   10(j) has
        been on the books for God knows how long
        and the Board goes to court under a 10(j)
        very rarely.

A: That is true, Your Honor, but that really
        can't be dispositive of this unique factual
        setting.

Q: Why is that?

A: As Mr. Edmundson made clear, this is a
        unique setting of professional employees.
        unlike anything the Board has con-
        fronted before. If we fail to enjoin this

[51]

dissolution we will effectively, if uninten-
tionally, be sending a signal to every professional employer in the country, that through
a swift and painless act, they can evade
their duty under the Act, to bargain. And,
that is why it's so essential in this case.
This Court is afforded a unique opportunity
to allow the Board to make a determination on
a full record, to resolve these complex
questions; to the extent that there are
questions about the standard here of reasonable cause, of jurisdiction, let us enjoin
this dissolution and allow the Board to make
its determinations with the structure still
intact.

Q: Isn't there an inconsistency in your
argument? You're saying, well, now you
must give this injunction because
the merger is really a sham. And, yet, on
the other hand, you are saying you must have
this injunction or the entity won't be here
any more. Isn't that inconsistent?

A: Oh, not at all Your Honor, although it
appears to be at first glance. If you
look at what Smith and Jones is doing,
indeed, there's going to be a shell of
Smith and Jones dissolving, but the essential
practice of Smith and Jones, as Mr. Edmundson
demonstrated, will continue. Uh, this is

[52]

not a dead law firm, it'll be a very lively
corpse embodied in Wind & Zephyr.

Q: Why can't it be reconstituted then a year
        or two from now? That's the point of Judge
        Kennedy's question, if you don't get an
        injunction, but you win at the Board?

A: Well, for simple efficiency terms,
        that would be less desirable than simply
        enjoining now, given the strong equities
        in favor   of the injunction. I'll sum up
        very briefly, Your Honor.

Q: Before you do that, you're not offended by
        the notion that you're telling someone to
        stay in business who doesn't want to stay
        in business?

A: Well, that argument is emotionally persua-
        sive, and Respondent will make it.

Q: Yes.

A: But, that would be allowing him to plead
        his own bad faith. He does not want to stay
        in business because he doesn't want to
        bargain. Relations are poor because he
        won't bargain with his associates.

Q: So what if it turns out that he's right?
    That there wasn't any anti-union animus.
    They have a Board hearing. It's
    found that the decision to try to close but
    which the Board has successfully kept them
    from doing, was made for economic reasons.
    Isn't that kind of an imposition on someone
    to make them stay in business and incur
    economic losses for a year or a year and
    a half?

A: Well, again, there's no indication in the
    record that losses will occur. This is
    just a firm that is not as profitable as it
    once was. Now, Rufus Smith had the
    opportunity to make as bleak a picture as
    possible of the economic circumstances and
    couldn't do much better, or worse, than this
    record. So that should not be that much of
    a concern of this Court. Those are purely
    speculative losses that might accrue to
    Smith and Jones. And to conclude, against
    those speculative losses, we must balance
    not only the impact upon these associates who
    will be terminated, and upon this union, which
    will evaporate, but on the National Labor
    Relations Act itself. There are national
    purposes at stake here. To allow profes-
    sional employers to escape their liability
    and their duty under the Act, under these

[54]

circumstances would be a manifestly bad
result. It would send that signal that I
indicated before to every professional
employer who simply seeks not to bargain.
For these reasons, Your Honors,
because jurisdiction is clear, because
the stakes are so high, we respectfully
urge that the District Court's injunction
be reinstated today.

Q: Thank you Mr. Masters.

Appendix C

CHECKLISTS FOR WRITTEN BRIEF AND ORAL ARGUMENT

No matter how extensively an advocate prepares a first draft of a brief or an oral presentation, it is necessary to review the draft or presentation before it is finalized. This is the essence of effective editing. To assist the advocate in this final revision, the following checklists are provided. These checklists have been adapted from the evaluation sheets used in the UCLA Moot Court Honors Program.

WRITTEN BRIEF CHECKLIST

1. OVERALL APPEARANCE
    Are all necessary sections in the brief? _____

    Is the typing and the physical presentation neat? _____

2. COVER OF THE BRIEF
    In compliance with the rules of the proper court? _____

3. TOPICAL INDEX
    Are the sections of the brief in proper sequence? _____

    Is the overall form correct (including even right hand margins)? _____

4. TABLE OF AUTHORITIES
    Does the table contain sensible division and arrangement of statutes and secondary source material; division of federal and state cases into separate categories? _____

    Are authorities properly cited? _____

    Should an appendix have been used? Are the items in the appendix the proper type of items? Is the appendix referred to in the body of the brief or was it added as an afterthought? _____

5. WHY THIS COURT HAS JURISDICTION
    A. OPINIONS BELOW
        Does the brief inform the court of the opinions below? _____

    B. JURISDICTION
        Does the brief contain the proper statement of jurisdiction? _____

6. QUESTIONS PRESENTED

Are the questions phrased such that an answer favorable to the advocate is naturally suggested? _____

Are the questions specific and tied to the facts of the case? _____

Is the wording active and assertive? _____

Is each question stated clearly and simply? _____

7. STATEMENT OF THE CASE

Is the nature of case described, relieving the court of speculating or spotting the issues? _____

Are the parties identified? _____

Are the lower court proceedings explained? _____

Which party is appealing from what? _____

Is the statement worded to favor the advocate's position without being overly argumentative in tone? _____

Are only those facts set forth which are relevant to the issues or which are needed for an understanding of the case? _____

Do the facts persuade the reader to the position of the advocate? Are the facts structured and sequenced in the most persuasive manner? Is clarity retained as to the chronology and interrelationships of the facts? Are subheadings used where appropriate? Are the facts stated in an interesting manner? Is a non-argumentative tone maintained? _____

8. SUMMARY OF ARGUMENT

Are the advocate's important arguments summarized in the most concise and persuasive manner? _____

Is the wording clear and simple? _____

Is the wording assertive and active? _____

9. ARGUMENT
   A. GENERAL CONSIDERATIONS

   Is the brief at all times persuasive? _____

   Are the results requested shown to be factually just? Are these results wedded to arguments which are technically sound, both legally and logically? _____

   Are all important issues addressed? _____

   Are the issues properly analyzed? _____

[57]

Is a theme developed for the brief from the facts which are most favorable to the advocate's position? Are any favorable facts omitted? Are any unfavorable facts included? ———————

Is the theme of favorable facts used to tie the separate issues into one stream of logically-related argument? ———————

Is the theme stated strongly, clearly, and positively with no hesitation or perceptible weakness? ———————

Are the issues structured and presented in a logical sequence? While maintaining a logical structure, is the sequence adopted the most persuasive pattern available? ———————

B. CAPTIONS

Are the captions clear, persuasive statements of each issue? Is each worded actively and assertively? Is each caption tied into the specific facts of the case? ———————

Does each caption make resolution of each issue in favor of the advocate seem logical and just? ———————

Do the captions when read together in the Topical Index provide a first-time reader with a succinct statement of the issues of the case and with a persuasive view of the advocate's positions on the issues? ———————

Are subheadings needed? Are they most appropriately used? ———————

C. TEXT OF ARGUMENT

Is the text easily readable? Is it concise and clear but interesting? Is it stripped of all irrelevancies and clutter? ———————

Is the argument low-keyed and subdued but relentless? Are bombast and extravagance avoided? ———————

Does each element of the argument fall logically within the scope of the caption? Is any information present which should be set forth under a different caption or subheading? Are thought-interrupting footnotes only used when the information is needed and logic and

[58]

continuity may only be preserved by use of them?   _____

Is the applicable legal principle clear? Is this principle tied to specific facts of the case? Does the combination of principle and fact persuasively suggest the desired conclusion?   _____

Is case law appropriately used? For cases principally relied upon, are the facts described in sufficient detail to place the holding in the proper framework to make the brief's reliance upon it logical and persuasive? If the case is relied upon in a lesser fashion, is a parenthetical factual statement used to provide sufficient context for the reliance?   _____

Is case law persuasively used? Are only appropriate, effective quotes used? Are string cites avoided where the principle is clear and established? If the principle is not clearly established but is the subject of confusion or is within a trend, are the numerous cases cited effectively used to show the case at bar to be within the holdings or trend? Is the requested result the logical product of such a showing?   _____

Is overreliance on certain cases avoided even where such cases are thought to be controlling? Are helpful policy arguments brought in effectively? Are policies and facts used together to buttress the case law and to compel the court to find the case law to be controlling?   _____

Are the points of the opposition anticipated and implicitly (or explicitly, where appropriate) rebutted or otherwise rendered ineffectual, irrelevant, or unpersuasive?   _____

Are unfavorable precedents effectively confronted?   _____

Is the overall argument sufficiently complete to enable a judge to read and absorb it without ever having to resort to looking up a cited authority or any other materials outside the record and the briefs?   _____

[59]

10. CONCLUSION

   Is the type of relief desired clearly requested?   ———

   If a Summary of Argument is part of the brief, does the Conclusion omit any resummarization of the arguments?   ———

ORAL PRESENTATION CHECKLIST

I. ORGANIZATION OF THE PRESENTATION

  1. INTRODUCTION

   Introduce himself, his party and if appropriate, his co-counsel?   ———

   Are the issues to be discussed and the highlights of the argument previewed for the court?   ———

  2. CLARITY OF ORGANIZATION

   Are the arguments presented in logical sequence?   ———

   Are smooth transitions made from one argument to another?   ———

   Does the organization aid and insure clarity and comprehension of the various arguments?   ———

  3. ALLOCATION OF TIME

   Is time allocated among arguments in an efficient manner?   ———

   Does the allocation of time anticipate and allot the most time to those specific issues which most concern the Court?   ———

  4. CONCLUSION

   Does the argument conclude with a concise and effective summary of the major points?   ———

II. DEVELOPMENT OF THE ARGUMENT

  1. PERSUASIVENESS

   Is maximum effective use made of the strongest points? Were weaker points made in such a way as to minimize any detrimental impact of such points?   ———

   Are the arguments presented in the most persuasive sequence?   ———

[60]

Are the arguments of the opposing side anticipated and minimized by proper selection of available arguments?   ———

2. ARGUMENT SUPPORT

Is the best case law authority used? Are the strongest policy arguments made and emphasized?   ———

3. APPLICATION OF LAW TO FACTS

Are the arguments and authorities effectively tied into the facts of the case?   ———

Are cases relied on properly analyzed and used to support arguments or show similarity to the facts of the case at bar?   ———

Is each step of the argument logical in its welding of facts, law and policy?   ———

III. RESPONSES TO QUESTIONS FROM THE BENCH

1. PREPARATION

Is the speaker adequately prepared to answer all questions?   ———

Are the facts and holdings of cited authorities and the details of policy arguments clearly recalled, understood, and applied?   ———

2. RESPONSIVENESS

Does the advocate answer the questions posed without first beating around the bush?   ———

Are the responses persuasive? Do they address the court's concerns and attempt to dispel those doubts with the best authority and logic possible?   ———

Do the responses evoke an empathy from the court toward the advocate's position and client?   ———

3. FLEXIBILITY

Is the advocate able to adjust his presentation to immediately address any persistent concern of the court over a specific issue?   ———

Is the advocate able to continue the presentation in an organized manner after each question is answered?   ———

[61]

4. PERCEPTION

Is the advocate able to understand the questions from the tribunal and perceive what elements the court considers troublesome or unpersuasive?

IV. SPEAKING ABILITY

1. ADVOCACY

Will the advocate's speech and manner at all times convey conviction and purpose on behalf of the client? Does the advocate avoid appearing overly scholarly or detached from the client's position?

2. SPEAKING TECHNIQUE

Does the advocate speak without undue hesitation and with proper diction?

Are inflection and modulation used appropriately —avoiding either a monotone or a distracting overuse of inflection or modulation?

Does the advocate choose appropriate words? Are bombast and extravagance avoided?

3. DEMEANOR

Does the advocate appear poised and relaxed?

Is composure and tact retained at all times, even under stress?

Are notes avoided or used effectively—e. g., unobtrusively, without excessive reliance?

Is eye contact frequent? Does it convey interest and conviction?

Are gestures used appropriately—avoiding either a wooden appearance or a distracting impression of hyperactive limbs and facial muscles?

4. OVERALL EFFECTIVENESS

Does the advocate's use of the above attitudes, techniques, and skills combine to make the advocate's arguments and responses to questions significantly more persuasive? Is great weight thereby added to the argument presented?

INDEX

References are to Pages

References are to Pages

†